REFERENCE

ED-R

Junior
Worldmark
Encyclopedia of
World Cultures

Junior
Worldmark
Encyclopedia of

World Cultures

VOLUME

Brazil to
Congo, Republic of

AN IMPRINT OF GALE

DETROIT · LONDON

JUNIOR WORLDMARK ENCYCLOPEDIA OF WORLD CULTURES

U•X•L Staff

Jane Hoehner, *U•X•L Senior Editor*
Carol DeKane Nagel, *U•X•L Managing Editor*
Thomas L. Romig, *U•X•L Publisher*
Mary Beth Trimper, *Production Director*
Evi Seoud, *Assistant Production Manager*
Shanna Heilveil, *Production Associate*
Cynthia Baldwin, *Product Design Manager*
Barbara J. Yarrow, *Graphic Services Supervisor*
Pamela A. E. Galbreath, *Senior Art Director*
Margaret Chamberlain, *Permissions Specialist (Pictures)*

Copyright © 1999
U•X•L
An Imprint of Gale
All rights reserved including the right of reproduction in whole or in part in any form.

Library of Congress Cataloging-in-Publication Data
Junior worldmark encyclopedia of world cultures / Timothy L. Gall and Susan Bevan Gall, editors.
p.   cm.
Includes bibliographical references and index.
Summary: Arranges countries around the world alphabetically, subdivides these countries into 250 culture groups, and provides information about the ethnology and human geography of each group.
ISBN 0-7876-1756-X (set   :   alk. paper)
1. Ethnology--Encyclopedias, Juvenile. 2. Human geography--Encyclopedias, Juvenile. [1. Ethnology--Encyclopedias. 2. Human geography--Encyclopedias.] I. Gall, Timothy L.   II. Gall, Susan B.
GN307.J85   1999
306' .03--dc21   98-13810
                                                                    CIP
                                                                    AC

ISBN 0-7876-1756-X (set)
ISBN 0-7876-1757-1 (vol. 1)   ISBN 0-7876-1758-X (vol. 2)   ISBN 0-7876-1759-8 (vol. 3)
ISBN 0-7876-1760-1 (vol. 4)   ISBN 0-7876-1761-X (vol. 5)   ISBN 0-7876-1762-8 (vol. 6)
ISBN 0-7876-1763-6 (vol. 7)   ISBN 0-7876-1764-4 (vol. 8)   ISBN 0-7876-2761-5 (vol. 9)

Printed in the United States of America
10   9   8   7   6   5   4   3   2

REFERENCE

Contents
Volume 2

Cumulative Contents vi
Contributors xi
Reader's Guide xv
Brazil 1
Brazilians 1
   Afro-Brazilians 11
   Kayapos 17
   Xavante 22
Bulgaria 31
   Bulgarians 31
Burkina Faso 39
   Burkinabe 39
   Mossi 43
Burundi 51
   Burundians 51
   Tutsi 57
Cambodia 61
   Khmer 61
   Hill Tribespeople 70
Cameroon 77
   Cameroonians 77
Canada 83
   Canadians 83
   French Canadians 89
   Inuit 94
Cape Verde 101
   Cape Verdeans 101
Central African Republic 105
   Central Africans 105

Chad 113
   Chadians 113
Chile 119
   Chileans 119
   Araucanians 126
China 131
   Chinese 132
   Dong 141
   Han 148
   Man (Manchus) 153
   Miao 157
   Tibetans 163
   Uighurs 168
   Zhuang 173
Colombia 177
   Colombians 177
   Páez 183
Congo, Dem. Rep. of the 189
   Congolese 189
   Azande 197
   Efe and Mbuti 201
Congo, Republic of the 209
   Congolese 209
   Aka 215
   Bakongo 221
Glossary 231
Index 235

Cumulative Contents

Volume 1

Afghanistan **3**
 Afghanis 3
 Hazaras...10
 Pashtun...13
Albania **19**
 Albanians 19
Algeria..**27**
 Algerians 27
Andorra **35**
 Andorrans...35
Angola..**39**
 Angolans 39
Antigua and Barbuda............................**49**
 Antiguans and Barbudans 49
Argentina **57**
 Argentines 57
Armenia..**65**
 Armenians 65
Australia...**73**
 Australians 73
 Australian Aborigines 80
Austria..**87**
 Austrians 87
Azerbaijan **95**
 Azerbaijanis 95
Bahamas **101**
 Bahamians...101
Bahrain...**107**
 Bahrainis 107
Bangladesh..**113**
 Bangladeshis 113
 Bengalis 121
 Chakmas..127
Barbados..**133**
 Barbadians 133
Belarus..**139**
 Belarusans 139
Belgium **145**
 Belgians 145
 Flemings...151
 Walloons 155
Belize **159**
 Belizeans..159
 Garifuna 166
Benin **173**
 Beninese 173
Bhutan..**179**
 Bhutanese..179

Bolivia **185**
 Bolivians...185
 Aymara 193
Bosnia and Herzegovina **201**
 Bosnians 201

Volume 2

Brazil **1**
Brazilians **1**
 Afro-Brazilians 11
 Kayapos 17
 Xavante 22
Bulgaria..**31**
 Bulgarians 31
Burkina Faso **39**
 Burkinabe 39
 Mossi 43
Burundi **51**
 Burundians 51
 Tutsi...57
Cambodia **61**
 Khmer 61
 Hill Tribespeople 70
Cameroon..**77**
 Cameroonians 77
Canada **83**
 Canadians 83
 French Canadians 89
 Inuit 94
Cape Verde...**101**
 Cape Verdeans...................................101
Central African Republic........................**105**
 Central Africans 105
Chad **113**
 Chadians 113
Chile **119**
 Chileans 119
 Araucanians 126
China...**131**
 Chinese 132
 Dong 141
 Han 148
 Man (Manchus) 153
 Miao 157
 Tibetans 163
 Uighurs 168
 Zhuang...173

CUMULATIVE CONTENTS

Colombia **177**
    Colombians 177
    Páez 183
Congo, Democratic Republic of the **189**
    Congolese 189
    Azande 197
    Efe and Mbuti 201
Congo, Republic of the **209**
    Congolese 209
    Aka 215
    Bakongo 221

Volume 3

Costa Rica **1**
    Costa Ricans 1
Cote d'Ivoire **7**
    Ivoirians 7
Croatia **13**
    Croats 13
Cuba **21**
    Cubans 21
Cyprus **29**
    Greek Cypriots 29
Czech Republic **37**
    Czechs 37
Denmark **43**
    Danes 43
Djibouti **51**
    Djiboutians 51
Dominica **57**
    Dominicans 57
Dominican Republic **63**
    Dominicans 63
Ecuador **69**
    Ecuadorans 69
    Jivaro 77
Egypt **83**
    Egyptians 83
El Salvador **91**
    Salvadorans 91
Equatorial Guinea **99**
    Equatorial Guineans 99
Eritrea **107**
    Eritreans 107
Estonia **113**
    Estonians 113
Ethiopia **121**
    Ethiopians 121
    Amhara 133
    Oromos 141
    Tigray 149

Fiji **157**
    Fijians 157
    Indo-Fijians 163
Finland **167**
    Finns 167
France **175**
    French 175
    Bretons 181
    French Guianans 185
Gabon **189**
    Gabonese 189
The Gambia **195**
    Gambians 195
Georgia **205**
    Georgians 205
    Abkhazians 214
    Adjarians 218

Volume 4

Germany **1**
    Germans 1
Ghana **9**
    Ghanaians 9
Greece **17**
    Greeks 17
Grenada **25**
    Grenadians 25
Guatemala **31**
    Guatemalans 31
Guinea **39**
    Guineans 39
    Fulani 46
Guyana **51**
    Guyanans 51
Haiti **57**
    Haitians 57
Honduras **67**
    Hondurans 67
Hungary **75**
    Hungarians 75
Iceland **81**
    Icelanders 81
India **87**
    Indians 88
    Andhras 96
    Gonds 102
    Gujaratis 107
    Marathas 112
    Oriya 117
    Rajputs 122

CUMULATIVE CONTENTS

Indonesia...129
   Indonesians 129
   Asmat 139
   Balinese...143
   Javanese 149
   Sundanese 155
Iran 161
   Iranians...161
Iraq...169
   Iraqis 169
   Ma'dan (Marsh Arabs)............................176
Ireland 181
   Irish 181
Israel..189
   Israelis 189
   Palestinians 198
Italy 207
   Italians..207
Jamaica..215
   Jamaicans 215

Liberia 159
   Malinke..159
Libya...167
   Libyans 167
Liechtenstein...175
   Liechtensteiners....................................175
Lithuania 181
   Lithuanians 181
Luxembourg..189
   Luxembourgers......................................189
Macedonia...193
   Macedonians 193
Madagascar..199
   Malagasy 199
Malawi 205
   Chewa and other Maravi Groups 205
Malaysia 213
   Malays 213
Mali 221
   Malians 221
   Songhay 227

Volume 5

Japan 1
   Japanese 1
   Ainu 14
Jordan...21
   Jordanians 21
Kazakstan..29
   Kazaks 29
Kenya..39
   Kenyans 39
   Gikuyu 50
   Gusii 60
   Kalenjin 67
   Luhya 74
   Luo 81
Korea, Republic of......................................91
   South Koreans 91
Kuwait..99
   Kuwaitis 99
Kyrgyzstan 107
   Kyrgyz 107
Laos 115
   Lao 115
   Kammu...125
Latvia..133
   Latvians...133
Lebanon...139
   Lebanese 139
   Maronites 145
Lesotho..149
   Sotho 149

Volume 6

Mauritania 1
   Mauritanians 1
Mexico...7
   Mexicans 7
   Maya 13
Micronesia...21
   Micronesians 21
Moldova 25
   Moldovans 25
Monaco 33
   Monégasques 33
Mongolia 39
   Mongols..39
   Ewenki 46
Morocco 53
   Moroccans 53
Mozambique 61
   Mozambicans 61
Myanmar 67
   Burman 67
   Karens 75
   Shans 83
Namibia...91
   Namibians 91
Nepal 99
   Nepalis 99
   Sherpas 107

CUMULATIVE CONTENTS

The Netherlands 115
   Netherlanders 115
   Frisians 122
New Zealand 127
   New Zealanders 127
   Maori 133
   Polynesians 139
Nicaragua 145
   Nicaraguans 145
   Sumu and Miskito 152
Niger 157
   Nigeriens 157
   Tuareg 164
Nigeria 171
   Nigerians 171
   Hausa 176
   Igbo 181
   Yoruba 186

Volume 7

Norway 1
   Norwegians 1
   Sami 9
Oman 17
   Omanis 17
Pakistan 25
   Pakistanis 25
   Baluchi 35
   Brahui 41
   Punjabis 46
Panama 57
   Panamanians 57
   Cunas 64
Papua New Guinea 71
   Melanesians 71
   Iatmul 79
   Melpa 84
   Motu 89
Paraguay 93
   Paraguayans 93
   Guaranís 98
Peru 105
   Peruvians 105
   Asháninka 113
   Quechua 119
Philippines 125
   Filipinos 125
   Hiligaynon 136
   Ilocanos 142
Poland 149
   Poles 149

Portugal 157
   Portuguese 157
Qatar 165
   Qataris 165
Romania 171
   Romanians 171
   Roma 178
Russia 187
   Russians 187
   Chechens 199
   Chukchi 206
   Mordvins 211
   Nentsy 216
   Tatars 221

Volume 8

Rwanda 1
   Rwandans 1
   Hutu 7
St. Kitts and Nevis 11
   Kittitians and Nevisians 11
St. Lucia 17
   St. Lucians 17
St. Vincent and the Grenadines 23
   St. Vincentians 23
San Marino 29
   Sammarinese 29
Saudi Arabia 33
   Saudis 33
   Bedu 41
Senegal 49
   Senegalese 49
   Wolof 56
Seychelles 61
   Seychellois 61
Sierra Leone 67
   Creoles of Sierra Leone 67
Slovakia 73
   Slovaks 73
Slovenia 81
   Slovenes 81
Somalia 87
   Somalis 87
South Africa 93
   Afrikaners 93
   Cape Coloreds 100
   English 105
   Xhosa 110
   Zulu 117
Spain 125
   Spaniards 125
   Andalusians 132

CUMULATIVE CONTENTS

Basques 138
Castilians 144
Catalans 150
Galicians 155
Sri Lanka **161**
Sinhalese 161
Tamils 169
Sudan **175**
Sudanese 175
Dinka 181
Suriname **185**
Surinamese 185
Swaziland **189**
Swazis 189
Sweden **195**
Swedes 195
Switzerland **205**
Swiss 205
Syria **213**
Syrians 213
Druze 219

Volume 9

Tajikistan **1**
Tajiks 1
Pamiri 7
Tanzania **13**
Tanzanians 13
Chagga 19
Maasai 25
Nyamwezi 34
Shambaa 39
Swahili 45
Thailand **51**
Thai 51
Trinidad and Tobago **59**
Trinidadians and Tobagonians 59
Tunisia **65**
Tunisians 65

Turkey **71**
Turks 71
Kurds 78
Turkmenistan **85**
Turkmens 85
Uganda **91**
Ugandans 91
Baganda 98
Banyankole 105
Ukraine **111**
Ukrainians 111
United Arab Emirates **117**
Emirians 117
United Kingdom **123**
English 123
Scots 130
Welsh 136
Uruguay **143**
Uruguayans 143
Uzbekistan **147**
Uzbeks 147
Karakalpaks 153
Vanuatu **159**
Ni-Vanuatu 159
Venezuela **163**
Venezuelans 163
Guajiros 170
Pemon 174
Vietnam **181**
Vietnamese 181
Cham 191
Western Samoa **197**
Samoans 197
Yemen **201**
Yemenis 201
Zambia **209**
Zambians 209
Bemba 215
Tonga 221
Zimbabwe **227**
Zimbabweans 227

Contributors

Editors: Timothy L. Gall and Susan Bevan Gall

Senior Editor: Daniel M. Lucas

Contributing Editors: Himanee Gupta, Jim Henry, Kira Silverbird, Elaine Trapp, Rosalie Wieder

Copy Editors: Deborah Baron, Janet Fenn, Jim Henry, Patricia M. Mote, Deborah Ring, Kathy Soltis

Typesetting and Graphics: Cheryl Montagna, Brian Rajewski

Cover Photographs: Cory Langley

Data Input: Janis K. Long, Cheryl Montagna, Melody Penfound

Proofreaders: Deborah Baron, Janet Fenn

Editorial Assistants: Katie Baron, Jennifer A. Spencer, Daniel K. Updegraft

Editorial Advisors

P. Boone, Sixth Grade Teacher, Oak Crest Middle School, San Antonio, Texas

Jean Campbell, Foothill Farms Middle School, Sacramento, California

Kathy Englehart, Librarian, Hathaway Brown School, Shaker Heights, Ohio

Catherine Harris, Librarian, Oak Crest Middle School, San Antonio, Texas

Karen James, Children's Services, Louisville Free Public Library, Louisville, Kentucky

Contributors to the Gale Edition

The articles presented in this encyclopedia are based on entries in the *Worldmark Encyclopedia of Cultures and Daily Life* published in 1997 by Gale. The following authors and reviewers contributed to the Gale edition.

ANDREW J. ABALAHIN. Doctoral candidate, Department of History, Cornell University.

JAMAL ABDULLAH. Doctoral candidate, Department of City and Regional Planning, Cornell University.

SANA ABED-KOTOB. Book Review Editor, Middle East Journal, Middle East Institute.

MAMOUD ABOUD. Charge d'Affaires, a.i., Embassy of the Federal and Islamic Republic of the Comoros.

JUDY ALLEN. Editor, Choctaw Nation of Oklahoma.

HIS EXCELLENCY DENIS G. ANTOINE. Ambassador to the United States, Embassy of Grenada.

LESLEY ANN ASHBAUGH. Instructor, Sociology, Seattle University.

HASHEM ATALLAH. Translator, Editor, Teacher; Fairfax, Virginia.

HECTOR AZEVES. Cultural Attaché, Embassy of Uruguay.

VICTORIA J. BAKER. Associate Professor of Anthropology, Anthropology (Collegium of Comparative Cultures), Eckerd College.

POLINE BALA. Doctoral candidate, Asian Studies, Cornell University.

MARJORIE MANDELSTAM BALZER. Research Professor; Coordinator, Social, Regional, and Ethnic Studies Sociology, and Center for Eurasian, Russian, and East European Studies.

JOSHUA BARKER. Doctoral candidate, Department of Anthropology, Cornell University.

IGOR BARSEGIAN. Department of Sociology, George Washington University.

IRAJ BASHIRI. Professor of Central Asian Studies, Department of Slavic and Central Asian Languages and Literatures, University of Minnesota.

DAN F. BAUER. Department of Anthropology, Lafayette College.

JOYCE BEAR. Historic Preservation Officer, Muscogee Nation of Oklahoma.

SVETLANA BELAIA. Byelorussian-American Cultural Center, Strongsville, Ohio.

HIS EXCELLENCY DR. COURTNEY BLACKMAN. Ambassador to the United States, Embassy of Barbados.

BETTY BLAIR. Executive Editor, Azerbaijan International.

ARVIDS BLODNIEKS. Director, Latvian Institute, American Latvian Association in the USA.

ARASH BORMANSHINOV. University of Maryland, College Park.

HARRIET I. BRADY. Cultural Anthropologist (Pyramid Lake Paiute Tribe), Native Studies Program, Pyramid Lake High School.

MARTIN BROKENLEG. Professor of Sociology, Department of Sociology, Augustana College.

REV. RAYMOND A. BUCKO, S.J. Assistant Professor of Anthropology, LeMoyne College.

JOHN W. BURTON. Department of Anthropology, Connecticut College.

DINEANE BUTTRAM. University of North Carolina-Chapel Hill.

RICARDO CABALLERO. Counselor, Embassy of Paraguay.

CHRISTINA CARPADIS. Researcher/Writer, Cleveland, Ohio.

SALVADOR GARCIA CASTANEDA. Department of Spanish and Portuguese, The Ohio State University.

SUSANA CAVALLO. Graduate Program Director and Professor of Spanish, Department of Modern Languages and Literatures, Loyola University, Chicago.

BRIAN P. CAZA. Doctoral candidate, Political Science, University of Chicago.

VAN CHRISTO. President and Executive Director, Frosina Foundation, Boston.

YURI A. CHUMAKOV. Graduate Student, Department of Sociology, University of Notre Dame.

J. COLARUSSO. Professor of Anthropology, McMaster University.

FRANCESCA COLECCHIA. Modern Language Department, Duquesne University.

DIANNE K. DAEG DE MOTT. Researcher/Writer, Tucson, Arizona.

MICHAEL DE JONGH. Professor, Department of Anthropology, University of South Africa.

GEORGI DERLUGUIAN. Senior Fellow, Ph.D., U. S. Institute of Peace.

CHRISTINE DRAKE. Department of Political Science and Geography, Old Dominion University.

ARTURO DUARTE. Guatemalan Mission to the OAS.

CALEB DUBE. Department of Anthropology, Northwestern University.

BRIAN DU TOIT. Professor, Department of Anthropology, University of Florida.

LEAH ERMARTH. Worldspace Foundation, Washington, DC.

NANCY J. FAIRLEY. Associate Professor of Anthropology, Department of Anthropology/Sociology, Davidson College.

GREGORY A. FINNEGAN, Ph.D. Tozzer Library, Harvard University.

ALLEN J. FRANK, Ph.D.

DAVID P. GAMBLE. Professor Emeritus, Department of Anthropology, San Francisco State University.

FREDERICK GAMST. Professor, Department of Anthropology, University of Massachusetts, Harbor Campus.

PAULA GARB. Associate Director of Global Peace and Conflict Studies and Adjunct Professor of Social Ecology, University of California, Irvine.

HAROLD GASKI. Associate Professor of Sami Literature, School of Languages and Literature, University of Tromsø.

STEPHEN J. GENDZIER.

FLORENCE GERDEL.

ANTHONY P. GLASCOCK. Professor of Anthropology; Department of Anthropology, Psychology, and Sociology; Drexel University.

LUIS GONZALEZ. Researcher/Writer, River Edge, New Jersey.

JENNIFER GRAHAM. Researcher/Writer, Sydney, Australia.

MARIE-CÉCILE GROELSEMA. Doctoral candidate, Comparative Literature, Indiana University.

ROBERT GROELSEMA. MPIA and doctoral candidate, Political Science, Indiana University.

MARIA GROSZ-NGATÉ. Visiting Assistant Professor, Department of Anthropology, Northwestern University.

ELLEN GRUENBAUM. Professor, School of Social Sciences, California State University, Fresno.

N. THOMAS HAKANSSON. University of Kentucky.

ROBERT HALASZ. Researcher/Writer, New York, New York.

MARC HANREZ. Professor, Department of French and Italian, University of Wisconsin-Madison.

ANWAR UL HAQ. Central Asian Studies Department, Indiana University.

LIAM HARTE. Department of Philosophy, Loyola University, Chicago.

FR. VASILE HATEGAN. Author, *Romanian Culture in America.*

BRUCE HEILMAN. Doctoral candidate, Department of Political Science, Indiana University.

JIM HENRY. Researcher/Writer, Cleveland, Ohio.

BARRY HEWLETT. Department of Anthropology, Washington State University.

SUSAN F. HIRSCH. Department of Anthropology, Wesleyan University.

MARIDA HOLLOS. Department of Anthropology, Brown University.

HALYNA HOLUBEC. Researcher/Writer, Cleveland, Ohio.

YVONNE HOOSAVA. Legal Researcher and Cultural Preservation Officer, Hopi Tribal Council.

HUIQIN HUANG, Ph.D. Center for East Asia Studies, University of Montreal.

ASAFA JALATA. Assistant Professor of Sociology and African and African American Studies, Department of Sociology, The University of Tennessee, Knoxville.

STEPHEN F. JONES. Russian Department, Mount Holyoke College.

THOMAS JOVANOVSKI, Ph.D. Lorain County Community College.

A. KEN JULES. Minister Plenipotentiary and Deputy Head of Mission, Embassy of St. Kitts and Nevis.

GENEROSA KAGARUKI-KAKOTI. Economist, Department of Urban and Rural Planning, College of Lands and Architectural Studies, Dar es Salaam, Tanzania.

EZEKIEL KALIPENI. Department of Geography, University of Illinois at Urbana-Champaign.

CONTRIBUTORS

DON KAVANAUGH. Program Director, Lake of the Woods Ojibwa Cultural Centre.

SUSAN M. KENYON. Associate Professor of Anthropology, Department of History and Anthropology, Butler University.

WELILE KHUZWAYO. Department of Anthropology, University of South Africa.

PHILIP L. KILBRIDE. Professor of Anthropology, Mary Hale Chase Chair in the Social Sciences, Department of Anthropology, Bryn Mawr College.

RICHARD O. KISIARA. Doctoral candidate, Department of Anthropology, Washington University in St. Louis.

KAREN KNOWLES. Permanent Mission of Antigua and Barbuda to the United Nations.

IGOR KRUPNIK. Research Anthropologist, Department of Anthropology, Smithsonian Institution.

LEELO LASS. Secretary, Embassy of Estonia.

ROBERT LAUNAY. Professor, Department of Anthropology, Northwestern University.

CHARLES LEBLANC. Professor and Director, Center for East Asia Studies, University of Montreal.

RONALD LEE. Author, *Goddam Gypsy, An Autobiographical Novel.*

PHILIP E. LEIS. Professor and Chair, Department of Anthropology, Brown University.

MARIA JUKIC LESKUR. Croatian Consulate, Cleveland, Ohio.

RICHARD A. LOBBAN, JR. Professor of Anthropology and African Studies, Department of Anthropology, Rhode Island College.

DERYCK O. LODRICK. Visiting Scholar, Center for South Asian Studies, University of California, Berkeley.

NEIL LURSSEN. Intro Communications Inc.

GREGORIO C. MARTIN. Modern Language Department, Duquesne University.

HOWARD J. MARTIN. Independent scholar.

HEITOR MARTINS. Professor, Department of Spanish and Portuguese, Indiana University.

ADELINE MASQUELIER. Assistant Professor, Department of Anthropology, Tulane University.

DOLINA MILLAR.

EDITH MIRANTE. Project Maje, Portland, Oregon.

ROBERT W. MONTGOMERY, Ph.D. Indiana University.

THOMAS D. MORIN. Associate Professor of Hispanic Studies, Department of Modern and Classical Literatures and Languages, University of Rhode Island.

CHARLES MORRILL. Doctoral candidate, Indiana University.

CAROL A. MORTLAND. Crate's Point, The Dalles, Oregon.

FRANCIS A. MOYER. Director, North Carolina Japan Center, North Carolina State University.

MARIE C. MOYER.

NYAGA MWANIKI. Assistant Professor, Department of Anthropology and Sociology, Western Carolina University.

KENNETH NILSON. Celtic Studies Department, Harvard University.

JANE E. ORMROD. Graduate Student, History, University of Chicago.

JUANITA PAHDOPONY. Carl Perkins Program Director, Comanche Tribe of Oklahoma.

TINO PALOTTA. Syracuse University.

ROHAYATI PASENG.

PATRICIA PITCHON. Researcher/Writer, London, England.

STEPHANIE PLATZ. Program Officer, Program on Peace and International Cooperation, The John D. and Catherine T. MacArthur Foundation.

MIHAELA POIATA. Graduate Student, School of Journalism and Mass Communication, University of North Carolina at Chapel Hill.

LEOPOLDINA PRUT-PREGELJ. Author, *Historical Dictionary of Slovenia.*

J. RACKAUSKAS. Director, Lithuanian Research and Studies Center, Chicago.

J. RAKOVICH. Byelorussian-American Cultural Center, Strongsville, Ohio.

HANTA V. RALAY. Promotions, Inc., Montgomery Village, Maryland.

SUSAN J. RASMUSSEN. Associate Professor, Department of Anthropology, University of Houston.

RONALD REMINICK. Department of Anthropology, Cleveland State University.

BRUCE D. ROBERTS. Assistant Professor of Anthropology, Department of Anthropology and Sociology, University of Southern Mississippi.

LAUREL L. ROSE. Philosophy Department, Carnegie-Mellon University.

ROBERT ROTENBERG. Professor of Anthropology, International Studies Program, DePaul University.

CAROLINE SAHLEY, Ph.D. Researcher/Writer, Cleveland, Ohio.

VERONICA SALLES-REESE. Associate Professor, Department of Spanish and Portuguese, Georgetown University.

MAIRA SARYBAEVA. Kazakh-American Studies Center, University of Kentucky.

DEBRA L. SCHINDLER. Institute of Arctic Studies, Dartmouth College.

KYOKO SELDEN, Ph.D. Researcher/Writer, Ithaca, New York.

ENAYATULLAH SHAHRANI. Central Asian Studies Department, Indiana University.

ROBERT SHANAFELT. Adjunct Lecturer, Department of Anthropology, The Florida State University.

TUULIKKI SINKS. Teaching Specialist for Finnish, Department of German, Scandinavian, and Dutch, University of Minnesota.

JAN SJÅVIK. Associate Professor, Scandinavian Studies, University of Washington.

CONTRIBUTORS

MAGDA SOBALVARRO. Press and Cultural Affairs Director, Embassy of Nicaragua.

MICHAEL STAINTON. Researcher, Joint Center for Asia Pacific Studies, York University.

RIANA STEYN. Department of Anthropology, University of South Africa.

PAUL STOLLER. Professor, Department of Anthropology, West Chester University.

CRAIG STRASHOFER. Researcher/Writer, Cleveland, Ohio.

SANDRA B. STRAUBHAAR. Assistant Professor, Nordic Studies, Department of Germanic and Slavic Languages, Brigham Young University.

VUM SON SUANTAK. Author, *Zo History.*

MURAT TAISHIBAEV. Kazakh-American Studies Center, University of Kentucky.

CHRISTOPHER C. TAYLOR. Associate Professor, Anthropology Department, University of Alabama, Birmingham.

EDDIE TSO. Office of Language and Culture, Navajo Division of Education.

DAVID TYSON. Foreign Broadcast Information Service, Washington, D.C.

NICOLAAS G. W. UNLANDT. Assistant Professor of French, Department of French and Italian, Brigham Young University.

GORDON URQUHART. Professor, Department of Economics and Business, Cornell College.

CHRISTOPHER J. VAN VUUREN. Professor, Department of Anthropology, University of South Africa.

DALIA VENTURA-ALCALAY. Journalist, London, England.

CATHERINE VEREECKE. Assistant Director, Center for African Studies, University of Florida.

GREGORY T. WALKER. Associate Director, Office of International Affairs, Duquesne University.

GERHARD WEISS. Department of German, Scandinavian, and Dutch, University of Minnesota.

PATSY WEST. Director, The Seminole/Miccosukee Photographic Archive.

WALTER WHIPPLE. Associate Professor of Polish, Germanic and Slavic Languages, Brigham Young University.

ROSALIE WIEDER. Researcher/Writer, Cleveland, Ohio.

JEFFREY WILLIAMS. Professor, Department of Anthropology, Cleveland State University.

GUANG-HONG YU. Associate Research Fellow, Institute of Ethnology, Academia Sinica.

RUSSELL ZANCA. Department of Anthropology, College of Liberal Arts and Sciences, University of Illinois at Urbana-Champaign.

Reader's Guide

Junior Worldmark Encyclopedia of World Cultures contains articles exploring the ways of life of over 290 culture groups worldwide. Arranged alphabetically by country in nine volumes, this encyclopedia parallels the organization of its sister set, *Junior Worldmark Encyclopedia of the Nations*. Whereas the primary purpose of *Nations* is to provide information on the world's nations, this encyclopedia focuses on the traditions, living conditions, and personalities of many of the world's culture groups.

Defining groups for inclusion was not an easy task. Cultural identity is shaped by such factors as history, geography, nationality, ethnicity, race, language, and religion. Sometimes the distinctions are subtle, but important. Most chapters in this encyclopedia begin with an article on the people of the country as a nationality group. For example, the chapter on Kenya begins with an article entitled "Kenyans." This article explores the national character shared by all people living in Kenya. However, there are separate articles on the Gikuyu, Kalenjin, Luhya, and Luo—four of the largest ethnic groups living in the country. They are all Kenyans, but each group is distinct. Many profiled groups—like the Kazaks—inhabit lands that cross national boundaries. Although profiled in the chapter on Kazakstan, Kazaks are also important minorities in China, Uzbekistan, and Turkmenistan. In such cases, cross-references direct the student to the chapter where the group is profiled.

The photographs that illustrate the articles show a wonderfully diverse world. From the luxury liners docked in the harbor at Monaco to the dwellings made of grass sheltering the inhabitants of the rain forest, people share the struggles and joys of earning a living, bringing children into the world, teaching them to survive, and initiating them into adulthood. Although language, customs, and dress illustrate our differences, the faces of the people pictured in these volumes reinforce our similarities. Whether on the streets

of Tokyo or the mountains of Tibet, a smile on the face of a child transcends the boundaries of nationality and cultural identity to reveal something common in us all. Photographer Cory Langley's images on pages 93 and 147 in Volume 6 serve to illustrate this point.

The picture of the world this encyclopedia paints today will certainly differ from the one painted in future editions. Indigenous people like the Jivaro in Ecuador (Volume 3, page 77) are being assimilated into modern society as forest lands are cleared for development and televisions and VCRs are brought to even the most remote villages. As the global economy expands, traditional diets are supplemented with Coke, Pepsi, and fast food; traditional storytellers are replaced by World Cup soccer matches and American television programs; and cultural heroes are overwhelmed by images of Michael Jordan and Michael Jackson. Photographer Cynthia Bassett was fortunate to be among a small group of travelers to visit a part of China only recently opened to Westerners. Her image of Miao dancers (Volume 2, page 161) shows a people far removed from Western culture . . . until one looks a little closer. Behind the dancers, in the upper corner of the photograph, is a basketball hoop and backboard. It turns out that Miao teenagers love basketball!

ORGANIZATION

Within each volume the chapters are arranged alphabetically by country. A cumulative table of contents for all volumes in the set follows the table of contents to each volume.

Each chapter covers a specific country. The contents of the chapter, listing the culture group articles, follows the chapter title. An overview of the composition of the population of the country appears after the contents list. The individual articles follow, and are organized according to a standard twenty-heading outline explained in more detail below. This structure allows for easy comparison between cultures and enhances the accessibility of the information.

Articles begin with the **pronunciation** of the group's name, a listing of **alternate names** by which the group is known, the group's **location** in the world, its **population**, the **languages** spoken, and the **religions** practiced. Articles are illustrated with maps showing the primary location of the group and photographs of the culture group being profiled. The twenty standard headings by which the articles are organized are presented below.

1 ● INTRODUCTION: A description of the group's historical origins provides a useful background for understanding its contemporary affairs. Information relating to migration helps explain how the group arrived at its present location. Political conditions and governmental structure(s) that affect members of the profiled ethnic group are also discussed.

2 ● LOCATION: The population size of the group is listed. This information may include official census data from various countries and/ or estimates. Information on the size of a group's population located outside the traditional homeland may also be included, especially for those groups with large scattered populations. A description of the homeland includes information on location, topography, and climate.

3 ● LANGUAGE: Each article lists the name(s) of the primary language(s) spoken by members. Descriptions of linguistic origins, grammar, and similarities to other languages may also be included. Examples of common words, phrases, and proverbs are listed for many of the profiled groups, and some include examples of common personal names and greetings.

4 ● FOLKLORE: Common themes, settings, and characters in the profiled group's traditional oral and/or literary mythology are highlighted. Many entries include a short excerpt or synopsis of one of the group's noteworthy myths, fables, or legends. Some entries describe the accomplishments of famous heroes and heroines or other prominent historical figures.

5 ● RELIGION: The origins of traditional religious beliefs are profiled. Contemporary religious beliefs, customs, and practices are also discussed. Some groups may be closely associated with one particular faith (especially if religious and ethnic identification are interlinked), while others may have members of diverse faiths.

6 ● MAJOR HOLIDAYS: Celebrations and commemorations typically recognized by the group's members are described. These holidays commonly fall into two categories: secular and religious. Secular holidays often include an independence day and/or other days of observance recognizing important dates in history that affected the group as a whole. Religious holidays are typically the same as those honored by people of the same faith worldwide. Some secular and religious holidays are linked to the lunar cycle or to the change of seasons. Some articles describe customs practiced by members of the group on certain holidays.

7 ● RITES OF PASSAGE: Formal and informal events that mark an individual's procession through the stages of life are profiled. These events typically involve rituals, ceremonies, observances, and procedures associated with birth, childhood, the coming of age, milestones in education or religious training, adulthood, and death.

8 ● RELATIONSHIPS: Information on greetings, body language, gestures, visiting customs, and dating practices is included. The extent of formality to which members of a certain ethnic group treat others is also addressed, as some groups may adhere to customs governing interpersonal relationships more or less strictly than others.

9 ● LIVING CONDITIONS: General health conditions typical of the group's members are cited. Such information includes life expectancy, the prevalence of various diseases, and access to medical care. Information on urbanization, housing, and access to utilities is also included. Transportation methods typically utilized by the group's members are also discussed.

10 ● FAMILY LIFE: The size and composition of the family unit is profiled. Gender roles common to the group are also discussed, including the division of rights and responsibilities relegated to male and female group members. The roles that children, adults, and the elderly have within the group as a whole may also be addressed.

11 ● CLOTHING: Many entries include descriptive information (design, color, fabric, etc.) regarding traditional clothing (or national costume) for men and women, and indicate the frequency of its use in contemporary life. A description of typical clothing worn in modern daily life is also provided, especially if traditional clothing is no longer the usual form of dress. Distinctions between formal and work attire and descriptions of clothing preferences of young people are described for many groups as well.

12 ● FOOD: Descriptions of items commonly consumed by members of the group are listed. The frequency and occasion for meals is also described, as are any unique customs regarding eating and drinking, special utensils and furniture, and the role of food and beverages in ritual ceremonies. Many entries include a recipe for a favorite dish.

13 ● EDUCATION: The structure of formal education in the country or countries of residence is discussed, including information on primary, secondary, and higher education. For some groups, the role of informal education is also highlighted. Some articles include information regarding the relevance and importance of education among the group as a whole, along with parental expectations for children.

14 ● CULTURAL HERITAGE: Since many groups express their sense of identity through art, music, literature, and dance, a description of prominent styles is included. Some articles also cite the contributions of famous individual artists, writers, and musicians.

15 ● EMPLOYMENT: The type of labor that typically engages members of the profiled group is discussed. For some groups, the formal wage economy is the primary source of earnings, but for other groups, informal agriculture or trade may be the usual way to earn a living. Working conditions are also highlighted.

16 ● SPORTS: Popular sports that children and adults play are listed, as are typical spectator sports. Some articles include a description and/or rules to a sport or game.

17 ● RECREATION: Listed activities that people enjoy in their leisure time may include structured pastimes (such as public musical and dance performances) or informal get-togethers (such as meeting for conversation). The role of popular culture, movies, theater, and television in everyday life is also discussed where it applies.

18 ● CRAFTS AND HOBBIES: Entries describe arts and crafts commonly fabricated according to traditional methods, materials, and style. Such objects may often have a functional utility for everyday tasks.

19 ● SOCIAL PROBLEMS: Internal and external issues that confront members of the profiled group are described. Such concerns often deal with fundamental problems like war, famine, disease, and poverty. A lack of human rights, civil rights, and political freedom may also adversely affect a group as a whole. Other problems may include crime, unemployment, substance abuse, and domestic violence.

20 ● BIBLIOGRAPHY: References cited include works used to compile the article, benchmark publications often recognized as authoritative by scholars, and other reference sources accessible to middle school researchers. Website addresses are provided for researchers who wish to access the World Wide Web. The website citation includes the author and title of the website (if applicable). The address begins with characters that follow "http://" in the citation; the address ends with the character preceding the comma and date. For example, the citation for the website of the German embassy appears as follows:

German Embassy, Washington, D.C. [Online]
    Available http://www.germany-info.org/, 1998.

To access this site, researchers type:
    www.germany-info.org

A glossary and an index of groups profiled appears at the end of each volume.

ACKNOWLEDGMENTS

The editors express appreciation to the members of the U•X•L staff who were involved in a number of ways at various stages of development of the *Junior Worldmark Encyclopedia of World Cultures.*

SUGGESTIONS ARE WELCOME: We appreciate any suggestions that will enhance future editions. Please send comments to:

Editors
*Junior Worldmark Encyclopedia
of World Cultures*
U•X•L
27500 Drake Road
Farmington Hills, MI 48331-3535
(800) 877-4253

Brazil

■ **BRAZILIANS** **1**

■ **AFRO-BRAZILIANS** **11**

■ **KAYAPOS** **17**

■ **XAVANTE** **22**

The original inhabitants of Brazil were Amerindians. When the Portuguese settlers arrived in the 1500s, they intermarried with the Amerindians. As a result, about 40 percent of the population is of mixed descent. About 54 percent of Brazil's population is white, and 5 percent is black. The Amerindian population is estimated at approximately 250,000, or less than 1 percent. Among the Amerindians, the cultures of the Kayapos and Xavante remain distinct and are profiled in this chapter.

Brazilians

PRONUNCIATION: brah-ZILL-yuhns
LOCATION: Brazil
POPULATION: Over 162 million
LANGUAGE: Portuguese
RELIGION: Roman Catholicism; Protestantism;
   Afro-Brazilian religions; indigenous beliefs

1 ● INTRODUCTION

Brazil was colonized (occupied and ruled) by the Portuguese. From the 1500s to the 1800s, Brazil provided nearly 75 percent of the world's supply of coffee. After independence from Portugal in 1822, Brazil expanded its production of rubber, sugar, and gold. Brazil also created manufacturing industries. As of the late 1990s, Brazil was the world's tenth-largest economy. However, not all Brazilians have prospered along with the economy; some Brazilians live in poverty.

2 ● LOCATION

Brazil is the fourth-largest country in the world in area. Its land mass is equal to the United States without Alaska and Hawaii. Nearly one-third of Brazil's land mass is taken up by the Amazon River basin. Most of the lowland areas in the north and west of Brazil are populated by native Amazonian tribes. The Amazon rain forest in Brazil is under threat as a result of extensive logging and deforestation. Many of the people who live in the rain forest are facing extinction.

Most Brazilians live in the densely populated south and southeast regions. The population (numbering more than 162 million)

includes immigrants from Europe, the Middle East, and Japan; Afro-Brazilian descendants of slaves; and native groups. Blacks have the same legal rights as whites, but most blacks live in poverty in the *favelas* (urban slums) of Brazil.

3 ● LANGUAGE

The official language of Brazil is Portuguese. Some examples of Portuguese greetings and the English equivalents appear in the table on the next page.

4 ● FOLKLORE

Each of the various ethnic groups in Brazil has its own tradition of folktales and myths.

5 ● RELIGION

The beliefs of many Brazilians reflect elements from African, European, and

Common Phrases

English	Portuguese	Pronunciation
Good morning	Bom dia	bone JEE-ah
Good afternoon	Boa tarde	BOH-ah TAHR-day
Please	Por favor	pore fah-VORE
Thank you (masculine)	Obrigado	oh-bree-GAH-doo
Thank you (feminine)	Obrigada	oh-bree-GAH-dah
1	um	OOng
2	dois	dOYs
3	trés	tRAce
4	quatro	KWAH-troo
5	cinco	SEEN-koo
6	seis	SAY-ees
7	sete	SEH-the
8	oito	OY-too
9	nove	NOH-veh
10	dez	dEHz

indigenous religions. A wide range of religious traditions and practices coexists in Brazil. These include the European religions of Catholicism and Protestantism as well as a multitude of spiritual sects of African origin.

While many Brazilians claim to be Roman Catholic, these beliefs are often infused by traditional practices. Offerings and gifts are made to saints and protective spirits for favors in this life. Self-sacrifice plays an important role in convincing saints to grant requests. To demonstrate their faith, fervent believers may crawl on their knees to sites of spiritual significance.

After Catholicism, Afro-Brazilian religions are the most important in Brazilian society. *Umbanda* is one of the most rapidly growing sects. It attracts both African and non-African Brazilians. Umbanda sects use music, dancing, and sometimes alcohol to reach a trancelike state that enables believ-

PhotoEdit

Dwelling in the Amazon River region. Nearly one-third of Brazil's land is taken up by the Amazon River basin.

ers to communicate with spirits. Also significant is *Condomble* of African origin. Condomble priestesses also seek to communicate with African spirits. Their ceremonies sometimes include the sacrifice of goats and chickens.

6 ● MAJOR HOLIDAYS

Carnival in Brazil is one of the world's most famous festivals. It is celebrated for the five days preceding Ash Wednesday (the start of the Christian period of Lent). Carnival virtually brings the country to a halt as Brazilians take off work to join street festivals, dance contests, and other activities. The major Carnival parade takes place in Rio de Janeiro. Elaborate costumes and floats are the result of many months' preparation. During Carnival, dance balls and samba contests are held. The festivities last well into the morning hours. Other Latin American countries also celebrate Carnival. However, only in Brazil is it done on such a grand scale.

7 ● RITES OF PASSAGE

Major life transitions (such as birth, marriage, and death) are marked by ceremonies appropriate to each Brazilian's religious tradition.

8 ● RELATIONSHIPS

Brazilians speak animatedly and use a variety of hand gestures for emphasis. For example, when a Brazilian speaker moves his or her fingers under the chin, this means "I don't know." Placing the thumb between the index and middle fingers is a sign of good luck.

Brazilians are accustomed to late-night dinners and parties. Many restaurants in the major cities do not open for dinner until 8:00 or 9:00 PM. People make up for lost sleep during the afternoon *siesta*. Stores and many businesses close for three or four hours during lunch. Many Brazilians go home to have lunch and a short nap before returning to work.

Not surprisingly, Brazilians are also heavy coffee drinkers. In many city plazas,

Cory Langley

A vendor sells hats at a public beach. Brazil is a land of contrasts. Its cities combine modern skyscrapers, suburban houses, and impoverished slums. Known as favelas, *Brazil's urban slums have been estimated to be home to as many as twenty-five million people.*

there are roving street vendors selling sweet espresso to passersby.

9 ● LIVING CONDITIONS

Brazil is a land of contrasts. Its cities combine modern skyscrapers, suburban houses, and impoverished slums. Known as *favelas,* Brazil's urban slums have been estimated to be home to as many as twenty-five million people. The inhabitants of favelas live in desperate poverty. Poor sanitation causes serious health problems. There is no garbage collection or sewer access. A life of crime is often the only alternative for unemployed youth with no economic opportunities.

In contrast, the upper and middle classes have a high standard of living. Brazil's major cities are very modern, with large shopping malls, restaurants, and superhighways. Luxury high-rise apartment buildings and large houses have all the amenities one would expect in the United States. Most middle- and upper-class families have servants to assist with housework.

There is a diverse range of housing and living conditions in rural areas. The type of housing depends largely on the weather. Adobe, stone, and wood are all used as housing materials. In the Amazon, reeds and palm are used to construct houses.

Susan D. Rock

A street in Alter do Chão, a town near the Amazon River in northern Brazil. Reeds and palm fronds are used for constructing walls and roofs in the Amazon River area.

10 ● FAMILY LIFE

A family in Brazil generally consists of parents and five to seven children. Some families continue to have as many as fifteen children. Both the nuclear families (parents and children) and extended families (a wider circle of relatives) play an important social role. Most socializing (drinking, dining, gambling, and so forth) is conducted with members of the extended family. Godparents remain extremely important in rural areas, but their importance may be declining in urban areas.

Gender differences are clearly marked in Brazilian society. Sexism is an ingrained feature of the culture. Limited educational opportunities, especially for lower-class women, keep females tied to traditional roles. Few middle- and upper-class women work outside the home, although in recent times this number has begun to increase.

Brazilian society has clearly defined roles for both women and men. Female beauty is highly valued, and young women commonly wear short skirts or shorts in an attempt to attract the attention of men. *Machismo* (an exaggerated show of manliness) is customary among Brazilian men. Interactions between the sexes typically have a flirtatious quality.

Cory Langley

Rio de Janeiro. Brazil's major cities are very modern, with luxury high-rise apartment buildings and all the coveniences one would expect in the United States. Most middle- and upper-class families have servants to assist with housework.

Marital infidelity is a serious social problem in Brazil. It is very common for men to take a mistress on a long-term or permanent basis. While this behavior is not completely sanctioned in Brazilian society, it is widespread and is tolerated.

11 ● CLOTHING

Brazilian dress in urban areas is very modern. Young people wear jeans and skirts. Among women short skirts and dresses are also very common. Business attire is very similar to that worn in the United States.

Dress varies more widely outside of urban areas. In the south plains regions near the border with Argentina, the *gaucho* (cowboy) style is still worn. This includes ponchos, wide straw hats, baggy pants known as *bombachas,* and boots. In the Amazon, native Amerindians wear face paint and traditional tunics. In the predominantly Afro-Brazilian region of Bahia, women wear bright, colorful skirts and head scarves.

12 ● FOOD

Brazil's cuisine is a unique melting pot of influences. It combines cooking styles and ingredients from the rain forest and the Portuguese and African cultures. African influences are particularly pronounced in the

Recipe

Copacabana Collards

Ingredients

2 pounds collard greens, tough stems removed and leaves rinsed well
4 ounces bacon, cut into ¼-inch cubes
1 Tablespoon minced garlic
Salt and coarsely ground black pepper, to taste
¼ cup canned chicken broth

Directions

1. Stack 4 to 6 collard leaves, one on top of the other, and roll them up on the diagonal. Thinly slice on the diagonal. Set aside.

2. Place the bacon in a large, heavy pot and cook, stirring, over low heat to render the fat, about 5 minutes. Add the garlic to the bacon and cook, stirring, for 2 minutes.

3. Add the collard greens, in batches if necessary, until they all fit. Combine well and season with salt and pepper.

4. Drizzle the greens with the chicken broth. Cover the pot and cook, stirring occasionally, over medium-low heat until just tender but still slightly crunchy, 10 to 12 minutes. Serve immediately.

Adapted from Lukins, Sheila. *Sheila Lukins All Around the World Cookbook.* New York: Workman, 1994.

southeastern region of Bahia. Spicy seafood dishes in that region may be flavored with peanuts, coconut, lime, or other tropical ingredients.

In Brazil it is a longstanding tradition to have *feijoada* for lunch on Saturday afternoons. Considered the national dish, feijoada is a stew of black beans with different types of pork—such as sausage, bacon, and salt pork—and an occasional piece of dried beef. (A recipe is included in the Afro-Brazilians profile in this chapter.) This dish was common among the slaves in Brazil who used discarded cuts of pork, such as the snout, tail, and feet to make the dish. These cuts are often still used. Feijoada is often accompanied by rice and/or vegetables such as collards or kale.

A recipe for a typical Brazilian collards dish accompanies this entry.

13 ● EDUCATION

Brazilian children are required to attend school for a minimum of eight years. In reality, however, a large percentage of the population fail to receive an adequate education. The national literacy rate (percentage able to read and write) is 83 percent for men and 80 percent for women, although these rates are much lower in some regions. School attendance at the secondary level is low. Brazilian schools are generally underfinanced and overcrowded. In order to cope with the large number of students, children attend classes either in the evening or in the morning.

Higher-level institutions of education are mostly attended by middle- and upper-class students. Places are limited and entrance exams are very difficult.

14 ● CULTURAL HERITAGE

Brazil has a wide variety of folk and modern music. Samba is perhaps the most popular and well-known internationally. However, samba is but one of Brazil's many

Cynthia Bassett

A scene at the waterfront of a major city.

rhythms and musical traditions. In the northeast, Portuguese guitar, introduced during colonial times, is still popular. African dances and percussion endure in Afro-Brazilian culture and are used in religious ceremonies. African influences are strongly felt in modern music as well.

Brazil has been the birthplace of musical forms that have become popular worldwide. In the 1950s, for example, a fusion of American jazz and samba rhythms known as bossa nova made international stars of singers such as Sergio Mendes. More recently, the *Lambada* topped the charts in the United States and Europe. The Lambada is in fact a

version of *carimbo,* a musical tradition of the northern regions, with strong Caribbean influences.

15 ● EMPLOYMENT

Brazil's economy is diverse. It has both an extensive raw material and agricultural sector as well as heavy industry and manufacturing. Brazil continues to be the largest coffee exporter in the world. It also produces sugar, soybeans, and corn for the export market. Many people in the northeast work in the sugar plantations and mills, while coffee laborers are found in the south. In addition, harvesting rubber, timber, and nuts provides a way of life for many inhabitants of the Amazon regions. Of all the South American countries, Brazil has been the most successful in exporting its manufactured products.

A significant proportion of urban Brazilians rely on small-scale, informal economic activities to survive. Women, for example, might become seamstresses or street vendors. A great many young women from the *favelas* (urban slums) find employment as servants in middle-class homes.

16 ● SPORTS

Soccer, popular throughout Latin America, is close to a national obsession in Brazil. The soccer stadium in Rio de Janeiro seats 200,000 people and is the largest stadium in the world. It is more than one mile (1.6 kilometers) in diameter, and has a nine-foot (three-meter) moat to keep the fans from running onto the field to disturb the soccer players or the officials. Brazil has won more World Cups than any other country. Its most famous soccer player, Pele, is a popular and highly regarded figure. It has been suggested that he might run for president of Brazil.

Volleyball is also very popular. The Brazilian men's volleyball team won the gold medal at the Barcelona Olympics in 1992, defeating the Netherlands.

17 ● RECREATION

In Rio de Janeiro and other seaside cities, the primary form of recreation is beach-going, including sunbathing. Brazil is the nation with the largest coastline in the world. People from all social and economic backgrounds flock to the beaches in the summer.

Samba schools are an important source of recreation in the *favelas* (urban slums). Similar to a community or neighborhood club, samba schools work all year long to prepare for Carnival festivities. They teach dancing, create costumes, and write songs for the annual Carnival song competition.

Televised soap operas are extremely popular with Brazilians of all social classes. *Telenovelas,* as they are called, are broadcast in the evenings and attract a huge following. Brazilian soap operas are so popular that they are successfully exported to other Latin American countries.

18 ● CRAFTS AND HOBBIES

A rich tradition of folk art and handicrafts arises from different regions in Brazil. In the mining region of Minas Gerais, goldsmithing and jewelry are the local art forms. Gemstones such as diamonds, opals, sapphires, and rubies are produced in Brazil. A popular piece of jewelry throughout Brazil is the *figa*. It is a pendant of a hand with the thumb between the first and index fingers— the symbol of good luck.

A unique traditional art form originates from the San Francisco River. This river was once believed to hold evil spirits. Nineteenth-century boaters took to carving fierce-looking figureheads, called *carrancas,* on their boats. These carvings were thought to provide protection from spirits and ward off bad luck. While most boaters no longer believe in these superstitions, many boaters still carry carrancas.

19 ● SOCIAL PROBLEMS

A serious social problem in Brazil is the number of homeless children living on the streets. It has been estimated that as many as eight to twelve million street children live in desperate poverty. Street children as young as seven and eight years old have been abandoned by parents who are too poor to provide for them. Drug abuse and glue-sniffing are serious problems among this group of young people. Street children are forced to resort to stealing, pickpocketing, and prostitution to survive. Although children have full protection under the law, thousands of street children have been murdered by Brazilian police. Many "death squads" were hired by shop owners who believed that the problem of street children could only be solved by eliminating them. In response, many community groups and the children themselves have organized to raise awareness of children's rights.

20 ● BIBLIOGRAPHY

Devine, Elizabeth, and Nancy L. Braganti. *The Traveler's Guide to Latin American Customs and Manners.* New York: St. Martins Press, 1988.

Lukins, Sheila. *Sheila Lukins All Around the World Cookbook.* New York: Workman, 1994.

Rojas-Lombardi, Felipe. *The Traveler's Guide to Latin American Customs and Manners.* New York: St. Martins Press, 1991.

Taylor, Edwin. *Insight Guides: Brazil.* Boston: Houghton Mifflin Company, 1995.

Weel, Thomas E. *Area Handbook for Brazil.* Washington, D.C.: American University: 1975.

WEBSITES

Brazilian Embassy, Washington, D.C. [Online] Available http://www.brasil.emb.nw.dc.us/, 1998.

Interknowledge Corporation. [Online] Available http://www.interknowledge.com/brazil/, 1998.

World Travel Guide. [Online] Available http://www.wtgonline.com/country/br/gen.html, 1998.

Afro-Brazilians

PRONUNCIATION: AH-frow brah-ZILL-yuhns
LOCATION: Brazil
POPULATION: About 16 million
LANGUAGE: Portuguese with some African terms
RELIGION: Afro-Brazilian sects such as Condomble; spiritualist sects

1 ● INTRODUCTION

Brazilians of African origin comprise nearly 10 percent of the total population of Brazil. As in the United States, their arrival can be traced back to the slave trade of the mid-1500s. It is estimated that nearly 4 million slaves were shipped to Brazil from Africa. This is higher than the estimated 600,000 slaves that were transported to the United States. Consequently, their cultural heritage is pervasive: Afro-Brazilian cooking customs and religion, for example, are practiced by Brazilians of all races and ethnic backgrounds.

Brazilian law prohibits discrimination on the basis of race. There is little open tension between people of different races in Brazil. However, there is subtle racial discrimination. For example, few Afro-Brazilians attend college and they have more difficulty finding good-paying jobs.

2 ● LOCATION

The population of Brazil is 162 million. There are indigenous Indians in the Amazon River region; immigrants from Europe, the Middle East, and Japan; and Afro-Brazilians. These ethnic groups have intermarried. As a result, the percentage of the population that considers itself to be Afro-Brazilian or black in the national census has declined, while the percentage of those who consider themselves brown has increased. This has been called the "bleaching" of Brazil.

Both sugar and cacao (plant whose seeds are used to make chocolate) were produced in Bahia, a state in northeastern Brazil. Bahia became the port of arrival for many slaves, and the center of Afro-Brazilian culture. In fact, most Bahia Brazilians are Afro-Brazilians. As of the late 1990s, Afro-Brazilians lived throughout the country. Many live in the major cities of Rio de Janeiro and São Paulo.

3 ● LANGUAGE

The official language of Brazil is Portuguese. Afro-Brazilians also speak Portuguese. They learned it to communicate with European Brazilians and with other Afro-Brazilians. Some words, such as *samba* (a Brazilian dance), have their roots in African languages. In Afro-Brazilian religion, the original African names of deities (gods), ceremonies, and dances are still used.

4 ● FOLKLORE

One of the most revered historical figures is Zumbi, a rebel slave leader. Many Afro-Brazilians celebrate November 20, the date on which Zumbi jumped off a cliff to avoid being captured by government forces.

5 ● RELIGION

Afro-Brazilian religions are popular with blacks and whites alike in Brazil. Some groups follow traditional African religious practices. An example is *Condomble*, a religion brought by the Yoruba people of Nigeria when they came to Brazil as slaves. Based in the state of Bahia, Condomble followers worship many different gods and goddesses of nature. One is *Iemanja,* the goddess of the sea. Condomble services, conducted late at night, feature pulsating drums and rhythmic music that encourage followers to reach a trancelike state.

Umbanda is a religion that combines African and non-African religious influences. It is common for the services to be led by a priestess. Followers of Umbanda invite spirits into their bodies as part of the services. Umbanda has many members in Rio de Janeiro, São Paulo, and Salvador.

6 ● MAJOR HOLIDAYS

In the state of Bahia, Afro-Brazilian festivals are celebrated. On February 2, people in the city of Salvador celebrate the Condomble goddess of the sea, Iemanja. Gifts and offerings are made to Iemanja and are floated out to sea in small, handmade sailboats. These offerings are usually sent by fishermen's wives in the hope that the goddess will protect the fishermen and ensure calm waters. Condomble rhythmic music accompanies the ceremonies.

An annual Afro-Brazilian festival to celebrate the liberation of slaves is held in the city of Cachoeira in the center of the country. Dancing, music, and prayer remind Afro-Brazilians of their slave ancestors.

All Brazilians celebrate *Carnival* during the week before the Christian observance of Lent begins.

7 ● RITES OF PASSAGE

Major life transitions, such as birth, puberty, and death, are marked by ceremo-

Cynthia Bassett

Afro-Brazilian boys with a Brazilian man.

music is incorporated into their traditional sports, *capoeira* (a martial art), and into religious services. Most Afro-Brazilians are deeply religious and these beliefs pervade every aspect of their lives. It is common, for example, for food and candles to be left on street corners as offerings to spirits.

9 ● LIVING CONDITIONS

Many Afro-Brazilians live in poverty in the urban slums that surround the major cities of São Paulo and Rio de Janeiro. Many of these slums, called *favelas,* are on steep hillsides. The first people to settle in these areas chose homes at the base of the hillside, which is more accessible and is likely to have electricity and running water. Further up the hillside are newer, less accessible communities. Pathways between houses are narrow and cramped. Often, large families live in a one-room dwelling. The lack of running water and accumulation of sewage in these crowded areas create health problems for residents. Clinics and other health care facilities, when they exist, are overcrowded and poorly equipped. The favelas surrounding Rio de Janeiro are also likely to flood. Heavy rains carry garbage down the hillsides and create landslides that wash away flimsy housing.

nies appropriate to each Afro-Brazilian's religious tradition.

8 ● RELATIONSHIPS

Afro-Brazilians are outgoing and gregarious. They speak animatedly and use a variety of hand gestures for emphasis. Afro-Brazilians are also accustomed to close personal contact. Women often walk hand-in-hand down the street. Male friends greet each other with a hug.

Music has been incorporated into many aspects of Afro-Brazilian life. Samba clubs that rehearse for Carnival are an important form of social organization. In addition,

10 ● FAMILY LIFE

Not everyone goes through a formal wedding in Brazil. Long-term relationships between couples who live together are common and socially accepted. This practice, known as *amasiado,* is also common among Afro-Brazilians. Couples in amasiado are viewed as married by the community. They may have children together without fear of being shunned.

Recipe

Feijoada

Ingredients

1 pound (2 cups) black beans, rinsed
¾ pound pork loin, butt, or shoulder
¼ pound bacon
½ pound smoked pork sausages
1 large yellow onion, chopped
2 ounces dried beef, chopped (optional)
3 garlic cloves, minced
6 green onions including tops, chopped
½ cup chopped parsley
2 bay leaves, crushed
1½ Tablespoons dried oregano
Parsley for garnish
Rice

Directions

1. Place the beans in a pot, cover with several inches of water, and soak overnight. Drain.
2. Return beans to pot, cover with three inches of water, and simmer until beans are tender (about 2 to 2½ hours); check periodically to be sure there is enough liquid. Add more water if necessary.
3. While the beans are cooking, preheat the oven to 375°F to roast the meats.
4. Dice the pork and the bacon into ½-inch cubes.
5. Place the pork, bacon, sausages, and chopped yellow onion in a large baking pan. Roast until well done. Check after 40 minutes, and remove the sausages if they are cooked through. All the meats should be well-done after one hour.
6. Cut the sausages into rounds and add them, the dried beef, bacon, and pork to the beans.
7. Add all the seasonings and green onions to the pot, and simmer for 30 minutes.
8. Garnish with parsley and serve with rice.

Adapted from Cusick, Heidi Haughy. *Soul and Spice: African Cooking in the Americas.* San Francisco: Chronicle Books, 1995.

The extended family provides assistance and support. Godparents, appointed when a child is christened, take their role and responsibilities seriously.

11 ●CLOTHING

There are regional differences in dress in Brazil. In the largely Afro-Brazilian region of Bahia, black women known as *Baianas* dress in clothing inspired by eighteenth century attire. Colorful, full-length skirts are worn with delicately embroidered white blouses, sometimes worn off the shoulder. Baianas also wear scarves or turbans wrapped tightly around their heads.

Brightly colored beads are worn by both men and women. These beads have religious symbolic meaning. The color of the beads reflects the African Condomble god that is special to the wearer, known as the person's *orixa*.

12 ●FOOD

Afro-Brazilian food combines African, Portuguese, and indigenous (native) ingredients and cooking traditions. African peppers and spices are now grown in the tropical northeastern state of Bahia. They are widely used in Afro-Brazilian cooking. *Dende* oil is extracted from an African palm grown in Brazil. Dende is used to make moqueca, a spicy mix of sautéed shrimp, tomato, and coconut milk.

The most distinctive Afro-Brazilian dish is *feijoada,* a black bean and pork stew, traditionally cooked in an African-style earthenware pot. Feijoada is considered the national dish of Brazil. Brazilian slaves created feijoada using the discarded pieces of pork (such as the tail, snout, and feet) they were given by their owners. These were stewed slowly with spices and beans. This dish was so tasty that it was soon copied by the slave owners. Feijoada is now made with prime cuts of pork and beef.

13 ● EDUCATION

Brazil has a serious problem of illiteracy (people unable to read or write). Approximately 20 percent of the Brazilian population is illiterate. Many others have only a rudimentary ability to read. The schools in the poorer neighborhoods where many Afro-Brazilians live have limited resources, and the quality of education is poor. Many Afro-Brazilian children don't attend school because they must begin work at a young age to help the family make ends meet. The low level of education most Afro-Brazilian children receive makes it difficult for them to find employment as young adults.

14 ● CULTURAL HERITAGE

Most of the slaves brought to Brazil from Africa were illiterate. Slave owners pre-ferred to keep it that way. As a result, an oral tradition of storytelling and history became very important in Afro-Brazilian culture. Family histories, stories, and myths continue to be passed down through successive generations.

Brazil's music traditions draw heavily from traditional African instruments, rhythm, and dance. Samba music, now popular around the world, is a direct descendant of African music. Afro-Brazilian music accompanies *afoxes,* dance groups that perform to music of the Condomble religion.

15 ● EMPLOYMENT

Brazil is the fourth-largest country in the world. Work varies by region. In the northeast, cattle-raising and ranching are important activities. In the southeast, sugarcane, cotton, and coffee are grown and exported. Many Afro-Brazilians work as field hands on ranches and large plantations. This is hard work and does not pay very well. In addition, many field workers must live away from their families at harvest time.

Brazil also has industry and manufacturing. Autos, shoes, textiles, and electronic equipment are all made in Brazil. The manufacturing sector does not generate enough employment for the millions of urban *favela* (slum) dwellers. Many favela residents work as self-employed street vendors or develop home-based enterprises. Many women, for example, work as seamstresses or hairstylists in their homes.

16 ● SPORTS

One of the most famous soccer players in the world is Pele (1940–), an Afro-Brazilian. (Pele's full name is Edson Arantes do

Nascimento.) Pele led the Brazil national team to World Cup championships in 1958, 1962, and 1970. He is so popular that some people think he should run for president of Brazil. Everyone in Brazil plays and watches soccer. The soccer stadium in Rio de Janeiro seats 200,000 people and is the largest stadium in the world.

A more distinctive Afro-Brazilian activity is *capoeira,* a martial art that is more like dancing than fighting. Brought over by slaves from Angola, this form of foot-fighting was banned by slave owners. In order to disguise this practice, slaves transformed foot-fighting into a rhythmic gymnastic dance form. Accompanied by music, capoeira dancers gracefully use arm and leg motions, designed to barely miss the opponent. Well-aimed high kicks skim over the head of the other fighter.

17 ● RECREATION

Most entertainment revolves around music and dancing. Preparations for Carnival can begin up to six months in advance of the festival. Samba schools are popular in the *favelas* (slums). They provide an outlet and form of recreation for many Afro-Brazilian young people.

The other central form of recreation for Afro-Brazilian youths is practicing the national sport—soccer. Brazil is probably the country most enthusiastic about soccer in the world. Both in urban and rural areas, playing soccer is the preferred after-school activity.

18 ● CRAFTS AND HOBBIES

In Bahia, the African tradition of cooking in ceramic pots is followed. As a consequence,

functional clay pots can be found in many markets. Intricately handcarved rosewood and handmade lace are art forms passed down from generation to generation. Banana leaf fibers are sometime used in place of thread for lacemaking.

In January in Bahia, colorful ribbons are sold that are believed to be good luck. These ribbons must be received as gifts—a person should never buy one for himself or herself. The ribbons are tied around the wrist with multiple knots. The wearer makes a wish as each knot is tied. When the ribbons fall off from daily wear, it is believed that the wishes will be granted.

Many Afro-Brazilian arts and crafts are closely linked to African religious traditions. Many objects used in Condomble rituals are produced by skilled goldsmiths in Bahia. Charms and other forms of jewelry traditionally once worn around the waist by slave women in Brazil are still popular today.

19 ● SOCIAL PROBLEMS

Drug trafficking and related violence are serious problems that are on the rise in *favelas* (slums). Organized gangs sell drugs and engage in other types of crime. In part, this is the result of high unemployment among youths.

Teenagers in the favelas probably did not finish high school, and their employment prospects are bleak. The lure of easy money by selling drugs has drawn many young people into this dangerous activity. Conflicts between competing gangs often lead to violence.

20 ● BIBLIOGRAPHY

Cusick, Heidi Haughy. *Soul and Spice: African Cooking in the Americas.* San Francisco: Chronicle Books, 1995.

Devine, Elizabeth, and Nancy L. Briganti. *The Travelers' Guide to Latin American Customs and Manners.* New York: St. Martins Press, 1988.

Page, Joseph A. *The Brazilians.* New York: Addison Wesley, 1995.

Reynolds, Edward. *Stand the Storm: A History of the Atlantic Slave Trade.* London: Allison and Busby, 1985.

Rojas-Lombardi, Felipe. *The Art of South American Cooking.* New York: HarperCollins, 1991.

Taylor, Edwin. *Insight Guides: Brazil.* Boston: Houghton Mifflin Company, 1995.

WEBSITES

Brazilian Embassy, Washington, D.C. [Online] Available http://www.brasil.emb.nw.dc.us/, 1998.

Interknowledge Corporation. [Online] Available http://www.interknowledge.com/brazil/, 1998.

World Travel Guide. [Online] Available http://www.wtgonline.com/country/br/gen.html, 1998.

Kayapos

PRONUNCIATION: kay-AH-pohs
LOCATION: Brazil (Amazon jungle)
POPULATION: A few thousand
LANGUAGE: Kayapo
RELIGION: Traditional indigenous beliefs

1 ● INTRODUCTION

The Kayapo Indians are one of the main Amerindian (native) groups that remain in the rain forest around the Amazon River in Brazil. The Kayapos resisted assimilation (absorption into the dominant culture) and were known traditionally as fierce warriors.

They raided enemy tribes and sometimes fought among themselves.

Their first steady contact with Europeans did not occur until the 1950s. Since then, they have had contact with squatters (settlers with no land rights), loggers, miners, and eventually Brazilian government officials. Logging and mining, particularly for gold, have posed threats to the Kayapos' traditional way of life. Other threats have included agricultural activities and cattle-ranching in cleared-out sections of the jungle. The increasing destruction of the rain forest threatens the delicate balance between humans, plants, and animals successfully maintained for thousands of years by Amazon Indians such as the Kayapos.

2 ● LOCATION

When the Portuguese conquerors first arrived in Brazil, there were about five million Amerindians. Today there are only about 200,000, of which a few thousand are Kayapos. They live along the Xingu River in the eastern part of the Amazon rain forest, in several scattered villages. Their lands consist of tropical rain forest and savanna (grassland). The Amazon basin, which includes the Amazon River and its tributaries such as the Xingu, is sometimes referred to as Amazonia. It includes parts of Venezuela, Colombia, Ecuador, and Peru.

3 ● LANGUAGE

The great diversity of Amerindian languages is partly due to groups of people living considerable distances from each other. Because of their relative isolation, groups developed distinct mythologies, religious customs, and languages. Even quite small groups such as the Kayapos are divided into smaller tribes with their own chiefs, although they all speak the Kayapo language. The pop star Sting (1951–) made the struggles of the Kayapo known to a wider world. One Kayapo chief, Raoni, left his Amazon homeland for a time and traveled widely with Sting. Another Kayapo who traveled with the musician was the panther-hunter N'goire.

4 ● FOLKLORE

There is an interesting legend among the Kayapos who live along a lagoon. They say that if one rises at dawn and looks across the lagoon, one can see the ghost of a white man on horseback galloping along the shore. This ghostly rider is said to wear a full suit of armor, rather like a European knight, or perhaps a Portuguese conqueror.

The Kayapos believe their ancestors learned how to live communally from social insects such as bees. This is why mothers and children paint each other's bodies with patterns that look like animal or insect markings, including those of bees.

The flamboyant Kayapo headdress with feathers radiating outward represents the universe. Its shaft is a symbol for the cotton rope by which the first Kayapo, it is said, descended from the sky. Kayapo fields and villages are built in a circle to reflect the Kayapo belief in a round universe.

5 ● RELIGION

The Kayapos believe that at death a person goes to the village of the dead, where people sleep during the day and hunt at night. There, old people become younger and children become older. In that village in the afterlife, Kayapos believe they have their own traditional assembly building. Kayapo women, it is thought, are permitted only short visits to deliver food to their male relatives.

6 ● MAJOR HOLIDAYS

Special days for the Kayapos revolve around the seasons. In the Amazon, these are the dry season and the rainy season. Kayapo ceremonies are also linked to their holidays. For example, an initiation rite is held when a boy reaches puberty or when he receives, as a small boy, his special ancestral name. The important dry-season celebration called *Bemp* (after a local fish) also includes marriage rites as well as initiation and naming ceremonies. Kayapos do not divide their time into secular and religious occasions. The religious, natural, social, and festive elements are all interconnected.

7 ● RITES OF PASSAGE

When children are born, the marriage ties between a husband and wife are formalized. A man may have two or three wives. Young children receive special ancestral names. Naming ceremonies are regarded as an important means of helping the child develop social ties and an identity as a Kayapo. The naming ceremonies are held in each dry or rainy season. Other seasonal rites include special dances or ceremonies related to the crops the Kayapos grow.

8 ● RELATIONSHIPS

The Kayapos have a traditionally hospitable way of greeting visitors to their homes. Food is prepared by the women, and a bed made of bamboo is laid out for a guest. On occasions body paint is worn (usually geometric designs in black or red paint). Adornments such as shell earrings or brightly colored feathers decorate the head.

Ceremonial life is very important and continues year-round. Kayapos are often either in the midst of a ceremony or making preparations for the next one.

9 ● LIVING CONDITIONS

The Kayapos live in thatched-roof huts without room divisions. The thatch for the roofs is made of palm leaves. The huts are quite roomy and large enough for an entire family. Instead of using mattresses, the bedding usually consists of hammocks. These are much cooler and more comfortable in a jungle environment.

Health protection is achieved through the use of medicinal roots and herbs. The Kayapos also have medicine men.

For transport the Kayapos use canoes to travel long distances in the Amazon. They can also trek for days or weeks at a time.

10 ● FAMILY LIFE

Teenage women of the village are prime candidates for marriage. They usually select partners who are suggested by their families. Only after the birth of a child is the marriage formalized. Traditional birth control has been discouraged in recent years in order to increase the tribe's numbers.

The Kayapos live in large family groups in villages. The women harvest the family's garden for vegetables. They also prepare body paint with the help of their children. Color dyes are created from mixed fruits and charcoal. The men hunt and fish. Every husband will usually have between two and three wives, each with several children.

11 ● CLOTHING

Traditionally men cover their lower abdomen with sheaths. The most striking ornamental addition to their attire is a light wooden lip disk about two-and-one-half inches (six centimeters) in diameter. The disk stretches their lower lip out to produce the Kayapos' extraordinary and very distinctive appearance. The usage of the lip disk is dying out among the younger men, who find it uncomfortable. In fact, younger men often wear Western-style shorts. This is due to increasing contact with Westernized Brazilians who have come to the Amazon to log, farm, or mine gold.

A Kayapo chief wears ceremonial feathers as part of his headdress. A headdress made out of bright golden-yellow feathers looks like the rays of the sun. Particular family links are indicated by the use of matching parrot feathers. The feathers signify initiation into adulthood. Other ornaments include beads, cotton bands, or shells, which women also wear.

Girls and boys wear colored cloth bands of various bright colors. These are tied and sometimes knotted below the waist or criss-crossed across the chest. They also wear ornaments such as beaded necklaces, wristbands, and armbands. Young Kayapos are usually barefoot. Some Kayapo chiefs occasionally wear Western-style thonged rubber sandals.

Body paint is an important addition for men, women, and children alike. It is not a casual form of make-up. The specific markings and occasions for wearing it are linked to particular rituals and activities.

12 ● FOOD

Fish is a main source of protein in the Kayapos' diet. Wild fruits and Brazil nuts are eaten. Vegetables are harvested, and animals such as monkey and turtle are hunted. Some animals are eaten rarely except during festivals. Kayapos are skilled hunters. They use blowguns and darts dipped in a type of poison called *curare,* which instantly paralyzes an animal.

Due to greater contact with the world outside their own culture, Kayapos are changing their diet. They can now purchase rice, beans, cookies, sugar, and milk from village stores that have cropped up in the Amazon to supply loggers, miners, and farmers.

13 ● EDUCATION

Most Kayapos continue to teach their young people the skills necessary to survive in the rain forest. These include hunting, fishing, trekking, and making and using canoes. Growing vegetables, beading, body paint preparations, and cooking are skills Kayapo girls are expected to know. Some missionaries in the Xingu River area have attempted to offer a more Western-style education, including reading and writing. However, many Kayapos have been extremely wary of accepting this type of schooling. They are concerned that their children will be lost to them and will forget traditional skills.

Recently, in a protected area of the Xingu Reservation, a school was set up to teach children from various tribes. They learn reading, writing, and arithmetic and receive information about the ways of people outside their own culture.

14 ● CULTURAL HERITAGE

Completing a full cycle of festivals is essential to Kayapo culture. Singing, chanting, and dancing are important to Kayapo life. Men and women also sing as they go out on a hunt or work the land. They use a type of rattle or *maraca* and sticks to beat rhythms.

15 ● EMPLOYMENT

Many Kayapos were pressured into taking part in gold mining in the Amazon River in the 1980s and 1990s. Gold mining is hard and often dangerous work. In addition, the mercury used in mining seriously pollutes the rivers.

Kayapo chiefs are helping direct their people in a variety of activities including harvesting nuts, fruits, and vegetables, as well as the construction of modern housing for recently arrived settlers. This means that the Kayapos no longer restrict themselves to traditional hunting and fishing. Because they earn money for their work they can purchase goods they did not have before.

16 ● SPORTS

Traditionally the Kayapos did not develop sporting skills separately from skills that were useful for work. Hunting, fishing, and trekking, for example, have now become sporting activities in white society. In Kayapo society they are survival skills; their recreational value is secondary. Some Kayapos obtain great pleasure from teaching these skills to younger members of the tribe. Acquiring prowess in any or all of them is a source of pride.

Kayapo children enjoy swimming along the shores of the Xingu River. Until the 1990s, this river was completely unpolluted. Villagers who have had more contact with people outside their own culture have learned to play soccer.

17 ● RECREATION

Storytelling is a significant aspect of Kayapo life. It is a way of transmitting Kayapo legends and history as well as a way of preserving the identity of a people. It is also a form of entertainment. Mostly, however, it forms part of the rituals that give structure and meaning to the life of the Kayapos. Storytelling is interwoven with dance rituals and ceremonies. These follow a definite cycle, linked to nature and to the changing seasons.

18 ● CRAFTS AND HOBBIES

Kayapos make beautiful beaded necklaces, some a brilliant blue or yellow. They also make bracelets and earrings using shells or stones, and headdresses made from the brightly colored feathers of various Amazon birds. The Kayapos are skilled in preparing and applying intricate designs as body paint. They weave sturdy and flexible hammocks. They also make their own canoes as well as fishing and hunting implements such as spears, clubs, blow guns, arrows, and darts.

19 ● SOCIAL PROBLEMS

Many activities in the Amazon threaten a way of life the Kayapos want to preserve. Poverty, a population explosion, and an unequal system of land ownership have driven many people into the Amazon region in search of land. Deforestation of the Amazon is occurring at a rapid rate. This destruction is accelerated by the activities of cattle ranchers who grow beef for export to fast food chains in the United States. Land that is over-grazed by cattle quickly becomes completely barren.

Commercial loggers have also contributed to the destruction of the Amazon jungle by providing tropical hardwood for construction in Japan, Western Europe, and the United States. The destruction of so many trees contributes to carbon dioxide pollution in the atmosphere and, therefore, to global warming.

Mining is yet another threat to the way of life of the Kayapos and other Amazon peoples. Smelting furnaces need charcoal, and much of it is taken from irreplaceable virgin forest. A harmful byproduct of the Amazon gold rush has been the introduction of new diseases to which the Kapayos have no natural immunity. Also, mercury poisoning affects Amerindian communities downstream from mining activities. Mercury released into the atmosphere is another form of pollution.

Some Amerindian groups, including the Kayapos, have been attacked and murdered in the search for land. Others have had their land forcibly taken away. In addition, many have had to work for very low wages in miserable conditions in some of the frontier towns.

The Kayapos are working hard to find ways of confronting the problems posed by the arrival of people who do not appreciate the delicate ecological balance of the Amazon region.

20 ● BIBLIOGRAPHY

National Geographic Index. Washington, D.C.: National Geographic Society, January–June 1984.

Sting, and Jean-Pierre Dutilleux. *Jungle Stories: The Fight for the Amazon.* Paris and London: Barrie and Jenkins, 1989.

WEBSITES

Brazilian Embassy, Washington, D.C. [Online] Available http://www.brasi1.emb.nw.dc.us/, 1998.

Interknowledge Corporation. [Online] Available http://www.interknowledge.com/brazil/, 1998.

World Travel Guide. [Online] Available http://www.wtgonline.com/country/br/gen.html, 1998.

Xavante

PRONUNCIATION: ZHAH-vahn-theh
ALTERNATE NAMES: Crixá; Curixá; Puxití; Tapacuá
LOCATION: Brazil
POPULATION: Population estimates not available
LANGUAGE: Gê
RELIGION: Indigenous beliefs

1 ● INTRODUCTION

In the late sixteenth century, Portuguese colonizers (foreigners who occupied and ruled the area) in Brazil named the Amerindians that inhabited the north of the Goiás region *Xavante,* for unknown reasons. The name the Amerindians used for themselves was Auwe, meaning people. The Xavante were numerous, strong, and rebellious. They resisted the invasion of their lands by attacking mining camps and raiding the settlers' cattle and crops. The Portuguese government managed to dominate them for the first time in 1784, when the Xavante were put into mission villages surrounded by military guards. Because the Xavante had resisted invasion and domination so fiercely, colonial governors called the period between 1784 and 1788 the "pacification" (when the Xavante were reduced to submission). Life in mission villages was not kind to the Xavante. A group of surviving Xavante eventually abandoned the missions and settled in eastern Mato Grosso. From that time until 1946, the Xavante repelled any attempt at contact by white people.

In the 1940s, the Brazilian government decided to encourage settlement on Xavante lands. Since then, the Xavante have made adjustments to deal with the settlers, who have different customs. However, the Xavante continue to preserve a strong sense of identity. Until 1988 the Xavante, like all Amerindians in Brazil, were not allowed to vote or make decisions for themselves. All Brazilian Amerindians are now regarded as full citizens.

2 ● LOCATION

The Xavante live in the state of Mato Grosso, in southwestern Brazil. It is the size of France, Germany, and Great Britain combined. *Mato Grosso* in Portuguese means "dense forest." Xavante villages used to be found at intervals for the entire length of the Rio das Montes (Montes River). When the land was sold to private companies during the 1960s, the new settlers pushed the Xavante to the vast wasteland of eastern Mato Grosso. The forest has been destroyed. Xavante land is referred to as savanna (grassland), which they prefer because open country offers more exciting hunting prospects. The savanna is not suit-

XAVANTE

0   250   500   750 Miles

0   250   500   750 Kilometers

ATLANTIC OCEAN

BRAZIL

BOLIVIA

PARAGUAY

ATLANTIC OCEAN

São Luís

Teresina

Tocantins

Juàzeiro

Salvador

São Francisco

Cuiabá

Xingu

Goiânia

Brasília

Belo Horizonte

Vitória

Paraná

São Paulo

Rio de Janeiro

Asunción

Curitiba

Resistencia

Florianópolis

Paraná

Pôrto Alegre

Salto

known by the names Crixá, Curixá, Puxití, and Tapacuá. Understanding their language leads to a deeper understanding of their culture. *Ro was'té-di,* for example, is what the Xavante call local jungle. *Ro* means "country" and *was'té* means "bad." They make no secret of their dislike of anything that is not open savanna, which they call *ro pse-di* or *ro we-de: pse* means "good," and *we* means "pretty" or "beautiful."

4 ● FOLKLORE

The Xavante tradition is rich in legends that try to explain natural phenomena and their history. Many legends highlight the value of the qualities the Xavante appreciate most—strength and courage. One tells of two young men who had the power to make new varieties of fruits grow, using only their words. But a time came when they started using their powers to frighten their friends. Finally, they were killed, and in the place where their blood was shed, two trees grew. The Xavante use the wood from those trees to make sticks that they place in their ears to protect themselves from dangers such as jaguars and bad dreams.

The Xavante believe that the stars are the eyes of heavenly people who are watching us from up above. It happened that once a young man fell in love with the beauty of a particular star. When he fell asleep, the star came to earth in the shape of a woman and found him. Their love grew, and so did the palm where they were sitting, taking them up to the sky. When the young man came back to earth, he told his family about his affair and then went back to heaven and stayed with his loved one forever.

able for growing crops because it is very poor country. Still, the Xavante prefer it to the tropical jungle.

Patches of tropical jungle exist all over their territory. These local jungles provide water and wild roots and fruits, which are the basis of the Xavante diet. Palms and other trees provide leaves and woods used to manufacture various artifacts.

3 ● LANGUAGE

The Xavante, though dispersed through a vast region, share a common language and culture. They are one of the Gê-speaking tribes of Amazonia. They have also been afterwards, as well as the whites and their towns. More detailed origin myths tell about people becoming human after being like animals. The beliefs and ceremonies of the Xavante revolve around their reverence for life and fertility.

6 ● MAJOR HOLIDAYS

Xavante holidays are full of joy and happiness. Some holidays are aimed at bringing back the good times, which are known as *Roweda*. Though in many of their holidays the men have a more active role than the women, some holidays have women as central figures. One of these is the ceremony of the naming of a child, in which many of the staged legends have women as protagonists. They tell about the female contributions to their cultural wealth.

7 ● RITES OF PASSAGE

The Xavante are divided into groups according to their ages—Babies; Not-Babies; Children; Boys and Girls; Bachelors; Young Men and Women; Mature Men and Women; and Elders. Passing from one group to the next is celebrated with special rites, songs, and dances. When a group reaches adolescence, the boys leave home and move into the Bachelors' hut. During this transition their ears are pierced and they take long baths in the river, receive presents, and take part in races. Through dramatic representations of legends, they learn the origins and significance of the new role they are about to take.

Among the Xavante, coupling is a process strictly regulated by laws. Marital relationships within families are discouraged. The marriage decisions are made mainly by

Laura Graham

A young girl removes urucum seeds from pods. Urucum is used in body paint and in other decorations.

5 ● RELIGION

Xavante are more concerned with change or discovery than with the question of creation. "The world was created because in the beginning there was nothing" was an explanation given to an interested academic. "Then Aiwamdzú came out of the earth. He was the creator and he was Xavante." By the time Aiwamdzú appeared, the earth already existed, but it was empty. The east—the beginning of the sky—had not been created yet. The north and the south were created

Laura Graham

When constructing a house, men put up the pole scaffold and women tie on the palm frond thatch.

parents. However, they do listen to their children and take their feelings into account.

8 ● RELATIONSHIPS

The Xavante are full of life. Their artistic, brightly-colored body painting, the joy and energy transmitted through their songs and dances, and the wisdom imparted through their rituals all communicate vitality and a commitment to survival.

The Xavante sense of community is evident in the way they organize their economy. They exchange goods and distribute their wealth to take care of both individual families and the entire tribe. This give-and-take system guarantees the survival of the entire group.

9 ● LIVING CONDITIONS

Since the middle of the twentieth century, the Xavante have ceased to be nomadic (wanderers who follow food sources). They now live in independent, horseshoe-shaped villages on the open savanna. The center of the horseshoe is the setting for meetings of the council of aldermen (representatives) where important decisions are made. Most Xavante live in "beehive" houses. Built by women, the round structures are made of sticks and cane and are covered with palm

Laura Graham

A father decorates his son before a ceremony.

also provides one of the few opportunities for women to go out and have a good time together.

It is quite common to find Xavante men married to more than one woman, a practice known as polygyny.

11 ● CLOTHING

Like many tribes of the eastern Brazil region, the Xavante originally went virtually naked. They decorated their bodies with an abundance of ornaments (such as earplugs), distinctive haircuts, body painting, and tattoos.

Traditionally, men always wore penissheaths from the moment they entered the Bachelors' hut. The sheath is a tiny conical spiral of palmito bark. It is worn over the folds of the foreskin, covering only the tip of the penis. Men would take it off only when urinating or having sex. Were it to fall off when they were running or bathing, it would be cause for great embarrassment.

Nowadays, though, men usually wear shorts, and most no longer wear their penissheaths or their ear-plugs. Women have taken to wearing clothes and even make-up when they can get it. In traditional Xavante communities, it was the men who did all the preening, but that has changed since contact with whites and with other tribes.

12 ● FOOD

The Xavante have a real passion for meat. The meat that is plentiful is that of deer and anteaters. Pigs, wild or domestic, steppe rats, monkeys, and armadillos, as well as most birds, are also part of their diet. Tur-

leaves all the way to the floor. Up to three families can share one house. Inside the houses, the light is perpetually dim, and the smoke and odor of cooking lingers while insects crawl or buzz around.

10 ● FAMILY LIFE

Women are the queens of Xavante homes. They build the houses, and inside they prepare the food and distribute it. Collecting, the most important economic activity, is primarily a woman's job. Though not regarded as a prestigious activity, it is essential to the household and the survival of the group. It tles are sought for their meat and their nourishing eggs.

Preferences aside, the Xavante live primarily on roots, nuts, and fruits, which are easier to acquire. The roots are boiled or roasted. Nuts and palmitos (edible shoots of a palm) are eaten year-round. Nuts, particularly babassú nuts, are a constant in the Xavante diet. Carob, *burití* (a fruit with a high vitamin-C content), and *piquí* are the most important fruits. The Xavante also eat honey anytime they catch sight of a beehive. As many bees are stingless, the Xavante simply climb the trees, open the hive, and eat the contents, bees and all.

13 ●EDUCATION

The level of formal education among the Xavante varies. In some villages only one or two of the younger men speak some basic Portuguese for the purpose of dealing with the outside world. In other villages most children and young Xavante are literate (able to read and write), and some have become teachers in their hometown.

Laura Graham

A man collects turtle eggs on a beach. Turtles are sought for their meat and their nourishing eggs.

The skills necessary to face life—such as learning how to overcome exhaustion, pain, and fear—are taught by the elders through traditional legends. Many bear the message: "Be strong and courageous, and multiply." The education of children is a shared responsibility. In the early years, the mother is the main figure. As they grow older, grandparents help to educate the girls. Boys are guided by their godfathers, a group of young men about ten years older.

14 ●CULTURAL HERITAGE

Music and dance are at the core of Xavante ceremonies. Groups of men sing from

morning through the day and the following night, hide gourd flutes for the girls to fetch, and beat time with rattles made of pigs' teeth. To make the melodies come to life, the Xavante choreograph dances in a series of highly formalized patterns. These are designed to inspire and delight both the performers and the spectators.

15 ●EMPLOYMENT

The Xavante practice shifting cultivation. Toward the end of the rainy season, a man fells an acre or two of trees and leaves them

Laura Graham

A Xavante runner carries a length of buriti palm in a log relay race.

to dry. Just before the next rainy season begins, he sets them on fire. The ashes add mineral nutrients to the soil. The Xavante plant crops that require virtually no tending, such as maize (corn), beans, and pumpkins. The primary basis of the Xavante's diet is wild roots, nuts, and fruits gathered in their wanderings.

Hunting is the passion of Xavante men. The traditional way of hunting is using darts with *curare* (a formula whose active ingredient comes from the sap of the vine *Strychnos toxifera*). It blocks nervous impulses to the muscles so they become flaccid (limp), and the animal simply falls to the ground. Modern Xavante hunt with guns.

Traditionally, fishing was also done with poison. Sap from forest vines dispersed through the water, paralyzing the breathing apparatus of the fish but leaving their meat edible. The introduction of metal hooks and nylon has simplified fishing a great deal.

16 ● SPORTS

The Xavante are superb runners. As often as once a week, teams of relay runners compete in a long race that may begin far out on the plain, ending with a dash into the village. Each runner carries a length of buriti palm weighing around 80 kilograms (175 pounds). They decorate their bodies with vegetable dyes and each ties a white cord around their neck, with the tufted ends in the front like a bow tie. The Xavante are reputed to be capable of catching game on foot.

In some communities, the Xavante have developed a passion for soccer. Everybody plays—young and old—and when all the men get tired of playing, the women take over.

17 ● RECREATION

Hunting provides not only a means of subsistence but also a source of entertainment. Xavante men spend hours planning treks and telling tales of fights and hunting exploits. Xavante men enjoy all aspects of hunting, especially since it allows them to make a public exhibition of their manliness.

Xavante ceremonies have been compared to classical ballet. Performers try to create a harmonious spectacle where beauty is most important. The Xavante word for "ceremony" is *dasïpse,* which translates as "something that makes oneself good." The performances are carefully prepared, enjoyed by players and spectators alike, and regarded as a major form of aesthetic expression.

18 ● CRAFTS AND HOBBIES

Among the first Xavante artifacts to become known to the outside world were the *uibro.* Characteristically used by young men, the uibro are war clubs that symbolize power. They are made from a young tree, with part of the root left as a knob at one end. The other end is sharpened to a point, and the club is exposed to the heat of the fire to make it hard.

Laura Graham

A young girl pretends to build a house. As modern development encroaches on the lands of the Xavante, their traditional way of life becomes harder to maintain.

Body painting is one of the most stunning art forms of the Xavante. Other crafts include making domestic objects out of wood, piranha teeth, and the claws of the great armadillo. Palm leaves and bark from trees are plaited (braided) to make most household utensils, such as baskets, mats, and fans.

19 ● SOCIAL PROBLEMS

Amerindian tribes in Brazil are still burdened by colonization. The groups that survived the European invasion and colonization of the Americas are now being pushed off their land by private companies. Contact with whites has also created the need for the Xavante to learn the national language and culture in order to function in the new, imposed way of life. However, education is not attainable by all. Many are left unable either to retain their traditional ways or to adapt to the new ones.

Nevertheless, the Xavante are recognized as one of the most forceful of the Brazilian tribes. They frequently send their representative to Brasilia (the Federal District of Brazil) to defend their rights and insist on better treatment. The Xavante Mario Juruna, the first Amerindian to become a deputy in Brazil's parliament, spoke of the dangers and the wishes of his people: "Indian wealth lies in customs and communal traditions and land which is sacred. Indians can and want to choose their own road, and this road is not civilization made by whites . . . . Indian civilization is more human. We do not want paternalistic protection [in the style of a more powerful father] from whites. Indians today . . . want political power."

20 ● BIBLIOGRAPHY

Bennett, Ross S., ed. *Lost Empires, Living Tribes.* Washington, D.C.: National Geographic Book Service, 1982.

Graham, Laura R. *Performing Dreams: Discourses of Immortality Among Xavante of Central Brazil.* Austin: University of Texas Press, 1995.

Maybury-Lewis, David. *Akwe-Shavante Society.* Oxford: Oxford University Press, 1974.

Steward, Julian Haynes, ed. *Handbook of South American Indians.* New York: Cooper Square, 1963

WEBSITES

Brazilian Embassy, Washington, D.C. [Online] Available http://www.brasil.emb.nw.dc.us/, 1998.

Interknowledge Corporation. [Online] Available http://www.interknowledge.com/brazil/, 1998.

World Travel Guide. [Online] Available http://www.wtgonline.com/country/br/gen.html, 1998.

Bulgaria

■ BULGARIANS 31

The people of Bulgaria are called Bulgarians. About 85 percent of the people trace their ancestry to Bulgaria. Turks account for about 10 percent of the total and Gypsies (Roma), a little more than 5 percent. To learn more about the Turks, see the chapter on Turkey in Volume 9; about the Gypsies, see the article on Roma in the chapter on Romania in Volume 7.

Bulgarians

PRONUNCIATION: buhl-GARE-ee-uhns

LOCATION: Bulgaria

POPULATION: 8.8 million (of whom 85 percent are ethnic Bulgarians)

LANGUAGE: Bulgarian

RELIGION: Eastern Orthodox; Islam; Protestant and Catholic minorities

1 ● INTRODUCTION

The first Bulgarian state (country with a government) was formed in AD 681. Over the following centuries, Bulgaria was ruled by three different royal families. In 1396, the Bulgarians were conquered by the Ottoman Turks, a Muslim people. They were ruled by the Turks for nearly five hundred years. Bulgaria finally became independent from the Turks near the end of the nineteenth century.

In 1944, troops from the Soviet Union entered the country and a Communist government was set up. Bulgaria was headed by a single leader—Todor Zhivkov—through nearly all of the communist era (1944–91). In 1991, Bulgaria elected its first non-Communist government.

Since 1991, Bulgaria has gone through a difficult period of political and economic change. But Bulgarians have not fought among themselves while adjusting to the changes. This is probably because most Bulgarians (about 85 percent) belong to a single ethnic group.

2 ● LOCATION

Bulgaria is located in the Balkan Peninsula in southeastern Europe. *Balkan* means "mountain" in Turkish. The Balkan Peninsula includes Albania, Greece, Bulgaria, Slovenia, Croatia, Macedonia, Yugoslavia, (Serbia and Montenegro), Bosnia and Herzegovina, and part of Turkey. Mountain

BULGARIANS

Russian. There are regional dialects, or variations, throughout the country.

Some common Bulgarian words are:

ENGLISH	BULGARIAN	PRONUNCIATION
hello	dobur den	DOH-bur den
goodbye	dovizhdane	doh-VEEZH-dan-eh
yes	da	dah
no	ne	neh

Basic number names are as follows:

ENGLISH	BULGARIAN	PRONUNCIATION
one	edno	ED-noh
two	dve	dvey
three	tri	tree
four	chetiri	cheh-TEH-rey
five	pet	pet
six	shtest	shest
seven	sedem	SEH-dehm
eight	osem	OH-sem
nine	devet	deh-VEHT
ten	deset	deh-SEHT

4 ● FOLKLORE

A favorite character of Bulgarian folktales for hundreds of years has been Sly Peter. He is known for outwitting others.

The *hajduks* (HIGH-dukes) are legendary freedom fighters, similar to the English folk hero Robin Hood.

Here are some Bulgarian proverbs that illustrate the practical side of the Bulgarian spirit:

A dog barks to guard itself, not the village.
Work left for later is finished by the Devil.

ranges, including the Balkan Mountains, cover much of the peninsula. More than half of Bulgaria is covered by the Balkan Mountains. North of the Balkans is a plain leading to the Danube River. The Black Sea lies to the east.

Approximately 85 percent (7.5 million) of Bulgaria's 8.8 million people are ethnic Bulgarians. Ethnic Turks account for about 10 percent of the total and Gypsies, a little more than 5 percent.

3 ● LANGUAGE

Bulgarian is the official language of Bulgaria and is spoken by everyone. Bulgarian is a South Slavic language. It is written with the Cyrillic alphabet, which is also used for

5 ● RELIGION

The Bulgarians are not strongly religious people. Religious observance is often a matter of tradition, rather than deeply held personal belief. The major organized

EPD Photos

The Bulgarian language uses the Cyrillic alphabet as shown in this Bulgarian newspaper.

religion in Bulgaria is Eastern Orthodox Christianity.

6 ● MAJOR HOLIDAYS

Official holidays include New Year (January 1 and 2); Liberation Day (March 3), which commemorates Bulgarian independence from the Ottoman Empire; Easter Monday (in March or April); Labor Day (May 1); Day of Letters (May 24), in honor of Bulgarian education and culture; and Christmas (December 25 and 26).

Many Bulgarians also observe the holy days of the Eastern Orthodox calendar, including a number of saints' days.

7 ● RITES OF PASSAGE

Religious ceremonies marking important life events include christening, marriage, the blessing of a new house, and the funeral service. By tradition, people usually avoid singing, dancing, or music-making for at least six months after the death of a relative or close friend.

It is customary for flower bouquets to have an odd number of flowers for all occasions except funerals. Funeral bouquets have an even number of blooms.

8 ● RELATIONSHIPS

Bulgarians greet each other by shaking hands. Close female friends may kiss one another on the cheek. The most common formal greetings are *Kak ste?* ("How are you?") and *Zdraveite* ("Hello"). The more informal forms, used with friends, relatives, and coworkers, are *Kak si?* and *Zdrasti* or *Zdrave*.

When talking, Bulgarians tend to stand or sit closer together than Westerners. They speak in louder voices and touch each other more often.

The Bulgarian gestures for "yes" and "no" often confuse people from other countries. For "Yes," one shakes one's head from side to side. "No" is signaled by one or two nods up and down (often accompanied by clicking the tongue).

9 ● LIVING CONDITIONS

Over 75 percent of Bulgarians own their own homes. Traditionally, Bulgarians lived in single-story houses made of wood, mud bricks, or stone and plaster. Most of these have been replaced by two-story brick houses with a plaster finish. In the cities, most people live in apartments rather than houses.

As protection against the cold winters in the North, some houses are built mostly underground. Only the roof shows above ground level.

AP/Wide World Photos

Folk dancers in traditional dress perform at a festival.

10 ● FAMILY LIFE

The three-generation extended family is common in rural areas. In cities, the nuclear family (just parents and their children) is usual. Single adults are expected to live with their parents until they marry. In addition, many young married couples live with one set of parents until they can afford their own home. Elderly parents are often cared for by their children.

Families in the cities usually have no more than two children each. Those in the country are often somewhat larger. Children are very close to their grandparents, who often provide child care so parents can work.

Bulgarian women have always had much freedom and responsibility. By the late 1990s, women made up almost half of the Bulgarian labor force. They held the same types of jobs as men.

11 ● CLOTHING

Bulgarians wear modern Western-style clothing. They dress with care, even for informal occasions. Parents choose their children's outfits with great care. They seem to like imported and hand-knitted clothing. Many women knit sweaters for their families.

Traditional Bulgarian costumes are worn only at festivals and for dance performances. They are colorful, with embroidered white shirts or blouses and fancy embroidered vests. Red is used in almost all costumes, either as a background color or in the embroidery. Black is also used in many costumes.

Recipe

Bulgarian Als-Ankara

Ingredients
Fruit juice (preferably a thick juice)
Vanilla ice cream or fruit sherbet
Fresh mint leaves

Directions
1. Place a small scoop of ice cream or sherbet into each glass.
2. Pour fruit juice over the ice cream or sherbet.
3. Decorate each glass with a sprig of mint and serve.

---

12 ● FOOD

Meat—especially pork or lamb—is an important ingredient in many Bulgarian dishes. Favorites include *kufteta,* a fried patty of meat and bread crumbs; *moussaka,* a casserole of pork or lamb with potatoes, tomatoes, and yogurt; *sarmi,* peppers or cabbage stuffed with pork and rice; and *shopska salata,* a salad of tomatoes, cucumbers, peppers, and feta cheese, which is called *sirene* in Bulgaria). :

Yogurt is a staple of the diet served at almost every meal. Bulgarians begin eating yogurt at the age of three months. Yogurt with water and ice cubes is a favorite summer drink.

Another important staple is bread, which is usually bought fresh every day. A popular snack is a slice of warm bread topped with feta cheese and tomato slices. A favorite dessert is *baklava* (flaky pastry dough with nuts soaked in sweet syrup). Bulgarians like to drink strong espresso and Turkish coffee.

13 ● EDUCATION

Students are required by law to attend school, which is free, until age fifteen. After the seventh or eighth grade, students decide which type of high school they want to attend. They must take an examination to get into the school of their choice. Most students finish high school.

Bulgaria has a number of universities. Students at public (government-run) universities traditionally did not have to pay tuition. However, in the 1990s tuition fees were charged in some cases. As of the late 1990s, several private colleges had been founded in Bulgaria, and these charged tuition.

Bulgarians board trams on the city streets of Sofia, the nation's capital.

14 ● CULTURAL HERITAGE

Bulgarian culture was reborn when Ottoman rule ended in the 1800s. The leading writers include poets Hristo Botev (1848–76), Dimcho Debelyanov (1887–1916), and Geo Milev (1895–1925). All three died violent deaths at a young age, either in battle or at the hands of the police.

Bulgaria's lively, rhythmic folk music is popular with folk dancers the world over. It is played on instruments that include the *gaida* (bagpipes), *kaval* (seven-hole reed pipe), *gadulka* (pear-shaped fiddle), *tambura* (fretted lute), and *tupan* (cylindrical drum).

The best-known Bulgarian folk dance is the *horo,* a fast, swirling circle dance. Another favorite is the *ruchenitza,* which is often performed in dance contests.

15 ● EMPLOYMENT

In the 1990s, Bulgaria suffered from a "brain drain," as skilled, educated workers left the country because of its economic problems. Over 450,000 Bulgarians left for Germany, France, Canada, the United States, and other countries. In addition, Bulgaria cannot provide jobs for many of the people left in the country. Unemployment in the mid-1990s was over ten percent. Nearly twenty-five percent of Bulgarians work in agriculture. Thirty-three percent hold jobs in industry.

16 ● SPORTS

The mountains of Bulgaria make skiing a very popular sport. Soccer and basketball are also important. Basketball is popular especially among young people in the cities. Volleyball, track, rowing, wrestling, and weight lifting are other favorite sports.

The resort city of Albena, on the Black Sea, hosts chess and volleyball tournaments.

17 ● RECREATION

Bulgarians like to spend their leisure time in practical ways. Women often sew or knit while they socialize. Bulgarian men spend some of their free time in making wine.

Gardening is another very popular hobby. Each year there is a rose festival in early June. Roses are also grown as a business in Bulgaria. It produces over seventy percent of the rose oil made in the world. Bulgarians are more likely to spend their time reading, or socializing in a coffee house, than watching television.

18 ● CRAFTS AND HOBBIES

The skills of many fine Bulgarian artisans can be seen in icons (religious paintings) and other church art. In most cases, the names of the individual artists are not known. Craftspeople of today weave intri-

Cory Langley

The major organized religion in Bulgaria is Eastern Orthodox Christianity. Orthodox churches feature beautiful mosaic icons like this one.

cately patterned cloth and carpets with complex designs.

19 ● SOCIAL PROBLEMS

There are some tensions between ethnic Bulgarians and the minority groups, Turks and Gypsies. Gypsies live mostly in poorly constructed housing on the edges of cities. Gypsies have very high unemployment rates. They live fewer years than average.

In the 1990s, the Bulgarians have struggled to adapt to lower living standards and an unpredictable political situation. These have developed since the end of the Communist era.

20 ● BIBLIOGRAPHY

Crampton, R. J. *A Short History of Modern Bulgaria.* Cambridge, England: Cambridge University Press, 1987.

Resnick, Abraham. *Bulgaria, Enchantment of the World.* Chicago: Children's Press, 1995.

Stavreva, Kirilka. *Bulgaria, Cultures of the World.* New York: Marshall Cavendish, 1997.

WEBSITES

Embassy of Bulgaria, Washington, D.C. [Online] Available http://www.bulgaria.com/embassy/wdc/, 1998.

European Travel Commission. [Online] Available http://www.visiteurope.com/Bulgaria/Bulgaria01.htm, 1998.

World Travel Guide. [Online] Available http://www.wtgonline.com/country/bg/gen.html, 1998.

Burkina Faso

■ **BURKINABE** 39

■ **MOSSI** 43

The people of Burkina Faso are known as the Burkinabe. The main ethnic group in Burkina Faso is the Mossi, who make up about 55 percent of the total population. They are mainly farmers and live in the central portions of the country. The Bobo, the second-largest ethnic group (about 1 million), are mostly farmers, artisans, and metalworkers living in the southwest around Bobo-Dioulasso.

Burkinabe

PRONUNCIATION: bur-kin-a-BAY
ALTERNATE NAMES: (former) Upper Voltans
LOCATION: Burkina Faso (formerly Upper Volta)
POPULATION: 10.6 million
LANGUAGE: French; Gur Group (Niger-Congo family of languages)
RELIGION: Islam; traditional religions; Christianity

1 ● INTRODUCTION

Burkina Faso is one of the poorest countries in Africa, and one that Americans know the least about. Until 1984, it was known as Upper Volta. Its new name was created from the combined words of three different languages to mean "country of upright or incorruptible men." The shorter form, Burkina, is often used. Burkinabe is the name for the country's citizens.

Burkina Faso was one of the last parts of Africa to be conquered by Europeans. The French claimed it in 1896–97. The colony became an independent nation in 1960, but it is still closely linked to France.

In the 1960s and 1970s, the country had two bloodless military coups, that is, the army took over the government without violent action. But power was eventually returned to civilians. Thomas Sanakara came to power in a violent coup in 1983. In 1987 Sanakara was killed by his followers, who continue to rule. Burkina has elections involving several political parties, but political parties that oppose the government have often boycotted, or refused to take part in, the elections.

2 ● LOCATION

Burkina Faso is located in west Africa, north of Côte d'Ivoire, Ghana, Togo, and

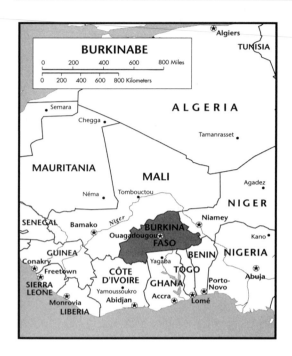

BURKINABE

Benin. It is slightly larger than the state of Colorado. Most of the country is gently rolling savanna (treeless plain). There are grasslands dotted with trees and areas of stunted brush.

The population of Burkina Faso was estimated at 10.6 milion in 1996.

3 ● LANGUAGE

French is the official language of the country. It is used in the schools and in official publications. Most Burkinabe also speak languages of the Gur group within the large Niger-Congo family of languages.

4 ● FOLKLORE

Most of Burkinabe history, law, and tradition has been passed down from one generation to another by word of mouth.

5 ● RELIGION

Current figures estimate the Muslim population of Burkina Faso at 50 percent. About 40 percent of Burkinabe follow traditional African religions, and 10 percent are Christian.

The traditional religion of the Burkinabe is similar to that of many other African peoples. The belief system has three main elements: a god, spirits, and ancestors. It is believed that an all-powerful god created the world. However, he is too high and too far away to have much interest in the activities of human beings.

Less powerful, but more important, are spirits of earth and air. They govern rainfall and fertile soil, affecting local conditions. Offerings and prayers are made to them at special places, such as sacred trees.

Third, and most important for daily life, is the influence of one's ancestors. Those who are living have a responsibility to their ancestors: they must take care of the family land; they must also marry and raise children to carry the family into the future. It is believed that the ancestors watch over their living descendents, and they can reward or punish their behavior.

6 ● MAJOR HOLIDAYS

Since the 1983 revolution led by Thomas Sankara, the most important secular (nonreligious) holiday has been the anniversary of the revolution, August 4. The government and schools also observe all the major Christian and Muslim holidays. These include Easter, Christmas, *Eid al-Fitr* (the end of the month-long fast of Ramadan), and *Eid al-Kabir* (the festival of Tabaski).

For this festival, Muslim households sacrifice a ram in memory of the story of Abraham. In the Old Testament (which Muslims accept as a holy book), Abraham was willing to sacrifice his beloved son Isaac at God's command.

7 ● RITES OF PASSAGE

The ethnic groups in Burkina Faso mark various stages in a person's life with public ceremonies. A baby's birth is announced to the community at a set time. There is also a formal ceremony for naming the baby. Boys are circumcised before they become adolescents. Marriage is viewed as the time when a person takes on full adult status. A funeral marks the transformation from a living elder to a watching ancestor. Burials must occur soon after death because of Burkina's hot climate. It is considered separate from the funeral. Funerals may be delayed for years, until the relatives can be present and can afford the cost of the funeral ceremony and feast.

8 ● RELATIONSHIPS

Most of the population lives in villages, surrounded by neighbors who usually are also relatives. People feel responsible for the well-being of those around them. As with other African peoples, respect for older persons is very important to Burkinabe society. Even city workers keep up ties to their families. They have a right to land to live on and to help from family members when they are old.

9 ● LIVING CONDITIONS

For those who live in rural villages, life has changed little over the centuries. Most people live in adobe houses with thatched roofs.

Electricity is available only in towns and cities, where some modern conveniences have been introduced. In rural areas, radios are battery powered. Water is carried from the well to the house in large pottery containers. Women carry these on their heads.

10 ● FAMILY LIFE

In most Burkinabe societies, descent is *patrilineal* (through the father). In the past, married sons and younger brothers were likely to live with their father or older brother. Today there is a tendency toward smaller households.

In the southwestern part of the country, some ethnic groups also transfer certain rights and goods through the female line. For example, a man's tools might be inherited by his sons, but his cattle may go to his sister's sons.

As in much of Africa, marriage in Burkina is primarily considered the means by which the entire family is perpetuated. Most marriages are arranged, and involve group meetings between both families.

11 ● CLOTHING

Traditionally, women wear a long cotton skirt wrapped at the waists. Tops were added to their costume in rural areas as well as cities. Men's traditional clothing is a cotton shirt and trousers. Some wear embroidered robes, showing a Muslim influence. City people tend to wear increasingly Westernized clothes. Farmers have taken to wearing used, American cut-off jeans as their work clothes.

EPD Photos

Millet, a grain important in the diet of Burkinabe, is available elsewhere in the world in packages like this.

12 ● FOOD

Throughout Burkina, millet and sorghum grains are the staple foods. The main food is a porridge made from millet flour, called *tô* in West African French. (It is also known as fufu in other parts of Africa.) It is cooked until it thickens into a firm mass. Then pieces are broken off with the right hand, dipped in sauce, and eaten. The stew-like sauce is made from vegetables, leaves, and spices, and may contain meat. Chickens and guinea fowl are the main sources of meat. A kind of beer somewhat like cider is brewed from sorghum. It is the main drink for everyone except Muslims and Protestant Christians.

13 ● EDUCATION

Not everyone can easily obtain an education. Consequently, the literacy rate is quite low: in 1995, it was estimated that 19.2 percent of the population over age fifteen could read and write. This 19.2 percent figure is an average; the figure for men was 29.5, and for women, only 9.2. After elementary school, it is even harder to continue education because of the smaller number of schools. There is one university, in Ouagadougou.

14 ● CULTURAL HERITAGE

The music of the Burkinabe is played on drums, flutes, and stringed instruments. In the western part of the country, there are many players of the *balophon*, a xylophone-like instrument made with dried gourds.

FESTPACO (Festival Panafricain du Cinéma d'Ouagadougou) is the leading film festival in all of Africa. Burkinabe filmmakers, such as Gaston Kaboré and Idrissa Ouédraogo, are making feature-length films that increasingly are seen in Europe and North America.

15 ● EMPLOYMENT

Most people in Burkina Faso still do the same sort of agricultural work their ancestors have done for centuries. The majority of the population are subsistence farmers, raising just enough crops and animals to meet their own needs.

16 ● SPORTS

Soccer and bicycle racing are the major sports. No holiday is complete without a bicycle race. There is a national basketball team, but few people are involved in this sport.

17 ● RECREATION

For the people of Burkina, radio is the most important link to the outside world. Local, national, and world news is broadcast. There are two television stations. They broadcast only two hours per weekday and five hours on weekends.

Movies are important, although theaters are found only in the larger towns and cities. Since relatively few movies are made in Africa, people usually see foreign films, especially films from India.

18 ● CRAFTS AND HOBBIES

The Burkinabe, especially in the western part of the country, produce some of the most famous African art. They carve wooden masks of animals or spirits, which dancers use in ceremonies. Patterned cloth is made by weaving and tie-dyeing. Leather bags, cushions, and hats are produced by many people.

19 ● SOCIAL PROBLEMS

Burkina has a shortage of jobs. There are also serious health problems, including malnutrition and river blindness. Almost half of all Burkinabe children are considered malnourished. Outbreaks of river blindness have been reported in over 80 percent of Burkina's land area, causing people to leave their villages to seek healthy, uninfected areas.

20 ● BIBLIOGRAPHY

Decalo, Samuel. *Burkina Faso*. Oxford, England and Santa Barbara, Calif.: Clio Press, 1994.

Skinner, Elliott P. *African Urban Life: The Transformation of Ouagadougou*. Princeton, N.J.: Princeton University Press, 1974.

WEBSITES

Internet Africa Ltd. [Online] Available http://www.africanet.com/africanet/country/burkina/, 1998.

World Travel Guide. [Online] Available http://www.wtgonline.com/country/bf/gen.html, 1998.

Mossi

PRONUNCIATION: MOH-say
ALTERNATE NAMES: Moose, Moshi, Mosi
LOCATION: Burkina Faso (formerly Upper Volta), Côte d'Ivoire (Ivory Coast)
POPULATION: 5 to 6 million in Burkina Faso, 1.2 million in Côte d'Ivoire
LANGUAGE: Moré
RELIGION: Traditional religions; Islam; Christianity

1 ● INTRODUCTION

The Mossi make up the largest ethnic group in Burkina Faso. They are the second-largest ethnic group in Côte d'Ivoire (Ivory Coast).

At one time the Mossi were organized into three kingdoms, Tenkodogo, Wagadugu, and Yatenga. It is not clear when these were founded. However, a Mossi raid on the city of Timbuktu in 1329 is described in Arab histories. Each Mossi village had its own chief, and groups of up to twenty villages were ruled by a district chief. The political system of the Mossi was very

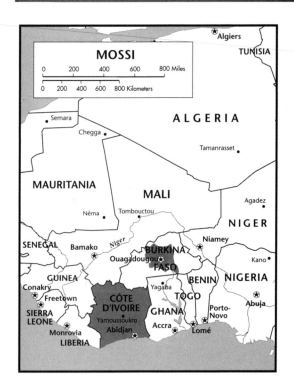

2 ● LOCATION

The Mossi homeland is the central portion of Burkina Faso, which was known until 1984 as Upper Volta. Burkina Faso has roughly the same area as the state of Colorado. The Mossi area, located in the center, runs from Tenkodogo in the southeast to Ouayagouya in the northwest. The country is mainly savanna, or grassland, with scattered trees. The few rivers and streams exist only in the rainy season. Only scattered pools keep water through the dry season. Most water used by the Mossi is drawn from wells.

In 1996, the estimated population of Burkina Faso was 10,623,323. Five to six million are probably Mossi; another 1.2 million Mossi live in Côte d'Ivoire.

3 ● LANGUAGE

The Mossi language is Moré. It belongs to the Gur group within the Niger-Congo language family. Like many African languages, Moré uses pitch (how high or low a tone is) to distinguish meanings. Also, as in other African languages, a verb form shows whether its action is continuing or happens only once.

A person's name shows something about his or her birth. As with many other West African peoples, there are Mossi names showing the day of the week when a person was born. *Arzuma* (for a boy) or *Zuma* (for a girl) means that a child was born on Friday; *Hado* was born on Sunday and *Larba* on Wednesday. *Lokre* is a name for someone born at the end of the month-long fast of Ramadan; *Kibsa* is the name for one born

closely connected to their religion. For this reason, the Mossi rulers resisted conversion to Islam, even though other African groups accepted the new religion (after about the tenth century). Even so, Mossi culture shows Muslim influences.

The Mossi were one of the last peoples in Africa to be colonized. They were conquered by the French in 1896–97. French taxes forced many Mossi to move to Côte d'Ivoire to earn money. Mossi men could go south between crop-growing seasons and bring money back to their families in the north. They also traveled around as traders and as soldiers in the French army.

As the economy of Côte d'Ivoire improved, more and more of the Mossi settled there. They became farmers or lived in the cities and towns.

during the festival of Tabaski, forty days after Ramadan.

4 ● FOLKLORE

There have been few written records in Mossi society. Special singers, called *griots,* were the keepers of oral traditions. The entire society used folktales and proverbs to pass on wisdom and experience to later generations.

The Mossi's account of their founding is handed down through the following myth: Over forty generations ago, a king named Naba Nedega had a daughter whom he would not allow to marry because she was a great warrior. So Princess Nyennega took a horse and fled north into what is now Mossi country. She married a local man. Their son, named *Ouedraogo* (stallion), was sent back to his mother's homeland to be raised by his grandfather, Naba Nedega. When he grew up, he returned to the north with cavalry from his homeland and conquered his father's people, the Bisa. The marriage of Ouedraogo and his troops with Bisa women produced the Mossi people. A statue of Princess Nyennega on horseback in the city of Ouagadougou commemorates the story.

5 ● RELIGION

The religion of the Mossi has three main components. There is a belief in an all-powerful creator, *Wende*; fertility spirits of the rain and the earth, which govern the soil and crops; and ancestors, who affect the lives of their descendants.

The fertility spirits are usually worshiped through animal sacrifices such as chickens or guinea fowl, which are held in sacred places. The ancestors watch over their descendants, punishing or rewarding them for their behavior. The yearly cycle of ceremonies is mainly about ancestors. Each household has a shrine to its ancestors, an upside-down pottery bowl with sacred plants and objects under it. This shrine is honored once a year, at the time of the harvest festival. Sacrifices and offerings are made to it and to the graves of male ancestors.

6 ● MAJOR HOLIDAYS

Basega is a festival of thanksgiving that comes in December, after the millet crop has been harvested. The Mossi thank the ancestors for helping with the successful harvest, and they ask for help with the coming year's crops.

The Muslim community celebrates its own holidays, and the Christians celebrate theirs.

Since the revolution of 1983, its anniversary, August 4, has been the official national day. National holidays are celebrated with parades and, in towns and cities, bicycle races.The anniversary of the date of independence from France, August 5, 1960, is a secular (nonreligious) holiday in Burkina Faso. So is December 11, the anniversary of the proclamation of the Republic in 1958.

7 ● RITES OF PASSAGE

From birth until death, major changes in a person's life are marked with formal rites of passage. A Mossi baby is formally presented to the community three days after birth for a boy, and four days after birth for a girl. At that time, the baby's name is announced. The child is formally welcomed into its family and takes the family name.

Before becoming adults, both boys and girls, in separate groups, are circumcised. Boys go in groups of fifteen to thirty to bush camps, where they stay for ninety to a hundred days to recover from the operation. At the same time, they are taught by older men the things they need to know to become members of society. Full adulthood is marked by marriage.

Mossi funerals are important family and religious events. Men are buried at the edge of their home, just west of the patio area outside the walled family compound. Women are buried in the fields of their husband's village, but the burial ceremony is performed by members of the deceased woman's own family (not by her husband's family). This symbolizes a woman's connection to her own family.

The funeral can occur up to a year after a burial and sometimes much later. The ceremony is what marks the passage of the dead person to the ancestors. The family must put on the funeral.

8 ● RELATIONSHIPS

Mossi greetings are more elaborate than those in other African societies. The persons greeting each other shake hands, and each asks how the other is. The questioning goes on to cover wives and children, and even the animals, such as cows and sheep. A full Mossi greeting for an honored elder can take half an hour. In any greeting, the person who is of lower status shows respect to the other by staying in a lower position. If a common person is formally greeting a chief,

he lies down in front of him and symbolically throws dirt onto his own head to show how much lower he is in status.

If two people of equal status meet, however, each tries to respect the other by slowly dropping from a standing position to a crouching one. The two people start out standing and shaking hands; they finish, still shaking hands, with both crouching low and sitting on their heels.

When visiting a household, guests stand outside the walls of the family's area and clap their hands to announce their arrival. The head of the household then comes out of the walled area to greet the visitors. Only a close friend or relative would go in unannounced.

9 ● LIVING CONDITIONS

The Mossi live in villages of extended families, that is, parents and children, plus other relatives. The village boundary may be a stream or other natural feature, but in general the village is a social unit more than a geographic one.

The traditional Mossi dwelling consists of a number of round adobe huts with cone-shaped, thatched roofs. They are surrounded with an adobe wall. (Today corrugated aluminum roofs are sometimes seen. They are something of a status symbol although they make the huts hotter and are noisier during rainstorms.) Each member of the extended family has a hut. Additional huts are used as kitchens, for storage, and as shelter for sheep, goats, and chickens. Each dwelling also includes a patio-like area of pounded, swept dirt with an awning. People rest there during the day and greet guests there. All houses face west.

10 ● FAMILY LIFE

Marriage is usually arranged between families. At the time of a marriage, the wife's family receives payments from her husband and his kin. Traditionally, this *bridewealth* was in the form of cattle and trade goods. Today, however, there are many possible types of payment. Nowadays it is not unusual for men and women who are in love to elope (run away and get married) if they cannot convince their families to agree to the marriage.

Within the walled area of the Mossi home, each wife has her own hut for herself and her children. There she prepares meals for herself and for them. If the husband has more than one wife, he joins each of them for meals in turn. Although many Mossi men have only one wife, there are two reasons wives often want their husbands to have more than one. First, it is useful to have another wife to help with laborious housework. In addition, another wife can give moral support and companionship.

Children have important roles in tending the family's sheep and goats. They also help haul water and gather firewood for cooking.

11 ● CLOTHING

Mossi women wear long skirts made of a cloth panel wrapped around the waist. It is common to wear a top as well, but until recently this was not the case in rural areas. It is more and more common for men to wear shirts and trousers of Islamic or European style. Wealthy men and chiefs still

David Johnson

A Mossi man from Yako, Burkina Faso, wearing traditional clothing. It is increasingly common for men to wear shirts and trousers, whether of Islamic or European style.

wear the traditional embroidered robes in the Muslim-influenced style of the savanna.

There is also a major business of selling used American clothing, even in rural markets. Today the everyday working outfit of a farmer is likely to be a woven shirt and a pair of cutoff blue-jeans. Rubber shoes and sandals have been added to the traditional leather ones.

12 ● FOOD

The staple of the Mossi diet is the millet grain, along with its relative, sorghum. Millet is ground into flour and made into por-

David Johnson

Mossi using traditional cultivating methods with oxen near Toma, Burkina Faso. Only recently have more modern techniques been integrated into the farming tradition.

ridge by boiling it in water. The bowl of thick, doughy food is called *sagabo* in Moré and *tô* in West African French. One eats it by breaking off a piece with the right hand and dipping it into a sauce made of vegetables, spices, herbs, and, sometimes, meat. Sorghum is used to brew a beer similar to cider that is drunk by all Mossi except Muslims and Protestant Christians.

Meat is a luxury and is usually added to sauces in small amounts. Grilled meat is for special celebrations.

Mossi often have food taboos, which tend to vary from clan to clan. Some families will eat dog meat, for example, and others will not.

13 ● EDUCATION

In traditional Mossi society, most education came from living with, watching, and helping more experienced, older people. The circumcision camps provided a few months of group schooling to boys. Muslims attended Koranic schools, where Arabic and the Koran (their holy book) were taught.

Modern education is becoming available, but not to everyone. In schools, classes are taught in French, the national language of Burkina Faso. The government has set standards for writing Moré, the Mossi language. Christian religious texts and agricultural information make up most of what is written in the Mossi language.

14 ● CULTURAL HERITAGE

Music has been important to Mossi society, not just as entertainment but also as work. It is used to set rhythms for agricultural tasks such as hoeing and threshing. The main musical instruments are drums. Some are large calabashes (a type of gourd) with leather drumheads and are played with the hands. There are also wooden drums played with sticks. The player can change a drum's pitch by changing arm pressure on the strings tying the head to the drum. There are also flutes and stringed instruments.

Some Mossi, but not all, have traditions of masked dancing at ceremonies such as funerals. More secular (nonreligious) dancing occurs at celebrations and festivals.

15 ● EMPLOYMENT

Modern Mossi have all the occupations of a modern nation open to them, but most are still farmers. Farming nowadays is a mix of subsistence farming (basic farming to feed the family) and cash crops. Some farmers grow vegetables or fruit for city markets and for export. Increasingly, farmers use modern technologies such as fertilizers and insecticides, as well as plows drawn by animals or tractors.

16 ● SPORTS

There was little leisure time for sports in traditional Mossi society. Military training required practice with swords, spears, and bows and arrows.

As part of modern Burkina Faso, the Mossi participate in soccer and bicycle racing, the two major national sports. Towns and cities have bicycle races on most holidays.

17 ● RECREATION

Aside from music, dance, and conversation, there were not many forms of entertainment or recreation in traditional Mossi society. *Griots* (traditional storytellers) recited family histories and traditions at weddings and other events. Radio is important to modern Mossi both for entertainment and for communication. Programming includes "personal notices" programs. These allow people in different parts of the country to pass messages to each other.

Television barely plays a role in Mossi life. In 1992 (the most recent year figures were available), there were only about 41,500 TV sets in this country of ten million people. Programming was broadcast only two hours a day during the week and five hours a day each on Saturday and Sunday.

Movies are popular, although theaters are only in the larger towns and cities. Full-length films by Mossi filmmakers such as Gaston Kaboré and Idrissa Ouédraogo are seen both at home and abroad.

18 ● CRAFTS AND HOBBIES

Pottery is made by only one clan of potters and drummers.

For the Mossi communities that have masked dancing, the carving and painting of masks is a major art form. Mossi masks are part of most major collections of African art.

The Mossi also produce metal earrings and jewelry, as well as hats, bags, and cushions from dyed leather.

Cowrie shells from the Indian Ocean were once used as money by the Mossi. They are still used as decorations for clothing and hats.

19 ● SOCIAL PROBLEMS

Burkina Faso shares with other countries the problems that come with the growth of cities. As more Mossi live and work in cities and large towns, traditional roles for men and women, and within families, are threatened. Some of the most powerful films by Mossi filmmakers have examined the pressures of city life.

The devaluation of Burkina Faso's currency, the CFA (Communauté Financière Africaine—African Financial Community) franc, in 1994 lowered wages and salaries. It also raised prices for imported products ranging from wheat flour to tires and radios.

20 ● BIBLIOGRAPHY

Decalo, Samuel. *Burkina Faso*. World Bibliographical Series, vol. 169. Oxford, England; Santa Barbara, Calif.: Clio Press, 1994.

Guirma, Frederic. *Tales of Mogho: African Stories from Upper Volta*. New York: Macmillan, 1971.

Skinner, Elliott P. *The Mossi of Burkina Faso: Chiefs, Politicians, and Soldiers*. Prospect Heights, Ill.: Waveland Press, 1989.

WEBSITES

Internet Africa Ltd. [Online] Available http://www.africanet.com/africanet/country/burkina/, 1998.

World Travel Guide. [Online] Available http://www.wtgonline.com/country/bf/gen.html, 1998.

Burundi

■ **BURUNDIANS** **51**
■ **TUTSI** **57**

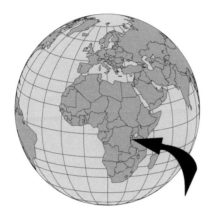

The people of Burundi are known as the Burundians. The largest group, the Hutu (also known as Bahutu), are traditionally farmers and make up about 85 percent of the population in both Burundi and the neighboring country of Rwanda. The Tutsi (also known as Watutsi, Watusi, Batutsi), a tall warrior people, make up less than 15 percent of the population, but dominate the government and military. For more information on the Hutu, refer to the chapter on Rwanda in Volume 8.

Burundians

PRONUNCIATION: buh-ROON-dee-uhns
LOCATION: Burundi
POPULATION: More than 6 million
LANGUAGE: Kirundi, French, Swahili
RELIGION: Christianity, indigenous beliefs

1 ● INTRODUCTION

Rwanda and Burundi are two African countries with long histories. Both were kingdoms centuries before Europeans arrived. It is believed that the Twa were the first people to inhabit the area. Hutus arrived between the seventh and fourteenth centuries. The Tutsi came into the region beginning in the fifteenth century.

European colonists ruled the Hutu and Tutsi kingdoms under one government. The Tutsi *mwami* (king) stood at the top of the social ladder, followed by the princes. At a lower level were the Tutsi and Hutu masses, whose members often married members of the other ethnic group. Hutu serfs, who were forced to work for the Tutsi upper class, were the lowest social class.

The Germans began to rule in 1899. During World War I (1914–18), The League of Nations gave the colony to the Belgians. The Belgians strengthened Tutsi political and economic power, using the Tutsi to rule for them.

Burundi became independent in 1962, Since then, Hutus have rebelled against their lower status and mistreatment. The Tutsi rulers have strongly resisted change in the balance of power. As a result, Burundi has had many episodes of violence between the groups on a massive scale; so has its neighbor, Rwanda. Since 1962, some 300,000 Burundians, mostly Hutus, have

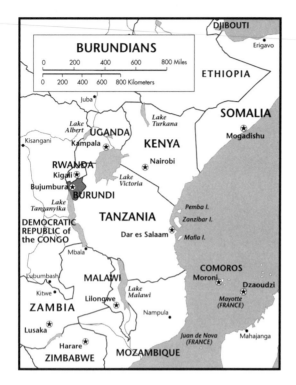

BURUNDIANS

| 0 | 200 | 400 | 600 | 800 Miles |
| 0 | 200 | 400 | 600 | 800 Kilometers |

dians along the western shore of Lake Tanganyika also speak Swahili. It is the language of East African trade. A traditional greeting in Kirundi is *Amashyo* ("May you have herds [of cattle]"). The reply is *Amashongore*, meaning, "I wish you herds of females." The language is full of references to cattle. Wishing a person "herds" means wishing them health and good fortune.

4 ● FOLKLORE

The Burundian literary tradition is passed down to younger generations in spoken poetry, fables, legends, riddles, and proverbs. There are epic poems about peasants, kings, ancestors, and cattle. Oral stories may be told through "whispered singing." Men sing quietly, accompanied by traditional instruments. The *inanga* is somewhat like a zither (a flat instrument with a number of strings stretched across it). The *idono* resembles a stringed hunting bow.

been killed. Nearly a million more have lost their homes.

2 ● LOCATION

Burundi is somewhat larger than the state of Maryland, but it has more than six million people. This makes it one of Africa's most densely populated countries, with 20.4 persons per square kilometer.

Most of the country is a high plateau. In the east, a mountain range rises to over 5,900 feet (1,800 meters). Lake Tanganyika and the Ruzizi river form a beautiful natural border with the Democratic Republic of the Congo.

3 ● LANGUAGE

Two official languages are spoken in Burundi: Kirundi and French. Many Burun-

5 ● RELIGION

Most Burundians are Christians. Over 60 percent of the population is Roman Catholic, and 5 percent is Protestant. The other 35 percent of the people follow traditional African religions.

6 ● MAJOR HOLIDAYS

The national holiday of Burundi is Independence Day, July 1. Sometimes, however, the government faction that has taken power by force most recently celebrates its own victory instead.

Burundians celebrate Christian and traditional holidays. The most important holiday is Christmas. It is an occasion for buying new clothes and wearing them to

Cynthia Bassett

Because of a preference given to boys, 60 percent of them learn to read and write compared to only 40 percent of girls.

church. After church, people return home to spend the day with family and friends, enjoying a good meal.

The Burundian traditional day is *umuco* or *akaranga*. The traditional games that have been part of it are no longer played. But Burundians still enjoy dancing, drinking, and traditional foods on this day.

7 ● RITES OF PASSAGE

As in much of Africa, rites of passage are important markers in the life cycle. Six days after birth, babies are presented to the family in the *ujusohor* ceremony. The mother receives flowers for her hair, and gifts of money and beer are given. Christian parents and their families usually baptize their children one month after birth. When the child becomes a toddler, it receives a name in the *kuvamukiriri* ceremony.

Initiation rites were once extremely important in Burundian society. However, the practice was discouraged by European missionaries. Today few Burundian children are initiated, although most of their grandparents were. The church has replaced initiation with the Christian rite of first communion. After a long period of religious instruction, young people are taken into the church as adults.

8 ● RELATIONSHIPS

Burundians are sociable people and visit each other without announcing it ahead of time. They typically greet each other by shaking hands with the right hand. Friends often greet by touching cheeks three times. Friends of the same sex give each other a firm hug, grasping each other's shoulders.

There is a set of gestures for pointing to people and calling people that is special to Central Africa. They point to someone by holding an arm out with the hand open and palm upward. Pointing at someone with the index finger is considered very rude. A person beckoning someone else extends an arm with the palm turned down and brings the fingers toward the wrist.

9 ● LIVING CONDITIONS

Traditional huts were made from reeds and canes. The tradition has given way in rural areas to houses of mud brick with thatched or tin roofs. Some are cylindrical in shape, and the mud walls may be whitewashed. In towns, houses built of hollow concrete blocks with galvanized iron or clay tile roofs are common.

Warfare has greatly affected living conditions in Burundi. People have been killed, homes have been burned, and cattle have been destroyed. Great numbers of people have become homeless. In 1994, the average number of years a person was expected to live was estimated at only about 40.3 years.

10 ● FAMILY LIFE

In Burundian society, the man is in charge of the home and makes the decisions. Women do the housework, raise the chil-dren, fetch water, collect firewood, cook the meals, and wash the clothes. Girls help with these chores and tend the younger children.

Some men have more than one wife, but this custom has been disappearing. Over-crowding and the cost of educating children have led to smaller families.

In Burundi, disciplining children is not just the parents' job. The extended family, friends, and acquaintances may correct another person's child. If they do not correct bad behavior, they may be accused of shirk-ing their duty to the community.

11 ● CLOTHING

Burundian traditional clothing consists of cloth wraparounds *(pagnes)*. Women, girls, and elderly men still wear them in rural areas.

Male herders wear two pieces of cloth, which hang down to the knees, with a cord around the waist. Many people go barefoot in the villages.

In Bujumbura, the capital, fashionable men and women, known as *sapeurs,* wear the latest fashions. The men dress up in suits and ties, and the women wear Western dresses and shoes. Young people are fond of blue jeans and T-shirts.

12 ● FOOD

The staple foods in Burundi are tubers, plantains *(matoke),* and beans. Burundians are most fond of sweet potatoes and cassava served with different types of beans, greens, and cabbage. They also enjoy cassava flour, boiled in water, and stirred to make a thick paste *(ugali).*

Cynthia Bassett

A mother and her child at the market.

school enrollment was only 7 percent for boys and 4 percent for girls.

Half of Burundians age fifteen and older can read and write, according to an estimate made in 1990. Because of the preference given to boys, more of them (61 percent) can read and write than girls (40 percent).

14 ● CULTURAL HERITAGE

Traditionally, Burundians played drums mainly for ceremonies. More and more, drumming has become a form of entertainment. As many as twenty-five men of all ages play huge drums carved from tree trunks. The drums are three feet tall. Men beat the drums with two sticks about eighteen inches long. They wear costumes of red and white cloth tied in the traditional way, one over each shoulder with a cord around the waist.

Burundian dancing is very athletic, with dancers leaping high into the air and spinning around. Sometimes dancers use wooden shields and spears and wear headbands and armbands made of beads.

Burundians make several traditional instruments that they play during family get-togethers.

15 ● EMPLOYMENT

Burundi is one of the world's twenty-five poorest countries. Most Burundians work in subsistence farming (producing the basic foods necessary to keep a family alive) and cattle herding. Those without steady jobs manage as best they can. Some set up sidewalk repair stands, repairing anything from watches to shoes. Unfortunately, these jobs pay very little.

Villagers usually rise early and do not eat breakfast. They return home for a large meal at noon. At night, they may eat leftovers or have tea. In the cities, French bread is very popular. European beverages such as coffee and tea have become common.

Burundians produce their own traditional drinks, including banana beer *(urwarwa)* and sorghum beer.

13 ● EDUCATION

From 1986 to 1992, most children dropped out of school after reaching grade five. High

16 ● SPORTS

Burundians are soccer fanatics. They play soccer wherever and whenever they can. Any kind of ball will do. Homemade goals mark parking lots, fields, streets, and any other flat surface. Schools have introduced other sports such as basketball, volleyball, and European handball.

17 ● RECREATION

In the cities, where electricity is available, people enjoy watching television on evenings and weekends. Whenever someone has money, they invite their friends to go out to a neighborhood bar (buvette) for a round of drinks.

Bujumburans really enjoy nightlife and are fond of a variety of popular music.

18 ● CRAFTS AND HOBBIES

Burundians produce many crafts of excellent quality. Among the best are mats and baskets. Papyrus roots, banana leaves, and bast (a strong, woody fiber) are the raw materials for the baskets. The Twa people are skilled in making pottery for their own use and for the tourist market. Wood carving has a long tradition. Carvers produce highly decorated drums for the tourist market.

Burundian craftsmen make fine instruments such as the thumb piano (ikembe). The ikembe is small and not like a Western piano. It has eleven metal bands for producing tones, and a sounding box. The indingiti is a traditional banjo or violin with a single string that is played with a bow. The inanga is an eight-stringed instrument with a large sounding board.

19 ● SOCIAL PROBLEMS

Burundi faces several serious environmental and health threats, including AIDS. However, making peace between the Hutu and Tutsi peoples is the most urgent problem. To have a stable nation, Burundians will have to deal with the inequalities in political power, land ownership, and wealth between these two ethnic groups.

20 ● BIBLIOGRAPHY

Lemarchan, Rene. *Burundi: Ethnocide as Discourse and Practice*. New York: Woodrow Wilson Center Press and Cambridge University Press, 1994.

Nyankanzi, Edward L. *Genocide: Rwanda and Burundi*. Rochester, Vt.: Schenkman Books, 1997.

Wolbers, Marian F. *Burundi*. New York: Chelsea House Publishers, 1989.

WEBSITES

Internet Africa Ltd. Burundi. [Online] Available http://www.africanet.com/africanet/country/burundi/, 1998.

World Travel Guide. Burundi. [Online] Available http://www.wtgonline.com/country/bi/gen.html, 1998.

Tutsi

PRONUNCIATION: TOOT-see
LOCATION: Rwanda, Burundi, northeastern
   Democratic Republic of the Congo (formerly
   Zaire)
POPULATION: Approximately 13 million
LANGUAGE: Kinyarwanda; Kirundi; French,
   English
RELIGION: Christianity combined with traditional
   beliefs

1 ● INTRODUCTION

The Tutsi are a people who live in Rwanda, Burundi, and the northeastern part of the Democratic Republic of Congo. They have much in common with the other groups of this region, the Twa and the Hutu. Their cultures are similar, and they all speak the same language.

In the past, the Tutsi were cattle herders. They were a minority of the population. However, most of the upper-class rulers were Tutsi. A system of cattle trading helped keep peace among the different groups. The wealthier people (often Tutsi) lent cattle to the poorer ones (often Hutu). In return they gained their labor, loyalty, and political support.

Social relations in Rwanda and Burundi were changed by European rule. The Germans held power from the 1890s until World War I (1914–18). Then the Belgians ruled until 1962. For most of this period, the Europeans treated the Tutsi better than the Hutu. In the 1950s, however, the Belgians urged the Hutu to challenge Tutsi power. In 1959 Hutu leaders overthrew the Tutsi monarchy in Rwanda. Many Tutsi fled to nearby countries. In Burundi, the change to independence was more peaceful. The *mwami* (the Tutsi king) helped the Tutsi and Hutu sides reach an agreement. However, the peace did not last. The Hutu tried to gain power by force, and they were defeated.

When the colonial period ended, opposite sides controlled Rwanda and Burundi. The Hutu held power in Rwanda until 1994. The Tutsi still rule Burundi. Hutu power in Rwanda ended in 1994 when Tutsi rebels overthrew the government. However, this Tutsi victory occurred at a great cost in human lives. As many as one million people were killed.

2 ● LOCATION

Rwanda and Burundi are mountainous countries in east-central Africa. Their combined total area is about 20,900 square miles (54,100 square kilometers). This is about the combined size of the states of Maryland and New Jersey.

Tutsi also live in the northeastern part of the Democratic Republic of the Congo (formerly Zaire). They live near the city of Bukavu in the Mulenge region. Here they are known as the *Banyamulenge*.

The combined population of Rwanda and Burundi was about 13 million in 1994. However, many refugees fled Rwanda that year. In addition, many Rwandese Tutsi returned from Uganda after the Hutu army was defeated in 1994.

3 ● LANGUAGE

The Hutu, Tutsi, and Twa all speak a Central Bantu language. It is called *Kinyarwanda* in Rwanda, and *Kirundi* in

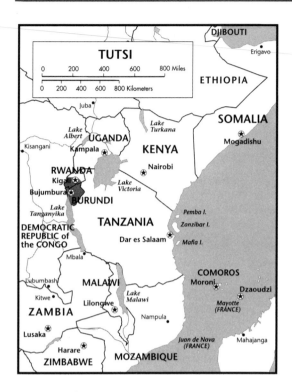

Burundi. Both are dialects of the same language. Like other Bantu languages, both use nouns with prefixes. For example, the word *Banyamulenge* ("Ba-nya-mulenge") can be divided into parts. The prefix "banya" means "people"; "Mulenge" is the name of a region. The whole word means "people of Mulenge."

Many Rwandese and Burundians speak French, the language of their former Belgian rulers. French is used in school. Also, many people in both countries have French first names. Tutsi who have been refugees in Uganda may also speak English.

Personal names may be based on events, poetry, or beliefs. The name *Ndagijimana* means "God is my herder." *Hakizumwami*

means "only the king can save." *Muvunanyambo* means "the defender of noble cows."

4 ● FOLKLORE

Tutsi folklore includes poetry, proverbs, folk tales, riddles, and myths. Some Tutsis used to know the names of their ancestors at least six generations back. Many believed they were descended from a mythical king named Gihanga.

One popular folk tale tells the story of Sebgugugu. He was a poor man who was helped by God. God performed miracles to provide food for him and his family. However, each time Sebgugugu wanted more. Through his greed, Sebgugugu lost everything in the end.

5 ● RELIGION

Today most people in Rwanda and Burundi are Christians. However, some traditional beliefs survive. These include the belief in a distant creator called *Imaana*. This god has the power to grant wealth and fertility. The king shares in this power. It can be seen in his sacred fire, royal drums, and rituals. Spirits of dead relatives, called *abazima*, carry messages between *Imaana* and the human world. However, the *abazima* may bring bad luck to those who do not respect them. People offer gifts to protect themselves from the *abazima*. They also try to learn the spirits' wishes by seeing fortune-tellers.

6 ● MAJOR HOLIDAYS

National holidays include Independence Day, May Day, New Year's Day, and the major Christian holidays. The Tutsis' traditional holidays were celebrated with dancing and sacred drumming. These holidays are no longer observed.

7 ● RITES OF PASSAGE

Hutu and Tutsi rites of passage are very similar. The first one, the naming ceremony, takes place seven days after a child's birth.

Marriage is made legal by payment of the bride wealth. It is paid by the groom's family to the bride's family because they are losing her labor. There is no ritual other than marriage to mark the beginning of adulthood.

Death is marked by prayers, speeches, and limits on many activities. Close family members are supposed to avoid physical labor and sex after a death. When the mourning period ends, the family holds a ritual feast.

8 ● RELATIONSHIPS

Social status is very important in both Rwanda and Burundi. Signs of status include a person's posture, body movements, and way of speaking. Upper-class people are supposed to act with dignity and not show their emotions.

The Tutsi have different greetings for morning, afternoon, and evening.

In the past, most people had arranged marriages to someone of the same social class. Today, Tutsi may choose the person they will marry. Group activities are more common than dating in couples. However, some young Tutsis in the cities practice Western-style dating and go out to night-clubs.

9 ● LIVING CONDITIONS

Traditional Tutsi houses were huts of wood, reeds, and straw shaped like beehives. Around them were high hedges that served as fences. Modern Tutsi build rectangular houses with Western-style building materials. These houses have corrugated iron or tile roofs.

10 ● FAMILY LIFE

Tutsi and Hutu families are patrilineal (the family name is passed on by males).

In the past, marriage in Rwanda and Burundi was based on the relations between the two families. Today most Tutsis choose the person they will marry.

11 ● CLOTHING

In the past, Tutsi men and women wore robes brought in from the African coast. A woman's costume included a white robe and white headbands. Today Western-style clothing is usually worn. Women wear dresses and scarves made from the printed cloth popular in East Africa. Men wear pants and shirts.

12 ● FOOD

Milk, butter, and meat are the most highly valued foods. However, people will only kill a cow on a special occasion. Goat meat and goat milk are also eaten. However, they are eaten secretly because it is against Tutsi customs. Tutsi in rural areas consume milk products, bananas, and sorghum beer. Meals are arranged around work schedules.

Alcoholic beverages are made from bananas and sorghum. People drink them on special occasions.

13 ● EDUCATION

No more than half of Tutsi in Rwanda and Burundi can read and write their native language. A smaller number can read and write French. There are teacher training schools in Burundi. Both Rwanda and Burundi have at least one university.

14 ● CULTURAL HERITAGE

Royal dancing and drumming groups performed for the kings of Rwanda and Burundi. For rituals, two dozen tall drums were placed around a central drum. The drummers moved around the drums in a circle. Each one took a turn beating the central drum. This style of drumming is still practiced, and it has been recorded.

Singing, dancing, and drumming are important in rural life. People compose many kinds of songs—hunting songs, lullabies, and *ibicuba* (songs praising cattle).

15 ● EMPLOYMENT

Cattle herding has always carried a higher status among the Tutsi than farming. In the past there was a special class of herders, called *abashumba*, who took care of the king's prize cattle (*inyambo*).

16 ● SPORTS

The main spectator sport in Rwanda and Burundi is soccer.

A game called *igisoro* is popular with children and adults. It is played on a wooden board with holes for beads or stones. Players line up their pieces in rows and capture as many of their opponents'

pieces as they can. In other parts of Africa the game is known as *mancala*.

17 ● RECREATION

Movie theaters in the capitals of Rwanda and Burundi show current European and American films.

18 ● CRAFTS AND HOBBIES

Traditional crafts of Rwanda and Burundi include basket weaving, pottery, woodworking, metal working, and jewelry making.

19 ● SOCIAL PROBLEMS

Since the early 1960s, the peoples of Rwanda and Burundi have lived through some of the worst violence in African history. The killings are usually called ethnic warfare between the Hutu and Tutsi. However, victims have often been killed for their political beliefs, not just their ethnic group.

20 ●BIBLIOGRAPHY

Lemarchand, Rene. *Burundi: Ethnocide as Discourse and Practice.* New York: Cambridge University Press, 1994.

Nyankanzi, Edward L. *Genocide: Rwanda and Burundi.* Rochester, Vt.: Schenkman Books, 1997.

Twagilimana, Aimable. *Hutu and Tutsi.* Heritage Library of African Peoples. New York: Rosen Publishing Group, 1998.

WEBSITES

Internet Africa Ltd. [Online] Available http://www.africanet.com/africanet/country/burundi/, 1998.

World Travel Guide. Burundi. [Online] Available http://www.wtgonline.com/country/bi/gen.html, 1998.

World Travel Guide. Rwanda. [Online] Available http://www.wtgonline.com/country/rw/gen.html, 1998.

Cambodia

■ **KHMER** **61**

■ **HILL TRIBESPEOPLE** **70**

Over 90 percent of the 10 million people in Cambodia are ethnic Khmers, descendants of the original population in the area. The largest minority groups are the Chinese (about 61,000) and Vietnamese (estimated at 56,000). Other minorities include small tribal groups known as hill tribespeople that live in the mountains of the country. More information on the ethnic Vietnamese may be found in the chapter on Vietnam in Volume 9. Information on the Chinese can be found in the chapter on China in this volume.

Khmer

PRONUNCIATION: kuh-MARE

ALTERNATE NAMES: Cambodians

LOCATION: Cambodia

POPULATION: about 9 million Khmer

LANGUAGE: Cambodian

RELIGION: Theravada Buddhism; Islam; Roman Catholicism; traditional beliefs; Taoism

1 ● INTRODUCTION

For much of the twentieth century, Cambodia has been largely unknown to most of the world except as the home of Angkor Wat (an elaborate three-story temple built in the twelfth century), one of the wonders of the world. Not until the Vietnam War (1954–75) did Cambodia come to the world's attention.

Cambodians are called Khmer. Their language, culture, and appearance reflect many centuries of influence from India, China, Malaysia, and Europe. Cambodia was once the heart of a great empire that stretched over much of Southeast Asia. In the late 1800s, the French colonized (invaded and occupied) Cambodia. In 1953, Cambodia gained independence from the French. For the next decade and a half, King Norodom Sihanouk tried to keep his country out of the war that was spreading in neighboring Vietnam. He was unsuccessful and was overthrown in 1970. General Lon Nol allowed the United States to fight the Vietnam War from Cambodia. As the war continued, corruption, bombing, economic disruption, and the displacement of over half the population destroyed much of Cambodia. This made it easier for the Communist rebels to overthrow the government in 1975.

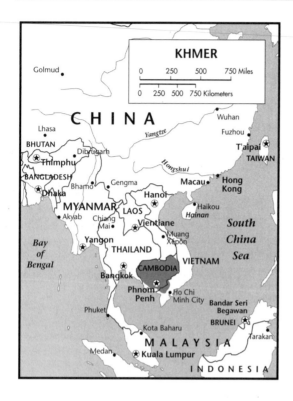

KHMER

0   250   500   750 Miles

0   250 500 750 Kilometers

The Communists, or Khmer Rouge (Red Cambodians), attempted to remake Cambodian society. They evacuated the cities, turned everyone into laborers, and dissolved banks, airlines, the postal service, and other institutions. They closed schools and hospitals and tore down temples and churches. In three and a half years of Khmer Rouge rule, at least one million Cambodians died from execution, starvation, torture, and disease.

In December 1978, Vietnam invaded and chased the Khmer Rouge to the Thai border. For the next decade the country was ruled by a government installed by the Vietnamese. Resistance armies, including the Khmer Rouge, attempted to take over the country. In 1993, the United Nations helped achieve reconciliation between resistance groups and the government and held elections. Cambodians are now experiencing more peace, security, and prosperity than most have since at least 1970.

2 ● LOCATION

Cambodia is a small country, about the size of the state of Oregon. Three-quarters of Cambodia lies in a flat basin that forms the center of the country, surrounded by plateaus and mountains.

Approximately 90 percent of the Cambodian population are ethnic Khmer. Another 5 percent of the population are Chinese-Cambodians. There is also a significant Vietnamese minority. Hill people, called "Khmer Loeu," also live in Cambodia. These are scattered tribes who live in remote plateaus and mountainous areas. There are also Cham, the descendants of a once-great empire that dominated central Vietnam. The Cham speak their own language and practice Islam.

A significant number of Khmer live in southern Vietnam and Thailand. Cambodians also live in more than twenty countries throughout the world.

3 ● LANGUAGE

The official language of the State of Cambodia is Cambodian. It is probable that as long as two thousand years ago the inhabitants of Cambodia were speaking a language related to the Cambodian language spoken today by the Khmer. The Cambodian script looks quite exotic to Westerners and is based on an ancient Brahmi script from South India.

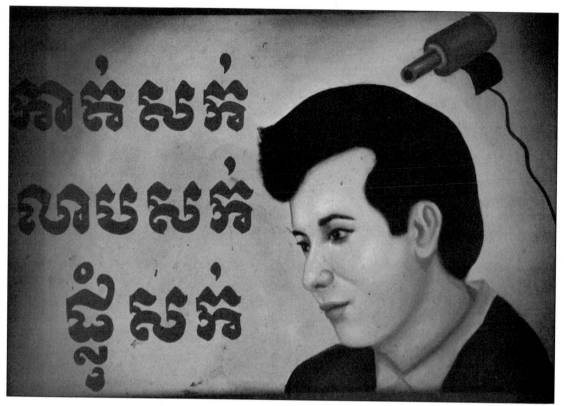

Cory Langley

An advertisement for a hairdresser shows the written Cambodian language.

Cambodian has borrowed extensively from the administrative, military, and literary vocabulary of Sanskrit (the ancient language of India and of Hinduism). Theravada Buddhism brought additional Pali (an Indic language) words. In addition, Cambodians have borrowed words from Thai, French, Chinese, and Vietnamese. Today, English words are becoming more common.

4 ● FOLKLORE

The first hero of Cambodia was *Kaundinya,* who is also the legendary first Cambodian. Cambodians trace their origin to the mar-

riage of a handsome prince who traveled with a magical bow to Cambodia. When a dragon princess rowed out to meet him, he shot an arrow at her boat. Frightened, she agreed to marry him. In exchange for the clothes he gave the naked princess, her father drank up the water that covered the land that became Cambodia.

5 ● RELIGION

Most Cambodians are Theravada Buddhist. Theravada Buddhism is one of the two main Buddhist sects and is practiced also in Thailand and Laos. Khmer Buddhists believe in *karma* and reincarnation—that is, they believe that today's actions will affect their lives in the future, either in this or future lives. The Buddhist religion allows Cambodians a way to gain merit so they may be reborn to a better life. They gain merit by good acts and religious deeds that include acting properly, celebrating holy days, and taking food to the monks at the temple.

Most Cambodians also believe in spirits who must be fed, made happy, and informed of family events. Thus, every wedding includes a ceremony to notify family spirits that a new member is joining the family.

Cambodian Cham are Muslim, many Vietnamese are Roman Catholic, the hill tribes are primarily traditionalist, and the Chinese Cambodians are Taoist or Buddhist.

6 ● MAJOR HOLIDAYS

The most important festivals in Cambodia are Buddhist. Among them are the celebration of the birth, enlightenment, and death of the Buddha; the monks' entry into and exit from the rainy season retreat; the Festival of the Dead; and offerings to the monks, called *Kathin.*

One of the most important holidays of the Cambodian year is New Year. It is celebrated at the beginning of the lunar year, usually in April. This is the time when most Cambodians begin preparing their rice fields for planting and begin sowing their rice seedbeds. The New Year celebration lasts several days, and includes religious ceremonies, dancing, music, and games.

The Festival of the Dead, or Prachum Ben, occurs in the fall. During the fortnight (two weeks) of celebration, offerings are made to the ancestors in the hope that they will protect their descendants.

7 ● RITES OF PASSAGE

The birth of a child is a wonderful and dangerous time for Cambodian families: They welcome the arrival of a new member of the family, but they also worry about spirits who are especially threatening to pregnant women, women in childbirth, and newborn babies. Women, and often their husbands, especially in rural areas, observe a number of rules to protect their family from these spirits.

For many Cambodian children, parents continue to exert almost complete control over them until they are married. Even then, the influence of their parents is heavy. Children are expected to show great respect to their parents and elders. They are severely punished for any disrespect or misbehavior. Children become full adults when they have jobs and their own households, spouses, and children. Even then, they are expected to follow the advice of their elders.

8 ● RELATIONSHIPS

When Cambodians meet, they greet each other with the *sampeah.* Joining their palms together, their fingers pointing up or slightly tilted toward the other person, they bring their hands up to their chest or forehead. The higher the status of the person they are greeting, the higher their hands go. They may also bow their head as they greet with the sampeah.

Cambodians place great importance on hierarchy and proper behavior. Women must respect men, children must respect their elders, and everyone must respect their

Cory Langley

Cambodian families typically have about five children. Many young couples live with the woman's parents until the birth of the first child. The young family then moves into their own house.

superiors. This includes anyone with higher status, greater wealth, or a more important job. Inferiors greet their superiors with greater respect, a deeper bow, or greater stoop when passing by or when offering food. Visitors, both familiar and strange, are treated to the best the household has to offer.

9 ● LIVING CONDITIONS

Most rural Cambodians live in small villages of two hundred or three hundred people. Houses are built on stilts to keep them above the floods of the rainy season. Poorer Cambodians live in single-room dwellings with thatched roofs and walls. Newer houses may have sheet metal roofs. The kitchen is attached to the side of the house.

Platforms under the house provide space for sitting and napping. Both humans and animals benefit from the shade during the hot season, and the protection from the rain during the rainy season. In the dry season, Cambodians work, visit, eat, and sleep under the house during the daytime, and retreat to their houses in the cool and darkness of the evening.

In the cities, Cambodians live in houses ranging from apartments to villas. Wealthier Cambodians live in two-and three-story houses and apartments with electricity and running water. Less-affluent Cambodians live in smaller apartments, often with many family members to a room. In the cities there are also homeless people, living on the sidewalks.

10 ● FAMILY LIFE

The husband is the head of the family and its public spokesperson. He is responsible for providing the family's shelter and food. The Cambodian wife controls her family's finances. In the countryside, her duties include caring for children, home, and garden, as well as transplanting, harvesting, and winnowing the rice. In the city, she may work outside of the home. The Khmer wife is also considered the ethical and religious heart of her family.

Cambodian families typically have about five children. Most men marry between nineteen and twenty-five years of age. Women marry at a slightly younger age. A young man commonly asks his parents' permission and assistance in obtaining a wife. It is still common for many young couples to spend the first year of marriage in the home of the woman's parents. After the parents are assured of their son-in-law's stability, or after the birth of the first child, the young couple moves into their own house.

11 ● CLOTHING

Many Cambodians continue to wear traditional clothing. Women wear a *sampot* and men a *sarong*. Both are wraparound cotton or silk skirts that fall to the knee. Khmer women wear a white blouse or shirt with the sampot. Men go bare-chested or wear a light-colored shirt. The quintessential Cambodian piece of clothing is a *krama,* a long slender scarf. Most commonly worn around the neck, the krama is also worn as a head turban or scarf, a skirt, blouse, purse, or baby sling.

Many Cambodians today prefer to wear Western trousers and shirts, particularly in urban areas. Children go barefoot, while their parents wear rubber thongs or sandals.

During the Khmer Rouge years (1975–78), people were forced to wear dark clothes and were punished or killed for wearing colors or jewelry. In the years following the Vietnamese takeover in 1978, the people were too poor to buy what they wanted. Since reconciliation was achieved in 1993, Cambodians have delighted in the return of a prospering economy and brightly colored and printed fabric and clothing in the marketplaces. Still, poverty is widespread, and most Cambodians can purchase only imported, second-hand clothing.

12 ● FOOD

Rice is the most important Cambodian food. Eaten at virtually every meal, it forms the basis of most Khmer dishes. Fish is almost as important and is eaten fresh, dried, or salted. Vegetables are also a vital part of the diet. Cambodians grow onions, peppers, eggplant, tomatoes, and potatoes in their gardens. Many homes are also surrounded by coconut and banana trees and other plants. A favorite treat is the durian fruit, horrid-smelling but delicious in taste. Other fruits include mangoes, papayas, jackfruit, and palm fruit.

The most traditional of Cambodian foods is *prahok,* fermented fish that is used as a thick sauce condiment with other dishes.

Traditional dances depict ancient folktales.

Betel nut is another favorite. It is a seed that is wrapped in leaves and chewed for its mild narcotic effect.

13 ● EDUCATION

Traditionally, education was provided primarily to boys at temple schools. They were taught religion and the religious language of Pali by Buddhist monks. After independence and before the 1970s, elementary and secondary schooling was expanded enormously for both boys and girls throughout the country.

In the 1970s, traditional and Western-style education came to a virtual standstill. Schools were destroyed, and teachers and students were severely punished or killed. After the Khmer Rouge were driven out in 1978, Cambodia had to begin again to build a system of education.

Today, most children begin school at age seven or eight and receive some schooling for at least several years. Parents want their children to become educated. However, families can barely afford the cost of schooling. It is also difficult for families to survive without their children at home to help with household chores. The literacy rate for adults is about 65 percent (80 percent for men, and 50 percent for women).

14 ● CULTURAL HERITAGE

During the Khmer Rouge regime from 1975 to 1978, Cambodians were not allowed to sing or dance on pain of death. It was a loss that hurt them deeply. Cambodians say that to dance and to listen to their music are among life's sweetest pleasures. Traditional instruments include guitars, xylophones, violins, gongs, and drums. Traditional dance has been the pride of Cambodians for a thousand years. Cambodian plays include both dance and music. They tell ancient stories of Hindu gods and heroes, folk tales about beautiful and wealthy royalty, greedy merchants, and noble youth; as well as comic stories that delight everyone.

Cambodian literature dates back to the seventh century. Traditional texts were memorized and performed by professional storytellers who traveled from place to place. Cambodian literature also includes tales of the Buddha's lives, verses that contain advice for daily life called *chbap,* and folk tales.

Traditional Cambodian literature is being overshadowed today by modern radio and movies, and especially by television and videos. Most Cambodian youth would rather watch a martial arts video from Hong Kong than listen to a storyteller relate ancient stories.

15 ● EMPLOYMENT

Most Cambodians are rice farmers who also grow vegetables and fruit in family gardens. Others cultivate cash crops. Most Cambodian farmers also raise domestic animals, most commonly water buffalo or oxen, which are used for plowing the fields. In the cities, Cambodians hold all the jobs seen in most cities of the world—government officials, construction workers, taxi cab drivers, waiters, maids, and retailers. Many Cambodians are also soldiers.

As the economy improves, colorful plastic utensils and long-lasting metal tools are replacing the wooden handicrafts Cambodians have practiced for centuries. A village that has long made earthenware pots now sells them for pennies to tourists.

16 ● SPORTS

The most popular spectator and participant sports are soccer and volleyball. Other sports include boxing, basketball, and bicycle races. A few Cambodians in urban areas also play tennis and swim. Canoe racing is enjoyed as well.

17 ● RECREATION

Children have a wide variety of family responsibilities and chores. Boys and girls both help with younger children, the care of animals, and a wide variety of other duties. Children usually turn these necessary activities into play and games. In addition, they enjoy swimming and running. A popular village game is played with rubber thongs. The boys draw a line in the dirt, then stand back and throw their sandals at the line. The boy who gets the closest is the winner. Girls and smaller children play a similar game with rubber bands. The winner wears her captured bands around her wrist. Girls also play hopscotch.

Movies, television, and videos are extremely popular in both the urban and rural areas. Karaoke is popular and can be found in the fanciest clubs in the capital of Phnom Penh to the humblest village. Cambodians also enjoy kite flying. In the villages, local festivals remain the most common and popular leisure activity. Eating, listening to music by local or traveling bands, playing videos and other games, drinking, and dancing fill the hours.

18 ● CRAFTS AND HOBBIES

The greatest handiwork of Cambodians was crafted during the Angkorean Period, from the ninth to the fourteenth centuries. Cambodian architects designed, and Cambodian slaves built, a number of temples and palaces in the Angkor region. Included in these is a priceless jewel of artistic work, the temple mausoleum of Angkor Wat.

Traditional crafts include carvings in stone and wood, jewelry making, and gold-and-silver working. Artists often copy ancient religious designs—statues of the Buddha, Hindu gods, scenes from the *Ramayana* (an ancient Hindu epic), and designs from the ancient temples of Angkor. Silk weaving is another craft practiced by many Cambodians.

19 ● SOCIAL PROBLEMS

During the Khmer Rouge regime (1975–78), human and civil rights in Cambodia were nonexistent. The inadequate food, cruelty, and horrors of those years had dreadful consequences on Cambodians, both physically and mentally.

In the late 1990s, as the government of the State of Cambodia increases its power relative to other parties, civil and human rights have decreased. With a limited ability to speak of their nation's problems, many Cambodians regret the loss of openness, maintain little hope for elections, and concentrate on survival. At the same time, although enormous economic, political, and social problems continue, Cambodians are experiencing more peace than they have for decades. For that, they say they are grateful.

20 ● BIBLIOGRAPHY

Chandler, David P. *A History of Cambodia.* Boulder, Colo: Westview Press, 1983.

Ebihara, M. M., C. A. Mortland, and J. Ledgerwood. *Cambodian Culture since 1975. Homeland and Exile.* Ithaca, N.Y.: Cornell University Press, 1994.

Edmonds, I. G. *The Khmers of Cambodia. The Story of a Mysterious People.* New York: The Bobbs-Merrill Company, Inc., 1970.

Ross, Russell R. *Cambodia. A Country Study.* Washington D.C.: U.S. Government Printing Office, 1990.

WEBSITES

Royal Embassy of Cambodia, Washington, D.C. [Online] Available http://www.embassy.org/cambodia/, 1998.

World Travel Guide. Cambodia. [Online] Available http://www.wtgonline.com/country/kh/gen.html, 1998.

Hill Tribespeople

PRONUNCIATION: Hill TRIBES-pee-puhl
LOCATION: Cambodia; Laos; Thailand; Vietnam
POPULATION: 70,000–100,000
LANGUAGE: Mon-Khmer; Austronesian
RELIGION: Traditional spirit-based beliefs

1 ● INTRODUCTION

Among the groups who live in Cambodia are the hill tribespeople. These tribespeople are not ethnic Khmer, as are the vast majority of Cambodians. They number less than 2 percent of the total Cambodian population, which is estimated at 8 million.

The tribespeople of Cambodia were originally called *phnong* or *samre,* meaning savage. The Cambodian government began calling them *Khmer Loeu* (Highland Khmer) in the 1960s, apparently to create unity among the highland tribal groups and the lowland Khmer. Most hill groups come from a very different cultural background than lowland Cambodians. Most have different language, customs, survival strategies, religion, and appearance.

During the 1960s, the Cambodian government sent the army to teach the Khmer language and culture to the hill tribespoeple in an effort to eventually assimilate (absorb) them into Cambodian society. Many tribespeople resented these efforts.

In the late 1960s and early 1970s, the Communist Khmer Rouge were able to recruit a number of young tribesmen to their cause. The illiterate tribal youth, unfamiliar with any element of civilization, became the prototype (model) of the Khmer Rouge army. Like other Cambodians, tribespeople were forced to abandon their traditional religious rituals, customs, and activities.

In 1978, the Vietnamese pushed the Khmer Rouge from power in Cambodia. The Khmer Rouge regained control of some areas of northeastern Cambodia in the 1980s. In most areas, however, the tribespeople live as they did before the Democratic Kampuchea years of the late 1970s. As of the late 1990s, the government was againg trying to teach the Cambodian language and culture to the hill tribespeople. The government claims that tribal languages and customs will continue to be respected.

2 ● LOCATION

The Khmer Loeu hill tribes live in remote highland areas in the plateaus and mountainous areas on the edges of Cambodia. The Khmer Loeu of Cambodia include thirteen distinct minority groups. The tribespeople live without regard to country borders, often in settlements that span both in Cambodia and in neighboring Laos or Vietnam. This is possible because of the isolation and ruggedness of the terrain, making political boundaries difficult to control. Hill people through the centuries have been able to avoid contact with lowlanders and to travel fairly freely across political boundaries.

The turmoil of the Vietnam War (1954–75) and Democratic Kampuchean rule that followed (1975–78) deeply affected the hill tribes. While some groups were recruited by the Khmer Rouge as soldiers, others fought to escape being drafted and controlled by the Communists. Many tribal people escaped the war and horrors of Cambodia by slipping over the border into neighboring countries where they lived with fellow tribespeople. When conditions were better in Cambodia, they moved back across the border.

3 ● LANGUAGE

The hill tribes of Cambodia belong to two very different language groups. One group speaks Mon-Khmer, an Austroasiatic language. The other group speaks an Austronesian language.

Names vary greatly from group to group. A person may carry an individual name, a nickname, and may change names frequently according to life situations and events. In some groups, people are called by the name of their father, mother, child, or spouse. Sometimes the name of a relative is added to the individual's name.

4 ● FOLKLORE

The heroes and myths of the hill tribes of Cambodia are religious and familial in nature. Heroes are actual or fictional ancestors whose deeds and characteristics are passed down from generation to generation. Many of these heroes are considered to have originated particular clans (large family groupings). They are respected, even worshiped, by their descendants both as great people and as the founders of their tribal group.

The myths of particular groups relate to these founding ancestors. Other myths relate stories of the spirits, landscape, animals, and plants of a group's environment. The myths of the highland groups thus form part of their traditional religious beliefs.

5 ● RELIGION

The people of the hill tribes continue the traditional beliefs and practices of their ancestors. They believe that magical spirits live in the natural world, inhabiting rocks, mountains, rivers, and trees.

Most religious leaders are also spirit healers who lead ceremonies to cure illness and other physical and mental problems. They do so by communicating with the spirits who have caused the difficulty or have allowed it to happen.

In some villages, there are two important sorcerers whose main duty is to control the weather. By so doing, they protect the com-

Cory Langley

This young girl is likely to change her name at least once during her lifetime. Among hill tribes, it is common for a person to change his or her name according to life situations and events.

munity from natural calamities and aid in the growth of crops.

6 ● MAJOR HOLIDAYS

The holidays of the tribal groups of Cambodia are primarily religious celebrations. Festivals are held to make the spirits happy and exorcise (drive out) evil spirits. The beginning of the lunar New Year is always an important festival. Life-cycle events such as birth, puberty, marriage, and death, are celebrated by families and villages. These are often major festivals involving multiple families and villages and considerable money and preparation.

7 ● RITES OF PASSAGE

Among most hill groups, infants and small children are greatly desired and are treated with great indulgence. Seldom scolded or punished, they are carried constantly by parents, siblings, or extended family members until around age three or four.

By the time girls are five or six years of age, they are assisting their mother in the home and with caring for younger siblings. By that age, boys are helping with garden duties and caring for the family's livestock. By the age of eight or nine, both boys and girls help in the fields.

Many youth marry while they are still teenagers. By the time most hill tribespeople have reached their early teens, they are fully socialized into adult life. The lives of adult hill people center on family, making a living, and dealing with the spirits or gods who rule the earth.

8 ● RELATIONSHIPS

For tribal people, like most traditional people living in small villages, interpersonal relations are based on fairly strict rules of etiquette (manners and proper behavior). Most villagers have known one another since birth and will continue living as neighbors for years to come. Consequently, they try to avoid conflict in their everyday relations.

With strangers, most tribespeople are modest and reserved. With family and fellow villagers, they are more open and expressive. Always, however, there is an emphasis on getting along with one another. Men and women, even closely related, seldom display affection openly. Visiting is a major activity and a common form of entertainment.

Young people do not date as do youth in the West. Courtship may be brief and involve little contact between the future bride and groom in some groups. Parents or matchmakers do most of the visiting and arranging. Contact between young men and women is generally careful, supervised, and understood to be leading to marriage.

9 ● LIVING CONDITIONS

Most hill groups live in regions far away from denser population areas of Cambodia. In Ratanakiri Province, for example, the only way into much of the province during the rainy season is by airplane and elephant.

The Khmer Loeu live in widely scattered villages near their fields. When they abandon their fields to seek new ones, they also abandon their village sites. Sometimes they return a generation or two later when the fields have regained their fertility.

Houses vary in size from huge dwellings in which many families live, to small, single-family structures. Multifamily houses generally are divided into sections, one per family. Each family also keeps its own hearth for cooking food. Houses may be built close to the ground or high on stilts. Most hill people live much as their ancestors did, without the electricity, running water, and appliances available to many Cambodians who live in the central plains.

10 ● FAMILY LIFE

Hill tribespeople observe a strict division of labor. Women have the primary responsibility for domestic chores, child care, carrying water, and looking after the domestic animals. They also gather food and weave. In agricultural villages, they are also involved in some rice cultivation chores. Men do the hunting and the heavy agricultural tasks. They also make and repair tools and build and repair houses.

Families tend to be large, and most hill people rely on their children to assist with chores. Marriages tend to remain traditional. In many groups, the choice of a mate and wedding arrangements are made by parents, often before the youth reach puberty.

Villages among the hill groups of Cambodia traditionally have been the basic political unit of social life. They are, therefore, independent and self-governing.

11 ● CLOTHING

Most Khmer Loeu continue to wear traditional clothing. Men wear a short loincloth and strings of beads. Women wear a variety of skirts.

The hill tribes of Cambodia weave their traditional colorful clothing on homemade looms. Each tribe has a different style of clothing and jewelry. Clothing is made of cloth that repeats thousands of tiny patterns, with decorations such as silver hoops added. One dress can take weeks to make. Some highland groups file their front teeth and wear tattoos just as their ancestors did.

The decrease in isolation from ethnic Cambodians has resulted in the use of imported clothing. Tribespeople increasingly wear a combination of traditional, Cambodian, and European clothing.

12 ● FOOD

Some hill groups who are primarily rice cultivators have rice as their central food. Groups who raise root crops, such as cassava, taro, and yams, depend primarily on those crops as well as maize (corn), eggplant, beans, sugar cane, bananas, and other fruits and vegetables.

Rice and vegetable crops are supplemented by greatly valued meat. This comes either from domestic animals, such as pigs and poultry, or game and birds from the neighboring forests. Additional valued foods include fish and eggs. Rice wine and cassava beer are common and are consumed primarily on ritual occasions.

Because modern appliances and packaged goods are few, much time and energy goes into the growing, preservation, and preparing of a family's daily meals. Women are primarily responsible for everyday food preparation. Men often bear the responsibility for making alcoholic beverages and cooking ritual foods.

13 ● EDUCATION

Schools and teachers from the lowlands are increasingly available for highland children. However, most highland children continue to be taught traditional skills in traditional ways by parents and relatives. The more contact a village has with Cambodians from the central plains, the more likely their exposure to schools and education in Cambodian subjects and language.

Traditionally, knowledge was passed on orally, rather than through writing. Recently, however, several of the hill languages have been put into written form.

14 ● CULTURAL HERITAGE

Music among hill people is played primarily in the service of religion. It is also played on ritual occasions such as marriage and funerals, and for popular entertainment. Musical instruments include drums, flutes, gongs, xylophones, and various kinds of horns. Instruments are traditionally made of wood, animal horn, and other natural materials. More recently, instruments have been made of modern metals.

The hill tribes have a strong oral tradition that consists of myths, legends, stories, and group knowledge. In the absence of writing and modern entertainment, youth learned the beliefs and events of their past from their elders. In turn, they passed them on to their children.

15 ● EMPLOYMENT

The hill people of Cambodia are either sedentary (staying in one place) or nomadic (migratory). Sedentary groups, which have larger populations, primarily cultivate rice in flooded fields known as paddies. Some are engaged in growing industrial crops.

Nomadic groups are farmers who use slash-and-burn agriculture. Land is cleared for agriculture by cutting down and burning the trees. Then the land is cultivated for several years, and finally abandoned to allow the forest to grow back. After a few decades, the original plot of soil has regained its nutrients and can again support crops.

In addition to growing crops, hill men also raise some domestic animals, including pigs, poultry, and buffalo. Some also raise ducks and geese. Men hunt game and birds in the surrounding forests, and they fish as well. Women do most of the vegetable and herb gathering.

16 ● SPORTS

Tribal children do not engage in organized sports. They spend much of their time assisting their parents in hunting, gathering, and growing crops. Boys learn from an early age to help their fathers. Recreation centers help teach boys what their fathers do. Boys practice with tiny bows, shooting small animals, trying to catch birds and fish, and in numerous ways imitating the activities of their elders.

Children who attend school may also play competitive games such as soccer or volleyball.

17 ● RECREATION

Music is a major form of entertainment. Musical instruments include flutes, mouth organs and harps, and percussion instruments, most made from bamboo. The bronze drum is both a musical instrument and a symbol of wealth and status used in important communal ceremonies.

Children spend many nighttime hours listening to the stories and legends of their people.

Movies, television, videos, and other popular entertainment of Westernized countries remain rare in much of highland Cambodia. Tribespeople rely on singing,

Cory Langley

Most hill people live much as their ancestors did, without the electricity, running water, and appliances available to many Cambodians who live in the central plains.

dancing, and playing musical instruments for much of their entertainment.

18 ● CRAFTS AND HOBBIES

Hill women weave clothing such as skirts and blouses for themselves, loincloths for their men, and blankets. Using cruder materials, men weave mats and baskets. Embroidery and appliqué work are also done. Hill tribespeople make a number of musical instruments, including gourd flutes, mouth harps, guitars, and banjos. Men make agricultural, hunting, and gathering tools. The Kuy of northern Cambodia have a reputation for being excellent blacksmiths. The

Brao are noted for their pottery-making skills.

19 ● SOCIAL PROBLEMS

The Khmer Loeu hill tribes continue to struggle for more independence from the lowland Cambodians. They continue to be viewed by many ethnic Khmer as inferior, with strange customs that are best done away with. Many Khmer Loeu fear that within a few years, their cultures will have disappeared along with their environment. Many are gradually being incorporated into lowland Cambodian life, adopting Khmer customs, clothing, and practices. Many of the youth are now being taught the Khmer language and are working on Cambodian farms.

20 ● BIBLIOGRAPHY

Chandler, David P. *The Tragedy of Cambodian History: Politics, War, and Revolution since 1945.* New Haven, Conn.: Yale University Press.

Hickey, Gerald C. *Shattered Worlds: Adaptation and Survival among Vietnam's Highland Peoples during the Vietnam War.* Philadelphia: University of Pennsylvania Press, 1993.

Kiernan, Ben. *How Pol Pot Came to Power: A History of Communism in Kampuchea, 1930–1975.* London: Verso, 1985

LeBar, Frank M., Gerald D. Hickey, and John K. Musgrave. *Ethnic Groups of Mainland Southeast Asia.* New Haven, Conn.: Human Relations Area Files, 1964.

WEBSITES

Royal Embassy of Cambodia, Washington, D.C. [Online] Available http://www.embassy.org/cambodia, 1998.

World Travel Guide. Cambodia. [Online] Available http://www.wtgonline.com/country/kh/gen. html, 1998.

Cameroon

■ **CAMEROONIANS** 77

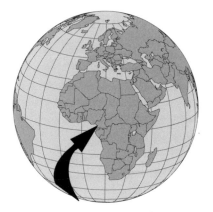

Cameroon has an extremely heterogeneous (mixed) population, consisting of approximately 200 ethnic groups. The principal groups are Bantus, mostly in the south, and the Fulani, in the north. For more information on the Fulani, see the chapter on Guinea in Volume 4

Cameroonians

PRONUNCIATION: kam-uh-ROON-ee-uhns
LOCATION: Cameroon
POPULATION: 13 million
LANGUAGE: English; French; twenty-four African languages
RELIGION: Islam; Christianity; indigenous beliefs

1 ● INTRODUCTION

Cameroon's present borders were drawn after World War I (1914–18). It had been a German colony in 1885 but was surrendered to the British and French in 1916. These colonizers divided the country in 1919. The British administered West Cameroon as part of Nigeria. The French made East Cameroon part of French Equatorial Africa (along with Chad, Gabon, and the Republic of Congo).

Cameroon won full independence in 1960. Cameroon's first president, Ahmadou Ahidjo, declared a one-party government in 1966. In 1972, a strong presidential government replaced the Federal Republic, and the country's name became United Republic of Cameroon.

2 ● LOCATION

Cameroon is slightly larger than California. It is one of Africa's most varied countries, physically and culturally. The climate varies with the latitude and the terrain. It is humidly tropical along the coastal plain, cool in the western mountains, and rather dry and hot on the flat and sometimes rolling northern savanna (treeless plains).

Cameroon's 13 million people come from seven major ethnic groups. However, by some counts, as many as 200 ethnic groups live within Cameroon's borders.

3 ● LANGUAGE

Cameroonians speak about twenty-four different African languages. In the North, people speak Saharan and Chadic languages. Bantu languages are spoken in the South. Cameroon is unique in having both English

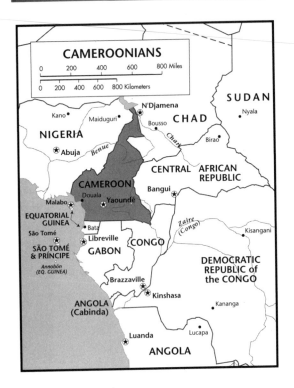

CAMEROONIANS

and French as official languages. French is dominant, and there is a movement to make it the only official language. However, the northwest and southwest provinces hold on to English.

4 ● FOLKLORE

Cameroonian folklore has many intriguing myths, legends, and proverbs from its varied cultural groups. Examples of proverbs are "Rain does not fall on one roof alone," "He who asks questions must be prepared to hear the answers," and "If you do not step on the dog's tail, he will not bite you."

An example of a myth recalls how traditional society once treated twins. It is said that in the past when a woman gave birth to twins, she presented them directly to the Sultan (ruler). A chicken was sacrificed to safeguard them and to ensure their good behavior. The mother then returned home with them and fed them meat. (Supposedly, twins from this group had an amazing ability to chew meat even before their teeth come in.) At age five, they returned to the palace to stay. The Sultan raised them as his own children and gave them a good education. As they grew older, the Sultan asked their advice on important decisions.

One of Cameroon's greatest heroes is Douala Manga Bell, who was hanged in 1914 for acting in opposition to German colonizers. Cameroonians remember his deeds and the bravery of his companions in songs and plays that are passed down from generation to generation.

5 ● RELIGION

Cameroon is mainly Catholic (34.7 percent) and Protestant (17.5 percent), but there is also a large Muslim population (21 percent), especially in the North. More than a quarter of the population follows native African beliefs. Like many other African peoples, Cameroonians combine parts of traditional animist (spirit) beliefs with their Christian or Muslim beliefs. For example, a *marabout* (traditional healer) may advise a sick person to write on a prayer board passages from the holy Koran. The patient then prays by reciting the words. Next, he dilutes the ink from the board and drinks it, taking in the holy words.

6 ● MAJOR HOLIDAYS

Holidays in Cameroon are treated differently by different groups. For example, National Day, May 20, which marks the change to a stronger government in 1972, is a great celebration for French-speaking Cameroonians. But the English speakers in the West see this holiday as a reminder of the power they gave away to the French-speaking majority at that time.

French speakers celebrate more on New Year's Day. English speakers emphasize Christmas. On Christmas Eve and Christmas Day, people put on their new clothes and go to church. Near Wum, people form large groups and go from village to village socializing, eating, drinking, and dancing. The feasting is so joyous that even Muslims join in the celebrations and go to church.

7 ● RITES OF PASSAGE

Traditional rites of passage such as initiation into adulthood, are losing the significance they once had in Cameroonian society. As Christian beliefs replace the traditional ways, baptisms, first communions, and weddings are more important. But, church ceremonies have not completely replaced traditional ways.

8 ● RELATIONSHIPS

The language of greeting depends on the region. In French one typically says, *Bonjour, comment ça va?* (Hello, how are you?). In Pidgin English one says "How na?"

People shake hands and some kiss on the cheek. Pointing to a person is considered rude. So is crossing one's legs at the knees or in the presence of someone with higher status. People use the right hand to pass or accept objects.

Visitors appear frequently and without warning, and relatives often stay and are fed for long periods.

David Johnson

A young boy with his scooter.

9 ● LIVING CONDITIONS

Cameroon has good conditions for farming, and oil is an important natural resource. But Cameroonians face many of the same challenges as other Africans. In the villages, most houses are still made of mud and thatch. However, these are gradually being replaced by houses made of concrete blocks and galvanized iron roofing. Still, many people travel from place to place, and many camp out in poor areas (shantytowns) at the edges of cities. Shantytowns often do not have basic services such as clean water.

10 ● FAMILY LIFE

Young people date more in the capital and big cities than in rural areas. Throughout the country, marriages are still arranged by families. Cameroonians usually have large families with at least six children. Families are larger if the head of household has more than one wife. Grandparents and great-grandparents live in the same compound, or group area, as their children. The male head of the family usually leads in important matters. Women must do much of the work, tending fields, gathering firewood, and hauling water besides taking care of the children and doing the housework.

11 ● CLOTHING

Traditional clothing is most often worn in the villages. In the North, Muslims wear colorful flowing robes and women cover their heads in public.

Pagnes (sarongs) are worn by women in all regions. A second piece of cloth can be used to attach a baby to one's back, provide shade for the head, or give warmth on chilly mornings. A turban, usually from the same fabric, covers the head.

In the towns, people sometimes wear traditional clothes, but the men are also likely to wear Western pants and shirts. The younger generation wears jeans and T-shirts. Women usually wear blouses over their sarongs.

12 ● FOOD

The staples are corn, millet, cassava, groundnuts (peanuts), plantains, and yams. One or more of these provide the ingredients for *fufu*, a stiff paste, that is rolled into small balls and dipped into stews. A favorite dish is *jamma*, spicy greens, served at the large noon meal. In rural areas, people eat out of shared bowls with the right hand. In the cities, people eat with kitchen utensils much as in the United States and other Western countries.

13 ● EDUCATION

Bilingual education, education in two languages, is provided by government, missionary, and private schools. Primary school begins at six years of age. Children begin high school at the age of twelve or thirteen, and continue until nineteen or twenty. The government has built five regional campuses of the University of Yaoundé. Each one has a different area of specialization.

14 ● CULTURAL HERITAGE

Cameroonian modern literature, film, and *makossa* (urban-style) music are very popular, thanks to Cameroon's rich and varied cultural past. Makossa music is heard all over the country, playing loudly from radios or being performed by live street musicians.

In traditional society, people still perform ancient rites with music, dance, masks, and statuettes. One group plays dirge (funeral-style) music at night when they want to accuse a person of a serious crime. With lifeless voices, singers march through the streets, striking bells and tapping on drums made of buffalo skin.

AP/Wide World Photos

Youngsters push a water cart, too heavy to be carried in the normal manner on their heads. They are traveling along a street near the main highway between Yaounde and Douala, the nation's two principal towns.

15 ● EMPLOYMENT

Most Cameroonians (about three-quarters) work in agriculture as subsistence farmers (growing the basic foods needed for the family), herders, or plantation workers.

16 ● SPORTS

Cameroonians are soccer fanatics, and rightly so. Cameroon qualified for the World Cup in 1982, 1990, and 1994, and went to the 1990 quarterfinals. Other popular European sports include basketball, tennis, and handball.

17 ● RECREATION

Cameroonian *makossa* music defines much of the popular culture. The music is hard-hitting, with a tight, fast-paced rhythm. People play it everywhere: on their transistor radios, at truck stops and taxi stands, in pubs and restaurants, and in nightclubs. Musicians such as Manu Dibango and Sam Fan Thomas are national celebrities.

Cameroonian television is limited to the government station, which has limited broadcast hours. Some men are fond of chess and checkers.

18 ● CRAFTS AND HOBBIES

Folk art objects include elephant masks; wooden, bronze, and bead-covered statuettes; carved pillars and bed posts; woven baskets; and pottery. The *Tso* dancers of the Kuosi perform in fabulous beaded elephant masks when a chief or an important person dies.

19 ● SOCIAL PROBLEMS

Cameroon is making political changes from a one-party system to democracy with several political parties, but the change has not come easily. Private newspapers carry stories claiming civil rights abuses, beatings, and even deaths related to demonstrations and strikes.

Cameroonians face serious economic and social challenges. The population grows at about 3 percent a year. The demand for education, health care, and jobs continues to increase. In addition, Cameroon's environment is endangered by destruction of forests, excessive grazing, illegal hunting, and heavy fishing.

20 ● BIBLIOGRAPHY

Carpenter, Allan. *Cameroon*. Chicago: Children's Press, 1977.

DeLancey, Mark. *Cameroon: Dependence and Independence*. Boulder, Colo.: Westview, 1989.

Hathaway, Jim. *Cameroon in Pictures*. Minneapolis, Minn.: Lerner Publications Co., 1989.

WEBSITES

InterGO Communications. [Online] Available http://www.teachersoft.com/Library/ref/atlas/africa/cm.htm, 1998.

World Travel Guide. [Online] Available http://www.wtgonline.com/country/cm/gen.html, 1998.

Canada

■ **CANADIANS** **83**
■ **FRENCH CANADIANS** ... **89**
■ **INUIT** **94**

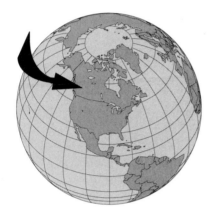

Nearly one-third of Canadians claim multiple ethnic origin. People who report British origin (including Irish) make up almost 45 percent of the population. Canada is also home to a large French minority (30 percent of the population) and a smaller number of native peoples, including the Inuit (Eskimos). Canadians also report origin from other European countries including Germany and Italy (about 3 percent each); and Ukraine, the Netherlands, and Poland (about 1 percent each).

Canadians

PRONUNCIATION: cuh-NAY-dee-uhns

LOCATION: Canada

POPULATION: 27.3 million (1991)

LANGUAGE: English and French (both official); Italian; German; Chinese; Spanish

RELIGION: Roman Catholicism, Protestantism (majority); Judaism; Buddhism; Sikhism; Hinduism; Bahaism; traditional religions of native groups

1 ● INTRODUCTION

Canada is the world's second largest country, surpassed in area only by Russia. It is also one of the least densely populated. Most of its population is concentrated in a strip 180 miles (290 kilometers) wide along its border with the United States.

Amerindian and Inuit peoples first migrated to present-day Canada from Asia across the Bering Straits around 10,000 BC. By the late seventeenth century, France and Britain were rivals for the region's rich fish and fur trade. This rivalry was ended in 1763 by the Treaty of Paris, which gave the British control over what had formerly been New France. The British North America Act created the Dominion of Canadian by 1867. By 1949, with the addition of Newfoundland, the Dominion had grown to include ten provinces.

The French Canadian separatist movement has grown since the 1960s. French became the province of Quebec's official language in 1974. Political independence for Quebec has been a controversial issue for both the province and the country as a whole.

2 ● LOCATION

Canada is a vast country with great geographical variety. Covering about two-fifths of the North American continent, it has an area of 3,849,650 square miles (9,970,594 square kilometers). The Canadian Shield, a rocky area of forests, lakes, and wilderness, covers roughly half of Canada, separating the eastern and western parts of the country.

The Atlantic provinces, to the east of the Shield, include two islands: Newfoundland and Prince Edward Island. The Great Lakes-St. Lawrence lowlands are home to the largest portion of Canada's population and the site of the nation's capital, Ottawa. The farmlands and ranching areas of the Western Plains lie west of the Canadian Shield and east of the Rocky Mountains. Still farther west lies the Western Cordillera (mountain range), which includes the Rockies. The northernmost part of Canada includes the tundra, which lies north of the tree line, and the country's Arctic islands.

Although Canada is 10 percent larger than the United States (including Alaska), it has only about 10 percent as many people. The 1991 census recorded just under 27.3 million. Three-fourths of Canadians are urban dwellers. Toronto is the most populous metropolitan area, with about 3.9 million people in 1991.

3 ● LANGUAGE

Both English and French are Canada's official languages. Canada is generally considered a bilingual country. However, only 16 percent of the population is actually bilingual. About 60 percent speak English only and 24 percent French only. Canada's native peoples speak between fifty and sixty different languages.

4 ● FOLKLORE

Canada's folklore tradition is generally divided into four main strains: native, French Canadian, Anglo-Canadian, and other ethnic groups. The native tradition includes creation and hero myths, such as the Raven and Thunderbird stories of the West Coast.

For many years the French Canadians had to transmit their culture orally across the generations, giving them a strong folklore tradition. Popular characters in French Canadian folklore include a hero named Ti-Jean (short for *petit Jean* or Little John) and a hunter named Dalbec.

Jokes and anecdotes, including "Newfie" jokes about Newfoundlanders, are popular among Anglo-Canadians.

5 ● RELIGION

Approximately 90 percent of Canadians are Christians. They are divided about equally between Catholics and Protestants. Protestant groups include the United Church of Canada and the Anglican, Presbyterian, Baptist, and Lutheran churches. Other religions include Judaism, Buddhism, and the traditional religions of native groups. Roman Catholics are in the majority in Quebec and New Brunswick. The other provinces are predominantly Protestant.

6 ● MAJOR HOLIDAYS

Canada's most important national holiday is Canada Day (formerly Dominion Day) on July 1. It commemorates the establishment of the Dominion of Canada in 1867. Canadians celebrate their nation's "birthday" with patriotic ceremonies, picnics, and fireworks. The holiday marking the beginning of summer in Canada is Victoria Day, the Monday preceding May 25. (It is called Dollard Day by residents of Quebec.) Canada's Labour Day, like that of the United States, occurs at the end of summer (the first Monday in September). Other legal holidays include New Year's Day and the major holidays of the Christian calendar. Canadians also have a Thanksgiving holiday similar to that of the United States, but it is held on the second Monday in October.

7 ● RITES OF PASSAGE

Canadians commemorate births, marriages, and deaths in ways similar to people of other western nations. Many mark these major life events within the traditions of their respective religions.

8 ● RELATIONSHIPS

Canadians' reputation for courtesy, tolerance, and cooperation is reflected in the traditional designation of their country as the "peaceable kingdom."

© Corel Corporation

Canadians celebrate Canada Day (July 1) at Parliament Hill in Ottawa, the nation's captial.

9 ● LIVING CONDITIONS

Two out of every three Canadians own their own homes. Single homes are the most common type of dwelling. However, the current trend is toward more multifamily structures. One in seven Canadian homes is heated by wood.

10 ● FAMILY LIFE

Nuclear families are the norm throughout Canada. The average age at marriage is mid-twenties for men and early twenties for women. In most families, children are separated from each other by only a few years. The majority of married couples share similar ethnic, religious, and educational backgrounds.

Currently, close to half of all Canadian marriages (four out of ten) end in divorce.

Women made up 45 percent of the labor force in 1992. However, they earned only two-thirds as much as men.

11 ● CLOTHING

Canadians wear modern, Western-style clothing. They may wear the traditional costumes of their ethnic groups on special occasions. In the western provinces, American-style cowboy gear is worn for special occasions and festivals, such as the Calgary Exhibition and Stampede in Alberta.

12 ● FOOD

Different foods are found in the different regions of Canada. "Brewis" (cod) is a favorite in Newfoundland. Clambakes are especially popular on Prince Edward Island. Quebec has a distinctive French-Canadian cuisine. Popular dishes include the *tourtière* (a meat pie), and *ragoût de boulettes et de pattes do cochon* (a stew made from meatballs and pigs' feet). Quebec is also known for its maple syrup.

Two of Ontario's favorite dishes are roast pheasant and pumpkin pie. Alberta is known for the quality of its grain-fed beef. Moose meat and fresh lake fish are widely eaten in the Northwest Territories. A recipe for wild rice, a delicacy in Manitoba, follows.

13 ● EDUCATION

Nearly the entire adult population of Canada is literate (can read and write). Education is administered by each province individually. In all cases it is compulsory from the age of about six to sixteen. Quebec has two parallel systems, one specifically for French-speaking, Catholic students. Most higher education is government-funded. Canada's best-known universities are the University of Toronto and McGill University in Montreal.

14 ● CULTURAL HERITAGE

Margaret Atwood (1939–), Robertson Davies, Mordecai Richler (1931–), and Margaret Laurence (1926–87) are among Canada's best-known modern writers.

Recipe

Wild Rice

Ingredients

1 cup wild rice
salt
¼ cup butter, cut up

Directions

1. Place rice in a sieve or colander. Rinse rice thoroughly several times under running water.
2. Put 2½ cups of water into a saucepan with ½ teaspoon of salt.
3. Cover and heat until water is boiling. Add rice and reduce heat. Cover the pan and simmer for 30 to 40 minutes, stirring occasionally. Rice is done when kernels split lengthwise so the white inside of the kernel is visible.
4. Add butter to hot rice and fluff with a fork. Celery, onion, or mushrooms, lightly cooked in butter, may be added to the rice if desired.
5. Rice may be prepared in advance and placed into a buttered casserole dish. Reheat in the oven at 350°F or in the microwave.

Classical musicians have included pianist Glenn Gould (1932–82) and vocal artists Jon Vickers and Maureen Forrester. Well-known popular performers include Joni Mitchell (1943–), Neil Young (1945–), Gordon Lightfoot (1938–), Jim Carrey (1962–) , and Alanis Morissette (1974–).

Well-known theatrical events include the Stratford Festival and Shaw Festival, both

© Corel Corporation

Canadians have a modern industrial economy.

held every year in Ontario, and the Festival Lennoxville in Quebec.

15 ● EMPLOYMENT

Like their neighbors in the United States, Canadians are finding themselves working harder for the same pay, as jobs become more competitive and less secure. About 70 percent of Canadians work in the service sector, 25 percent work in industry, and about 3 percent work in agriculture.

16 ● SPORTS

Ice hockey is Canada's national sport, and its stars are worshiped as national heroes.

Professional games draw thousands of fans on Saturday nights. Youngsters often rise as early as 4:00 or 5:00 AM on weekends to play on little-league hockey teams. Other popular winter sports include skiing, ice-skating, snowshoeing, and tobogganing. Favorite summer sports include baseball, volleyball, and soccer. Lacrosse was originated by the native population before the arrival of Europeans. Curling, a sport where a heavy "stone" is slid across the ice, was adopted from the Scots.

17 ● RECREATION

Like their U.S. counterparts, Canadian families spend much of their evening time watching television. Many are regular newspaper readers. Their scenic land provides many Canadians with recreation. Many own weekend and vacation cottages on lakeshores or in wooded areas.

18 ● CRAFTS AND HOBBIES

Amerindian artists produce jewelry, beaded moccasins, baskets, and leather goods. The Inuit are known for their soapstone, ivory, and serpentine carvings as well as prints, paintings, drawings, and wall hangings.

19 ● SOCIAL PROBLEMS

Canada has a relatively low level of violent crime. Its cities are generally clean, efficiently run, and have little homelessness and illegal drug dealing. Canada has a large national debt and faces growing demands for decentralization from many of its regions. A most serious problem is the threat that Quebec will secede and become a sovereign state.

20 ● BIBLIOGRAPHY

Kalman, Bobbie. *Canada: The Culture.* New York: Crabtree Publishing, 1993.

Malcolm, Andrew. *The Land and People of Canada.* New York: HarperCollins, 1988.

Shepherd, J. *Canada.* Chicago: Children's Press, 1987.

Weihs, Jean. *Facts about Canada, Its Provinces, and Territories.* H. W. Wilson Co., 1995.

WEBSITES

Canada. [Online] Available http://www.informatik.uni-kiel.de/~car/Canada.html, 1997.

Canadian Tourism Commission. Canada. [Online] Available http://206.191.33.50/tourism/, 1998.

Embassy of Canada, Washington, D.C. [Online] Available http://www.cdnemb-washdc.org, 1998.

World Travel Guide. Canada. [Online] Available http://www.wtgonline.com/country/ca/index.html, 1998.

French Canadians

PRONUNCIATION: frEHnch cuh-NAY-dee-uhns
ALTERNATE NAMES: Cajuns (in the United States)
LOCATION: Canada (mainly Quebec); United States (mainly Louisiana and New England)
POPULATION: 6.5 million in Canada; 2–5 million in the United States
LANGUAGE: French
RELIGION: Roman Catholicism

1 ● INTRODUCTION

French Canadians are descendants of Canada's colonial-era French settlers. Most live in the province of Quebec, where they form a majority of the population. The past thirty-five years have seen a strong rebirth of the French Canadians' sense of cultural identity. It has been accompanied by a political separatist movement with far-reaching implications not only for Quebec, but for all of Canada.

The French presence in Canada began in 1534, but permanent settlement did not begin until Samuel de Champlain founded Quebec City in 1608. The French eventually carved out an enormous territory stretching as far east as the Maritime provinces and south to the Gulf of Mexico.

After France's defeat in the French and Indian Wars, Britain won control of New France, formalized by the Treaty of Paris in 1763. Under British rule, the French Canadians remained a distinct cultural group. The preservation of their cultural identity was aided by the influence of the Catholic Church, the tendency to marry within their own community, and the tradition of having large families. When the Dominion of Can-

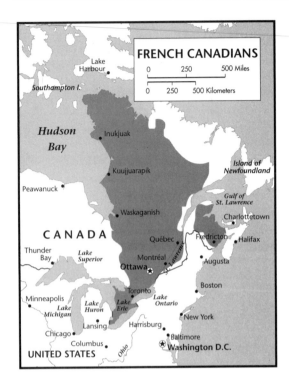

FRENCH CANADIANS

0   250   500 Miles

0   250   500 Kilometers

Lake Harbour

Southampton I.

Hudson Bay

Inukjuak

Kuujjuarapik

Island of Newfoundland

Peawanuck

Waskaganish

Gulf of St. Lawrence

Charlottetown

CANADA

Québec

Fredricton

Halifax

Thunder Bay

Lake Superior

Montréal

Augusta

Ottawa

Boston

Minneapolis

Lake Michigan

Lake Huron

Lake Erie

Toronto

Lake Ontario

New York

Lansing

Harrisburg

Chicago

Columbus

Baltimore

Washington D.C.

UNITED STATES

Ohio

ada was established in 1867, French Canadians accounted for one-third of the new country's population.

After World War II, there were growing demands for political autonomy (self-rule) in Quebec. French was recognized as Quebec's official language in 1974. The separatist Parti Québécois came to power in the province in 1976. A proposal for political independence from the rest of Canada was defeated at the polls in 1980. However, French Canadian separatism has remained a contentious issue for both the province and the nation as a whole.

2 ● LOCATION

The 6.5 million French Canadians living in Canada represent about a quarter of the country's total population. The majority—5.1 million—live in the province of Quebec. There are also French Canadians—known as Acadians—in the Maritime provinces of New Brunswick, Nova Scotia, and Prince Edward Island. They account for about 15 percent of the population in those provinces. There are also French Canadian communities in Ontario and the western provinces, as well as in the United States.

3 ● LANGUAGE

French Canadians are the largest group of Francophones (French speakers) in North America.

The vocabulary and pronunciation of Canadian French differ from those of the French spoken in France. Québécois is based on an older form of French and also contains many English expressions. For example, "to marry" is *marier* instead of the French term, *épouser*. Similarly, "appointment" is *appointement* instead of *rendezvous*, and "ignore" is *ignorer* instead of *négliger*.

The Acadians speak a distinctive form of French characterized by many old-fashioned expressions preserved from the seventeenth-century dialects of western France. In Moncton, New Brunswick, contact with English speakers has produced a French-English called Chiac.

4 ● FOLKLORE

The French-Canadian folklore tradition was strengthened by colonial laws that made it crucial for French Canadians to transmit their culture orally across the generations. Popular characters in French Canadian folklore include a hero figure named Ti-Jean (short for *petit Jean*, or Little John) and a hunter named Dalbec.

5 ● RELIGION

The majority of French Canadians are Roman Catholic. Until the 1960s, the church was central to French Canadian life. Since that time, however, the French Canadian community has become more secular. Church attendance has declined, and the influence of the church on daily life has decreased.

6 ● MAJOR HOLIDAYS

French Canadians celebrate Dollard Day on the Monday preceding May 25. The day honors a seventeenth-century French war hero. On that same day, the rest of Canada celebrates Victoria Day in honor of Britain's Queen Victoria. The most important religious holidays for French Canadians are Christmas and Easter. Many—especially those in rural areas—still observe the traditional Christmas celebration. It includes a large midnight supper (*Réveillon*) of *tourtières* (meat pies), *ragaut* (stew), and other dishes. On St. Jean Baptiste Day (24 June), the Québécois celebrate their patron saint with parties, bonfires, and fireworks. The Acadians' patron saint is Our Lady of the Assumption, and Assumption Day (August 15) is their day of celebration.

7 ● RITES OF PASSAGE

Most French Canadians observe the major life cycle events, such as birth, marriage, and death, within the traditions of the Roman Catholic church. The government of Quebec, the home of Canada's largest French-speaking population, recognizes common-law marriage in cases where couples have lived together for two years.

8 ● RELATIONSHIPS

Like their English-speaking neighbors, French Canadians are hospitable, friendly, and polite. It is common for men to open doors for women or give up a seat if a woman is standing. French Canadians use the common greeting of *Bonjour* (Good day) for "Hello" and *Au revoir* for "Goodbye." Adults use first names and informal forms of address (such as *tu* rather than *vous*) only with people they know well, such as close friends or relatives. Both men and women may exchange kisses on both cheeks in a European-style greeting. Close women friends often greet each other by embracing.

9 ● LIVING CONDITIONS

Housing in Canada varies by region, depending on the local availability of building materials. Two out of every three Canadians own their own homes. Single homes are the most common type of dwelling although the current trend is toward greater numbers of multifamily structures. The homes of the Acadians, like most of those in the Maritime provinces, are mostly built of wood.

10 ● FAMILY LIFE

Until the 1960s, the family lives of French Canadians were heavily influenced by the Roman Catholic Church. Large families were the norm. Today the average couple has only two children. The French Canadian divorce rate is comparable to that among other groups in North America. Roughly half of all newly married couples eventually

Recipe

Tourtière

Ingredients

1½ to 2 pounds pork, ground or finely chopped
1 clove of garlic, crushed
1 medium onion, chopped
½ cup hot water
¼ teaspoon celery salt
¼ teaspoon ground cloves
salt and pepper to taste
double 9-inch pie crust

Directions

1. Mix the water, pork, and seasonings in a saucepan.
2. Cook over a low flame for 20 to 25 minutes and then cool. (Optional: ¼ cup dry bread crumbs may be added at this point.)
3. Cover the bottom of a 9-inch pie pan with bottom layer of pie dough, add pork filling, and cover with top layer of dough.
4. Seal the crust by pinching the edges together. Preheat oven to 350°F. Bake pie about 35 minutes, or until browned.

divorce. The increased divorce rate has raised the number of single-parent families.

Since the 1970s, educational and employment opportunities for Canadian women have expanded. They have entered the professions and other traditionally male areas of the economy in increasing numbers. The government of Quebec established a program to encourage employment opportunities for women in the early 1980s.

11 ● CLOTHING

French Canadians wear modern Western-style clothing. The traditional costume of the Acadians is still worn on special occasions. Women wear white bonnets and blouses, black skirts, and white aprons. Men wear white shirts, black vests, and knee-length black pants. White stockings and black shoes are worn by both men and women.

12 ● FOOD

Quebec has a rich, distinctive French-Canadian cuisine. Popular dishes include *tourtière* (a meat pie), and *ragoût de boulettes et de pattes do cochon* (a stew made from meatballs and pigs' feet). Other favorites include French onion soup, pea soup, and *poutine*, a traditional dish made with French fries or grated potatoes. Quebec is also known for its maple syrup. Children enjoy eating *tourquettes*, a natural candy made by pouring boiling maple syrup onto fresh snow.

13 ● EDUCATION

Education in Canada is administered by each province individually. In all cases school attendance is compulsory from the age of about six to sixteen. Quebec has two parallel systems, one of which is specifically for French-speaking, Catholic students. The Acadian populations of New Brunswick, Nova Scotia, and Prince Edward Island are legally guaranteed access to French-language schools in predominantly French-speaking areas.

Most higher education in Canada is government-funded. Laval University in Quebec is Canada's oldest university, and

McGill in Montreal is one of its most prestigious.

14 ● CULTURAL HERITAGE

French Canadian radio stations must allot 75 percent of their programming to music by French recording artists. Folk and country music are especially popular with Acadians.

Leading contemporary French Canadian authors include playwright Michel Tremblay (1942–) and short-story writer Mavis Gallant (1922–). Perhaps the most renowned French Canadian author of the twentieth century was Gabrielle Roy (1909–83). Her first novel, *The Tin Flute* (1945), drew a stark portrait of Quebec's urban poor.

15 ● EMPLOYMENT

Before the 1980s, management positions in Quebec tended to be dominated by English speakers. However, after the separatist Parti Québécois came to power in 1976, many English speakers left the province. Since then the gap between the two groups has narrowed substantially. Today the French Canadian middle class occupies a prominent position in industry, finance, and other key economic areas. French Canadians work in government and the professions and own small businesses. There is still a French-speaking working class in both unionized and nonunionized fields. Many Quebecois have performed hazardous work in the province's asbestos mines.

Before the twentieth century, the French-speaking Acadians in the Maritime provinces engaged in farming, fishing, and forestry. Today many engage in commercial farming and fishing.

16 ● SPORTS

Hockey, the Canadian national sport, is popular among French Canadians. Every team in the National Hockey League (NHL) includes French Canadians. Quebec has had five professional teams since the NHL began in 1917—three in Montreal (Canadiens, 1917–present; Wanderers, 1917–18; and Maroons, 1924–38) and two in Quebec City (Bulldogs, 1919–20; and Nordiques, 1979–95). The Montreal Canadiens—popularly known as the "Habitants" or "Habs"—have won the Stanley Cup, which is awarded to League champions, more than twenty times.

17 ● RECREATION

The Canadian Broadcasting System (CBC) broadcasts French-language news programs, dramas, films, and sports events. Quebec also has a large audience for English-language television and radio programming and magazines. *Le Journal de Montréal* and *La Presse* are the most widely read French-language newspapers.

Like Canadians of all backgrounds, French Canadians enjoy the beautiful scenery of their native land on vacation trips. Many families own small cottages in the country, which they visit on weekends and during vacations. Others travel to distant parts of the country for camping or other outdoor activities.

A time-honored pastime among French Canadian families in Quebec is "sugaring off." Early in the spring, they head for the woods to tap maple trees for sap that is then boiled down in *cabines à sucre* ("sugar shacks") to make maple syrup and maple sugar.

18 ● CRAFTS AND HOBBIES

Traditional crafts among the Acadians include knitting and weaving. Colorful hooked rugs are a specialty.

19 ● SOCIAL PROBLEMS

The social status of French Canadians has historically been lower than that of the English-speaking majority. Traditionally, they have not been as well educated and have suffered widespread discrimination.

A major concern of French Canadians today is the preservation of their culture and language against the threat of assimilation into English-speaking North America. In both Quebec and the Maritimes, the drain of resources caused by emigration to other parts of Canada and to the United States is also a concern.

20 ● BIBLIOGRAPHY

Lemco, Jonathan. *Turmoil in the Peaceable Kingdom: The Quebec Sovereignty Movement and Its Implications for Canada and the United States.* Toronto: University of Toronto Press, 1994.
Richler, Mordecai. *Oh Canada! Oh Quebec! Requiem for a Divided Country.* New York: Knopf, 1992.
Wartik, Nancy. *The French Canadians.* New York: Chelsea House, 1989.

WEBSITES
Canada. [Online] Available http://www.informatik. uni-kiel.de/~car/Canada.html, 1997.
Canadian Tourism Commission. Canada. [Online] Available http://http://206.191.33.50/tourism/, 1998.
Embassy of Canada, Washington, D.C. [Online] Available http://www.cdnemb-washdc.org/, 1998.
World Travel Guide. Canada. [Online] Available http://www/wtgonline.com/country/ca/index. html, 1998.

Inuit

PRONUNCIATION: INN-oo-eht
ALTERNATE NAMES: Eskimo
LOCATION: Canada (Greenland); United States (Alaska); Aleutian Islands; Russia (Siberia)
POPULATION: 90,000
LANGUAGE: Inuit
RELIGION: Traditional animism; Christianity

1 ● INTRODUCTION

The Inuit, or Eskimo, are an aboriginal people who make their home in the Arctic and sub-Arctic regions of Siberia and North America.

The word "Eskimo" was bestowed upon these hardy, resourceful hunters by their neighbors, the Algonquin Indians of eastern Canada. It means "eaters of raw meat." Recently, it has begun to be replaced by the Eskimos' own name for themselves, "Inuit," which means, "real people."

The Inuit are descended from whale hunters who migrated from Alaska to Greenland and the Canadian Arctic around 1000 AD. Major changes in Inuit life and culture occurred during the Little Ice Age (1600–1850), when the climate in their homelands became even colder. European whalers who arrived in the latter part of the nineteenth century had a strong impact on the Inuit. The Westerners introduced Chris-

Cynthia Bassett

Inuit women gathered firewood, butchered the animals, and erected tents in summer and igloos in winter.

tianity. They also brought with them infectious diseases that substantially reduced the Inuit population in some areas. When the whaling industry collapsed early in the twentieth century, many Inuit turned to trapping.

Wherever they live, the Inuit today are much involved in the modern world. They have wholeheartedly adopted much of its technology, as well as its food, clothing, and housing customs. Their economic, religious, and government institutions have also been heavily influenced by mainstream culture.

2 ● LOCATION

The Inuit live primarily along the far northern seacoasts of Russia, the United States, Canada, and Greenland. All told, there are more than 100,000 Inuit, most of whom live south of the Arctic Circle. The majority, about 46,000, live in Greenland. There are approximately 30,000 on the Aleutian Islands and in Alaska, 25,000 in Canada, and 1,500 in Siberia. The Inuit homeland is one of the regions of the world least hospitable to human habitation. Most of the land is flat, barren tundra where only the top few inches of the frozen earth thaw out during the summer months. The majority of Inuit have always lived near the sea, hunting aquatic mammals such as seals, walrus, and whales.

3 ● LANGUAGE

The Inuit language is divided into two major dialect groups: *Inupik* and *Yupik*. Inupik speakers are in the majority and reside in an area stretching from Greenland to western Alaska. Speakers of Yupik inhabit a region consisting of southwestern Alaska and Siberia.

4 ● FOLKLORE

According to a traditional folktale told by the Tikigaq Inuit of north Alaska, the raven (a traditional trickster figure in Inuit folklore) was originally white. It turned black in the course of a deal it made with the loon. The two birds agreed to tattoo each other but ended up in a soot-flinging match that turned the loon gray and the raven black.

5 ● RELIGION

Christianity, first introduced by missionaries, has largely replaced traditional Inuit religious practices. However, many of native religious beliefs still linger.

Many traditional Inuit religious customs were intended to make peace with the souls of hunted animals, such as polar bears, whales, walrus, and seals.

6 ● MAJOR HOLIDAYS

Today the Inuit observe the holidays of the Christian calendar. Traditionally, a feast called a potlatch was held whenever a new totem pole was raised. The Inuit who held the potlatch would often give away his most valuable possessions at the ceremony.

7 ● RITES OF PASSAGE

Traditionally, a feast was held when an Inuit boy killed his first seal or caribou. Women were married when they reached puberty, and men when they could provide for a family. The Inuit believed in an afterlife thought to take place either in the sea or in the sky. After people died, their names were given to newborn infants, who were thereby believed to inherit the personal qualities of the deceased.

8 ● RELATIONSHIPS

Unlike many aboriginal cultures, traditional Inuit society was not based on the tribal unit. Instead, the basic social unit was the extended family, consisting of a man and wife and their unmarried children, along with their married sons and their families.

9 ● LIVING CONDITIONS

The Inuit had several different forms of traditional housing. In Greenland, they often lived in permanent stone houses. Along the shores of Siberia, they lived in villages made up of houses built from driftwood and earth. Summer housing for many Inuit was a skin tent, while in the winter the igloo, or house made of snow, was common.

Today many Inuit live in single-story, prefabricated wooden houses with a combined kitchen and living room area and one or two bedrooms. Most are heated with oil-burning stoves. However, since the Inuit are spread across such a vast area, their housing styles vary.

Cynthia Bassett

Inukshuk (like a person)— towers of stones—were built to trick herds of caribou or to serve as landmarks. The caribou, thinking the inukshuk was human, would change direction and move toward an ambush by Inuit hunters. These young Inuit pose for a photo with an inukshuk, a traditional symbol of their people.

In recent years, dogsleds have been replaced by snowmobiles as the main mode of transportation for many Inuit.

10 ● FAMILY LIFE

Family ties—both nuclear and extended—have always been of great importance to the Inuit. Having a large family was always considered desirable.

Traditionally, women have often assumed a secondary role in Inuit society. At mealtime, an Inuit woman was required to serve her husband and any visitors before she herself was permitted to eat. But at the same time, a common Inuit saying extolled women in this way: "A hunter is what his wife makes him." The women were the ones who gathered firewood, butchered the animals, and erected tents in summer and igloos in winter.

11 ● CLOTHING

Traditional Inuit clothing was perhaps the most important single factor in ensuring survival in the harsh Arctic environment. Its ability to keep the wearer alive in sub-zero temperatures was of prime importance. The Inuit made all their clothing from various animal skins and hides. In winter they wore two layers of caribou skin clothing. The outer layer had the fur facing out, while the fur of the inner layer faced in. The outer garment was a hooded parka.

Today a variety of shops sell modern Western-style clothing to the Inuit. Like their counterparts in cultures throughout the world, young people favor jeans, sneakers, and brightly colored sportswear. However, both old and young still rely on traditional Inuit gear when confronting the elements in any extended outdoor activity.

12 ● FOOD

The traditional Inuit dietary staples were seal, whale, caribou, walrus, polar bear, arctic hare, fish, birds, and berries. Because they ate raw food, and every part of the animal, the Inuit did not lack vitamins, even though they had almost no vegetables to eat. With the introduction of modern Western-style food, including fast food, over the past two to three decades, the Inuit diet has changed, and not for the better. The consumption of foods rich in sugar and carbohydrates has resulted in tooth decay and other diet-related medical problems.

A tradional bread, bannock, was made while trapping or living in camps. The dough could be wrapped around a stick and cooked over an open fire. A recipe for bannock that can be prepared in an oven accompanies this article.

13 ● EDUCATION

Most Inuit children ski or ride snowmobiles to get to and from school. They are taught standard subjects, including math, history, spelling, reading, and the use of computers. However, Inuit teachers are also concerned

---

Recipe

Bannock

Ingredients
4 cups flour
½ teaspoon salt
5 teaspoons baking powder
1½ cups water

Directions
1. Mix ingredients together to form a stiff dough.
2. Sprinkle flour on a clean work surface. With very clean hands, knead the dough. Dust hands and dough with flour if the dough is sticky.
3. Form in a round loaf about 1 inch high. Bake on a greased baking sheet at 350°F for 30 minutes.
4. Serve warm with butter and jam or honey.

Adapted from Shlabach, Joetta Handrich. *Extending the Table.* Scottsdale, Penn.: Herald Press, 1991.

---

that the students learn something about their culture and traditions.

14 ● CULTURAL HERITAGE

Considering that the Inuit inhabit an area covering more than 5,000 miles (8,000 kilometers), their culture is amazingly unified. From Siberia to Greenland, Inuit economic, social, and religious systems are much the same.

In addition to the prints and carvings for which the Inuit have become famous, dancing, singing, poetry, and storytelling play important roles in their native culture.

Cynthia Bassett

Traditional Inuit winter clothing consists of two layers of caribou skin. The outer garment, a hooded parka, has the fur facing out, while the fur of the inner layer faces in toward the wearer's skin.

15 ● EMPLOYMENT

Today most Inuit live a settled existence in villages and towns. They obtain wage employment or receive some form of social assistance. Major employers include the government, the oil and gas industry, and the arts and crafts industry. In addition, many Inuit are still involved in subsistence hunting and fishing at some level.

16 ● SPORTS

The Inuit enjoy games that enable them to display their physical strength, such as weightlifting, wrestling, and jumping contests. They also play a ball game that is sim-ilar in many ways to American football. Ice hockey is popular as well.

17 ● RECREATION

At traditional Inuit gatherings, drumming and dancing provide the chief form of entertainment. Quiet evenings at home are spent carving ivory or bone, or playing string games like cat's cradle. A traditional Inuit game similar to dice is played on a board, using pieces in the shape of miniature people and animals. The Inuit also enjoy typical modern forms of recreation such as watching television and videos.

18 ● CRAFTS AND HOBBIES

Traditional Inuit arts and crafts mostly involve etching decorations on ivory harpoon heads, needlecases, and other tools. Over the past decades, the Inuit have became famous for their soapstone, bone, and ivory carvings, as well as their prints and pictures. Another artistic tradition is the creation of elaborate wooden masks.

Inukshuk, towers of stone in the form of a human, were built as landmarks or as decoys for herds of caribou.

19 ● SOCIAL PROBLEMS

Social problems include unemployment, underemployment, alcoholism, drug abuse, and a high suicide rate.

20 ● BIBLIOGRAPHY

Condon, Richard. *Inuit Youth: Growth and Change in the Canadian Arctic.* New Brunswick, N.J.: Rutgers University Press, 1987.

Hahn, Elizabeth. *The Inuit:* Rourke Publications, 1990.

Philip, Neil. *Songs Are Thoughts: Poems of the Inuit.* New York: Orchard Books, 1995.

Shlabach, Joetta Handrich. *Extending the Table.* Scottsdale, Penn.: Herald Press, 1991.

WEBSITES

Canada. [Online] Available http://www. informatik. uni-kiel.de/~car/Canada.html, 1997.

Canadian Tourism Commission. Canada. [Online] Available http://http://206.191.33.50/tourism/, 1998.

Nortext. Exploring Nunavet. [Online] Available http://www.arctic-travel.com, 1998.

Cape Verde

■ **CAPE VERDEANS** 101

The people of Cape Verde are called Cape Verdenas. About 70 percent are descendants of Portuguese colonists and their African slaves, who came, most often, from what is today Guinea-Bissau. Another 28 percent of the inhabitants are entirely African.

Cape Verdeans

PRONUNCIATION: kayp VUHRD-ee-uhns
LOCATION: Cape Verde; United States
POPULATION: 300,000
LANGUAGE: Portuguese (official language), Crioulo
RELIGION: Catholicism with *Crioulo* aspects

1 ● INTRODUCTION

The Cape Verdean archipelago (island chain) had no known inhabitants before colonial times. It is believed that Arab sailors were aware of the islands by the tenth or eleventh century.

From 1455 until its independence in 1975, Cape Verde was a colony of Portugal. The islands were first reached around 1455 by captains sailing for Portugal's Prince Henry "The Navigator." They were looking for new trade routes and African gold, and they began to sail along the upper West African coast in the early fifteenth century.

The Portuguese based their slave-trading economy on these islands in the seventeenth to nineteenth centuries. Slaves worked on Cape Verdean sugar plantations, and they did general labor and household work. It was common for slave owners to have children with their servants. That is largely how today's native *Crioulo* (Creole) population evolved.

Since 1975, Cape Verde has been governed by a National Assembly. A single party, the African Party, was in power from independence until Cape Verde's first elections involving several parties in 1991.

2 ● LOCATION

The Republic of Cape Verde is an archipelago nation of nine main islands. It lies about 300 miles (483 kilometers) off the west coast of Senegal. The horseshoe-shaped archipelago consists of two island groups. They are the northern Barlavento islands and the southern Sotavento islands. Some islands are flat and sandy. Others have mountains (notably Mount Fogo) that rise

CAPE VERDEANS

more than 9,000 feet (2,743 meters) above the sea. The capital, Praia, is located on the largest island, São Tiago.

Today, more Cape Verdeans live in far-away communities than in the homeland. Cape Verdeans are found throughout Africa, Brazil, and Portugal, as well as in Senegal, Italy, and Holland, and in the United States, in southeastern New England.

3 ● LANGUAGE

Although Portuguese is the official language, *Crioulo* (Creole) is most widely spoken in Cape Verdean homes and clubs. Like other Creole languages, Cape Verdean is unique and follows its own grammar, vocabulary, and style. Women play an important role in preserving the Crioulo language from one generation to the next.

4 ● FOLKLORE

Cape Verdean folklore is a rich combination of Portuguese and African sources. One popular set of tales relates to *Nho Lobo*. The folksy wisdom of this clever wolf is used to teach basic values and lessons about life.

5 ● RELIGION

Most Cape Verdeans are devout Catholics. Religion is an important source of stability and basic values in their communities. Important saints' days are observed widely. (Many of the islands are named for the saints' days on which they were discovered.) A unique Cape Verdean religious tradition is the *mastro* ceremony, which involves a post or mast that is colorfully decorated with fruits to honor a saint.

6 ● MAJOR HOLIDAYS

Important holidays include January 20, the anniversary of the assassination of President Amílcar Cabral (1924–73), and July 5 (Independence Day). Religious holidays include Christmas, Easter, and various saints' festivals. Cape Verdeans also celebrate Carnival in the days preceding Lent. The *tabanka* festival combines African-style shrines with a Portuguese religious parade.

7 ● RITES OF PASSAGE

The stages in life are marked by the ceremonies of first communion, marriage, and cemetery burial at death. Additionally, farewell parties for people about to travel and for returning visitors have become so important that they are almost like a rite of passage.

8 ● RELATIONSHIPS

Social networks based on the family and the community are essential to finding a job, obtaining loans, seeking marriage partners, and carrying on social life in general. Cape Verdeans are deeply involved in social clubs, volunteer and service organizations, and community affairs.

9 ● LIVING CONDITIONS

Architectural styles in Cape Verde are strongly influenced by Portuguese culture. In appearance the structures are much like those found in coastal Brazil. Houses showing an African influence feature the round *funco* style from West Africa. They are built with Cape Verdean stone, but may have an African-style, cone-shaped thatched roof. Piped water and electricity are common in the main towns, but not always found in rural areas.

10 ● FAMILY LIFE

The warmth and generosity of Cape Verdean family life is deeply rooted in culture and history. It is common for families to share a pot of *cachupa* (stew) with relatives, neighbors, and any visitors who may drop in.

Parents make great sacrifices to educate their children. Families take great pride in children's academic achievement and in success in their jobs.

AP/Wide World Photos

Two women watch as a volcano on the Cape Verdean island of Fogo smolders in the distance.

11 ● CLOTHING

Western-style clothing is standard, especially for men and children. Women sometimes wear outfits that include their unique *panos* (strips of a cloth woven on the West African narrow loom). These panos are used as sashes for dancing and also can be used as a wrap for carrying babies. Used clothing from Europe and the United States is also used to meet local needs.

12 ● FOOD

Cape Verdean foods include *cachupa* (stew), *conj* (soup), *djagacida* (chicken with rice), and *gufong* (cornbread). Recipes often involve corn, rice, and couscous (crushed grain, especially a certain type of wheat) as a starchy base. The most common meats are pork, chicken, and fish (especially tuna). A wide variety of tropical fruits are readily available, including mangoes and bananas.

13 ● EDUCATION

Cape Verdeans have a relatively high standard of formal education. This is partly because of the tradition of seminary education on the island of São Nicolau. There are high schools in the major towns and elementary schools throughout the islands. There are also teacher-training and technical schools, but there is no university in Cape Verde.

14 ● CULTURAL HERITAGE

Cape Verde has a rich variety of popular music, some of it imported from the communities where Cape Verdeans have settled abroad. Styles range from European-style *mazurkas* and *valzas* to the rhythmically complex *batuko*. Most famous of all are the *coladeiras* and *mornas*.

15 ● EMPLOYMENT

Farming and fishing in Cape Verde are conducted at subsistence level (to provide a basic diet) or for small-scale exports. Cape Verde workers often travel to other countries as contract laborers. They are found in every walk of life, including education, major sports, medicine, the arts, banking, business, and construction.

16 ● SPORTS

Many sports are popular in Cape Verde, especially soccer. Basketball is gaining popularity. Swimming, surfboarding, scuba diving, track and field, and long-distance running also are growing in popularity.

17 ● RECREATION

Cape Verdean entertainment is centered in the home, where dances, parties, and receptions are often held. A favorite board game in Cape Verde is *ouri*, a "pit and capture" game that can be traced to ancient Egypt.

18 ● CRAFTS AND HOBBIES

A wide array of folk arts are found in Cape Verde. Women crochet and weave. Men build ship models, carve wood and cow horn, and make musical horns from shells.

19 ● SOCIAL PROBLEMS

Cape Verde suffers from a rising use of illegal drugs and alcohol and an increase in cases of AIDS. Many skilled and educated Cape Verdeans leave the country to seek employment overseas.

20 ● BIBLIOGRAPHY

Halter, Marilyn. *Between Race and Ethnicity.* Urbana: University of Illinois Press, 1993.

Lobban, Richard A., Jr. *Cape Verde.* Boulder, Colo.: Westview Press, 1995.

Lobban, Richard A., Jr., and Marlene Lopes. *Historical Dictionary of the Republic of Cape Verde.* 3rd ed. Lanham, Md.: Scarecrow, 1995.

WEBSITES

Embassy of the Republic of Cape Verde, Washington, D.C. [Online] Available http://www.capeverdeusembassy.org/, 1998.

World Travel Guide. Cape Verde. [Online] Available http://www.wtgonline.com/country/cv/gen.html, 1998.

Central African Republic

■ **CENTRAL AFRICANS** 105

Central Africans, the people in the Central African Republic, belong to more than 80 ethnic groups, which are classified according to geographic location. The Banda (34 percent) in the east central region and the Baya (27 percent) to the west are estimated to be the largest groups.

Central Africans

PRONUNCIATION: SEN-truhl AFF-ri-kuhns

LOCATION: Central African Republic

POPULATION: 3.2 million

LANGUAGE: French and Sango (official languages); Ubangian group (Niger-Congo family of languages)

RELIGION: Christianity; Islam; Baha'ism, Jehovah's Witness; animism

1 ● INTRODUCTION

The Central African Republic (CAR) is a landlocked country the size of Texas. It is located at the center of the African continent and became an independent country in 1960. Before the arrival of the French and Belgians in 1887, the peoples of the CAR were divided among numerous small kingdoms and sultanates. From 1899 to 1960, the CAR was known as Ubangi-Shari. The

CAR is one of the least developed and least-known parts of Africa.

When the Europeans arrived in the late 1800s, they took large parcels of land and turned them over to private companies. All of the natural wealth of the land was considered the property of these companies. The people who inhabited these lands did not like being controlled by the Europeans. Led by Barthélemy Boganda, a former priest and schoolteacher, Central Africans were finally able to establish their own government and end French colonial rule in 1960. The CAR has a democratically elected president. In the late 1990s, the president was Ange Félix Patassé.

2 ● LOCATION

The CAR spans all three of Africa's major types of landscape. To the extreme south is the dense, equatorial, tropical rain forest. Over the middle portion of the country,

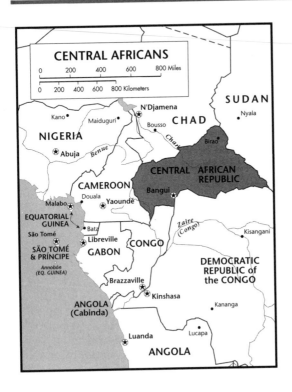

CENTRAL AFRICANS

where the bulk of the population lives, is savanna (grassland with scattered trees). To the extreme north of the country the savanna gives way to the Sahel, which is semi-desert. The terrain of the CAR consists primarily of gently rolling hills with a few small mountains in the northwest and the northeast. In the middle portion of the country, the savanna is occasionally broken up by rocky outcroppings called *kagas*.

The CAR is home to approximately forty different ethnic groups. With a population of only 3.2 million in an area of 240,535 square miles (622,986 square kilometers), the CAR is one of the most sparsely populated countries in the world.

3 ● LANGUAGE

The forty ethnic groups of the CAR are unified by a single national language, Sango. When the French arrived in Ubangi-Shari, the people living in the region spoke a number of different languages. The French colonists adopted Sango, both for communicating with the local population and for speaking among themselves. They were responsible for spreading the use of this one language throughout the region.

Sango and French are both official languages of the CAR. About 98 percent of the population speaks Sango on a day-to-day basis, but French is the language of government and education.

4 ● FOLKLORE

Each of CAR's forty ethnic groups has its own mythical heroes. However, the central figure in the national folklore is *Tere*. He is a clever man of supernatural powers who uses tricks to outsmart his opponents.

5 ● RELIGION

Most Central Africans are Christians, with 35 percent of the population being Protestant and 18 percent Catholic. The remainder are either Muslim, Baha'i, or Jehovah's Witnesses.

Many Central Africans still observe the traditional religion of ancestor worship, or animism. Each person is assigned a *totem*. This is an animal spirit that is passed on from generation to generation. One may never eat the animal associated with one's totem. When people die they pass on their totems to young children, usually a son or grandson.

Central Africans consult traditional priests, or witch doctors, called *nganga*, who relay messages from their ancestors' spirits. Often the nganga will order a ritual sacrifice (usually a chicken) to placate the spirits.

6 ● MAJOR HOLIDAYS

There are two major holidays in the CAR: Independence Day (December 1), known as *Premier Décembre*, and Mother's Day (held on the last Sunday in May or the first Sunday in June). The first honors the day that Barthélemy Boganda declared the independence of the country. It is celebrated with parades and official ceremonies. School-children and members of many organizations parade before local and national dignitaries. Afterward people feast on special dishes, such as roasted goat, gazelle, or pork.

Mother's Day has grown into a celebration of all women. It serves to recognize the labor and sacrifice that all women make in CAR society. On this day, men do all the cooking and cleaning, while the women sit in the shade and are served by men. Some men add humor to the occasion by wearing women's clothing as they carry the duties normally assumed by women.

7 ● RITES OF PASSAGE

The most important rite of passage among Central Africans is circumcision. It serves as a symbol of initiation to both adulthood and the various ethnic groups. Many ethnic groups practice circumcision on both boys and girls when they enter puberty, around the age of thirteen. As part of the ritual, groups of up to thirty boys or girls are iso-lated from their villages. For three months they live in a secret camp in the forest or on the savanna. Here they receive intensive training and education in the spiritual beliefs and practices of their ethnic group. They also are taught about the responsibilities they will bear as full-fledged members of society. When the initiation period is over, they are marched back into the village where they are greeted with much celebration, dance, and fanfare. As the newest members of society, they are given presents, and special feasts are held in their honor. Once they have completed this rite of passage, they have the right to take a spouse.

In modern CAR society male circumcision increasingly takes place in a hospital and the practice of female circumcision is discouraged by the government. Even if circumcision does not actually take place, the removal from society for educational purposes and initiation does take place. However the period often is only a matter of a few weeks rather than months.

Honoring the deceased also plays a very important role in Central African society. Death is treated as the transition from the living to the spiritual world. Periods of mourning may last anywhere from a few days to years. In the first few hours after the death of a close relative, male family members are expected to display their grief by shaving their hair off. During this time, women are expected to abstain from any type of personal grooming and adornment. An all-night vigil around the corpse will be held the first night. There is much singing and dancing to help coax the spirit into the other world. The body is promptly buried at sunrise the next day, with the head pointing north for men and south for women. At the end of the mourning period, there is a celebration with dancing and festive food. The day after this celebration the family will symbolize the return to normal life by putting on a new set of clothing.

8 ● RELATIONSHIPS

Central Africans begin each day by greeting the members of their families with a handshake. Each family member asks the others how they slept.

Whenever a new person enters a group of people, the newcomer is expected to first greet the most important person (for example, the oldest person or an honored guest) with a handshake. He or she then greets every person in the group in the same way. When leaving a group, a second handshake is required of each person. Close friends, especially men, may follow the handshake with a snap of the fingers, produced jointly by both parties. Women and men both shake hands, but increasingly women are adopting the French practice of kissing on both cheeks.

Sharing a meal, even if it is just a few boiled peanuts, is an important aspect of Central African culture. Even if one is not hungry, it is considered rude to refuse a meal when offered. Instead, one should eat at least a few bites to be polite.

9 ● LIVING CONDITIONS

The CAR is one of the poorest countries in sub-Saharan (southern) Africa. It is plagued with a low standard of living and high death rate from disease and malnutrition. Most Central Africans live in mud-brick huts with grass roofs, without running water and elec-

tricity. In large villages, each home or group of homes has a latrine (pit-style toilet). This helps ensure that the supply of drinking water will not be contaminated by human waste. However, it is not uncommon for the builder to make the mistake of constructing the latrines too close to the well or stream that supplies the drinking water.

10 ● FAMILY LIFE

For most couples, there is no formal marriage ceremony. However, the man's family must pay a bride-price to the family of the bride. Bride-price may range anywhere from a few goats and chickens to large sums of money. No marriage is considered official until a child has been born. If the marriage fails because there are no children or the wife is unfaithful, the family of the man can demand a return of the money.

Once children have been born, a younger sister or cousin of the wife will often come and live with the family to help out. The young assistant is in many respects an apprentice, learning how to keep house and to care for babies and children. Children of the husband's or wife's siblings often join the household. The children live together to make better education possible, or to share the same caregiver. Then other parents can spend more time working to make a living.

11 ● CLOTHING

Most women today wear a *pagne,* a cotton cloth tied around the waste like a skirt and worn with a matching blouse made of the same fabric. Clothing is a powerful symbol of wealth, and fabrics from Europe are status symbols.

Jason Lauré

Many Central African women and girls wear a pagne, *a cotton cloth tied around the waste like a skirt.*

For casual wear, men may wear a matching shirt and pants made from colorful printed cloth. However, for important occasions they wear European-style clothing. Increasingly, men and women are wearing West African-style outfits known as *shada*. Made of colorful batik cloth and adorned with elaborate embroidery, shada may cost hundreds of dollars apiece. Less fortunate Central Africans wear secondhand European and American clothing bought for a few cents apiece at local markets.

12 ● FOOD

The staple food of the Central African diet is cassava, which is a starchy root. After the plant is soaked in water for three days, the roots are peeled and broken into pieces to be dried in the sun. Just before eating, the dried cassava is ground into a fine flour used to make the mainstay of Central African cuisine, called *gozo*. This is a firm paste made by adding the cassava flour to boiling water.

Most Central African meals consist of gozo served with a sauce made with meat, fish, and vegetables. A typical meal consists of one bowl of sauce accompanied by one ball of gozo. A favorite everyday dish called *ngunja* is made with the dark green leaves of the cassava plant. Most sauces, including ngunja, are thickened with peanut butter, which gives them added protein and flavor.

EPD Photos

A xylophone, made by attaching pieces of wood to rows of gourds, is a common type of musical instrument.

Everyone eats with their fingers from a central common dish. Men and women who are not relatives do not ever eat together. Men and women relatives may eat together, but only in private and never in public. In public, men and women eat separately.

Usually only one meal is cooked per day and served at the noon hour. In the evening and for breakfast the next day, leftovers are eaten.

13 ● EDUCATION

Parents are expected to pay a fee for every stage of education of their children, including primary school. Most Central Africans born since 1960 have at least attended primary school. Very few, however, have gone beyond that. To earn a high school diploma, students must take an exam called a baccalaureate. Very few Central Africans are able to pass this exam. All those who pass—and

who have the money—are able to go on to the one university in the country, the Université de Bangui.

The official language in government-sponsored schools is French, but the earliest grades are taught in Sango and French. Young people begin their education in Sango and gradually make the transition to French. By the time they reach high school, classes are conducted entirely in French.

14 ● CULTURAL HERITAGE

The CAR has a rich tradition in music and dance, which are part of every major holiday and event. The primary musical instrument is the conga drum. It is made by stretching a piece of wet leather over a hollowed-out length of log. These drums come in all shapes and sizes. Some stand up to a yard (meter) tall and can be heard several miles away. Xylophones made with wood and gourds are another common type of musical instrument.

By the late 1990s, electric guitars, keyboards, and snare drums were common in urban areas. Popular recorded music sung in Sango is heard all over the country. In buses, taxis, restaurants, and bars, there is almost always a radio or a cassette player providing background music.

15 ● EMPLOYMENT

The majority of Central Africans are subsistence farmers. They grow most of the food they consume, and just a bit more that they sell in order to pay for necessities such as soap and cloth. A limited number grow cash crops such as coffee or cotton. There is almost no manufacturing in the CAR.

16 ● SPORTS

Central Africans are avid sports enthusiasts. Soccer and basketball are among their greatest passions. Athletic clubs in almost every city and town sponsor soccer teams that compete for regional and national championships.

Basketball was introduced in the 1970s by American Peace Corps workers, who built courts at high schools throughout the country. In 1988 the CAR national team astounded the continent by winning the African championship.

17 ● RECREATION

In Bangui, the capital, there are television programs in Sango and French. In the evening those rare individuals who have both electricity and a television will place the set outside so that all the neighbors can watch. It is not unusual to find forty or fifty people gathered around a television in the evening watching storytellers, the local news, or an old French movie. Radio is a major source of entertainment for those lucky enough to have shortwave radios and batteries to operate them.

One of the most popular activities for Central Africans of all ages is dancing. In even the smallest towns there is at least one gathering place with a cement dance floor and a cassette player. In the evening such places are popular with young adults who come to listen to the latest music from the Central African Republic and its neighbor, the Democratic Republic of the Congo.

Visiting other people plays a prominent role in Central African society. Sunday afternoons and holidays are given over to this activity. On these days many Central Africans will put on their finest clothing and set out to call on friends or relatives either at home or in public places.

18 ● CRAFTS AND HOBBIES

Traditional art in the CAR takes a variety of forms including ebony carvings, pottery, weaving, and hair braiding. Skilled artisans produce a host of ebony products that are popular with Central Africans and tourists alike. Statuettes, figurines, and animal carvings are the most common.

In the savanna region of the CAR, the weaving of mats and baskets is a common activity. Elaborate patterns may be woven into the mats and baskets by dyeing the grasses and reeds different colors.

19 ● SOCIAL PROBLEMS

Government corruption and AIDS are the two biggest social problem facing the CAR in the late 1990s. AIDS is wiping out a significant portion of the generation aged twenty to forty. This is putting a strain on older people, who are being forced to care for orphan children. Rapid population growth is contributing to declining living standards.

Successive Central African governments have claimed to respect human and civil rights, but have done very little to ensure that these rights are guaranteed.

20 ● BIBLIOGRAPHY

O'Toole, Thomas. *The Central African Republic in Pictures*. Minneapolis, Minn.: Lerner Publications Co., 1989.

Strong, Polly. *African Tales: Folklore of the Central African Republic*. Mogadore, Ohio: Telcraft, 1992.

WEBSITES

Internet Africa Ltd. Central African Republic. [Online] Available http://www.africanet.com/africanet/country/car/, 1998.

World Travel Guide. Central Africa Republic. [Online] Available http://www.wtgonline.com/country/cf/gen.html, 1998.

Chad

■ CHADIANS 113

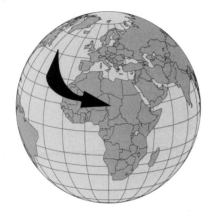

The people of Chad are called Chadians. The majority trace their origins to African groups, but the population has been influenced over the years through successive invasions from the Arabic north. The population can be broadly divided between those who follow the Islamic faith in the north and the people of the south.

Chadians

PRONUNCIATION: CHAD-ee-uhns
LOCATION: Chad
POPULATION: 6.1 million
LANGUAGE: French, Arabic (official languages); more than 100 local languages
RELIGION: Traditional African religion; Islam; Christianity

1 ● INTRODUCTION

In the eleventh century, traders from north Africa were searching for gold and slaves. They came to the area that is Chad, and introduced the religion of Islam. In the early twelfth century, one region of present-day Chad had a Muslim king. His kingdom, known as Kanem, remained powerful until the French explorers arrived in the late 1800s.

French won control over Chad in the Battle of Kousseri in 1900. But Chad was a low colonial priority for the French. They made only halfhearted attempts to develop it. Chad won its independence in 1960. A few years later, Muslims from the north fought against the government. France sent troops to support the Christian government, but neither side has won control. Chad remains in turmoil.

2 ● LOCATION

Chad is a landlocked country, far from oceans and seas. It has an area roughly equal to Idaho, Wyoming, Utah, Nevada, and Arizona combined, stretching over 1,100 miles (1,770 kilometers) from north to south. The middle of the country is a region called the Sahel. The Sahel is semi-desert. Lake Chad forms part of Chad's border with its neighbors, Niger and Nigeria, and is the fourth-largest lake in Africa. Magnificent sand dunes cover the land in the north. Mountain ranges cover stretches of the southwest, east, and far northwest.

The population of Chad is over 6 million. There are about 200 ethnic groups that

CHADIANS

| 0 | 200 | 400 | 600 | 800 Miles |
| 0 | 200 | 400 | 600 | 800 Kilometers |

ALGERIA
LIBYA
EGYPT
NIGER
CHAD
SUDAN
NIGERIA
CENTRAL AFRICAN REPUBLIC
CAMEROON
DEMOCRATIC REPUBLIC of the CONGO
GABON
CONGO

The earliest settlers around Lake Chad were the *Sao*. Legends held that the Sao were giants possessing great strength. They could run long distances in just hours and pull up trees like blades of grass. Sao women could lift huge ceramic *granaries* (jugs to hold grain), holding an entire year's harvest with a single hand.

5 ● RELIGION

Chadians follow three religious traditions: traditional African religion that focuses on ancestors (35 percent), Islam (55 percent), or Christianity (10 percent). In Chad, Islam and Christianity have absorbed a number of beliefs from traditional African religion. Although Islam has been influenced by traditional African religion, Chadian Muslims are strict in their beliefs. For example, during the holy month of Ramadan, all Muslims fast (don't eat or drink) during daylight hours. Chadian Muslims do not even swallow their own saliva from sunrise to sunset during Ramadan.

6 ● MAJOR HOLIDAYS

Traditional holidays having to do with seasons and harvesting are festive occasions. For example, in the southern farming region, festivals are held during the millet harvest in September to November and again during the New Year in December. At New Year, the chief appears after a month of confinement in his lodge. In his regal dress, the chief marches slowly, accompanied by dignitaries. Musicians play long horns made from gourds, and dancers perform. Afterward, the local hosts serve a splendid meal to visitors who come from great distances to join the celebration. Secular (nonreligious) holidays such as

speak more than one hundred distinct languages.

3 ● LANGUAGE

French and Arabic are Chad's official languages, but more than one hundred local languages are spoken. Chadian Arabic includes more than thirty dialects that people throughout the country use to communicate with each other.

4 ● FOLKLORE

Many Chadians revere the World War II (1939–45) hero Félix Eboué (1884–1944), in whose memory was erected a magnificent monument in the city of N'Djamena.

Independence Day generally hold less interest for Chadians than do Muslim and Christian holidays.

7 ● RITES OF PASSAGE

The *Sara yondo* is a ceremony held to help a young man from southern Chad achieve adulthood. Every six or seven years, older men gather with boys for several weeks during school vacations. During these meetings, the men teach the youths about authority so that they can assume the men's role. When the process is complete, the boys are considered men. They no longer associate with their mothers and sisters as before, and must eat and live separately. Similar ceremonies for girls teach them household responsibilities and respect for male authority.

8 ● RELATIONSHIPS

As in other regions of Africa, greeting and leave-taking are important parts of human relations. Muslims exchange a standard series of greetings. They ask about the other person's well-being, and that of his wife and family, too. After each exchange, the listener touches a hand to his or her chest. This signals gratitude that all is well with the other person.

It is an honor to receive visitors. Chadian hosts always offer the visitor something to eat—or at least a glass of water—as a sign of hospitality. In the dusty Sahel region, hosts usually offer visitors water to wash their faces, hands, and feet. In the south, visitors may be welcomed by a large container of millet beer. It is considered impolite to leave before the beer has been drunk.

AP/Wide World Photos

Chadian women wear robes that cover the entire body except face, hands, and feet. Women in the south often wear colorful wraparound skirts and tailored shirts.

9 ● LIVING CONDITIONS

Living conditions are very harsh in most rural areas of the country. In 1995, life expectancy in Chad was forty-seven years.

In towns in the semi-desert region, the Sahel, homes are built inside walled compounds. Mud bricks held together with straw and camel dung are used to make the walls and the roofs. Houses consist of one or two rooms. The interior is dark, because the houses typically have only one or two small windows. Houses are used mainly only for sleeping in the cooler and rainy seasons, and for storage. Kitchen rooms are often separate. Meals may be cooked outdoors.

10 ● FAMILY LIFE

The Toubou and Daza people of the Sahara Desert are nomads (people who move frequently, carrying their homes with them). The main social unit of nomads is the clan. It is not uncommon for people from more than one clan to live together in groups of around one hundred people. Camps—groups of families—form when they need to work together during the growing season, and they disband later. Clan members are scattered everywhere, so people usually find kinsmen (relatives or others from their clan) in most camps.

By contrast, the more settled people of the Sahel identify with the *kashimbet*. This is a unit composed of an elder male or group of males, their wives, and descendants. Unlike the nomads, these extended families stay together.

11 ● CLOTHING

Clothing styles vary according to climate zone and ethnic group. The sun, heat, and blowing sand in the north require clothing that covers the entire body except for the face. Men often wear light cotton pants under white cotton robes. They wrap a white or red-and-white scarf around their heads in the form of a turban. Women wear robes that cover the entire body except face, hands, and feet. Boys wear simply cut cloth shirts and pants, while girls may wear cotton shirts with wraparound cloth skirts.

Recipe

Millet Porridge

Ingredients

1 cup millet (available at health food stores)
1¾ cups water
½ teaspoon salt
sugar or honey

Directions

1. Place millet in a strainer and rinse. Allow to drain until water is no longer dripping.
2. Heat water and salt in a saucepan until it boils. Add millet.
3. Lower heat and simmer, stirring constantly, until millet is soft (about 20 to 30 minutes).

Serve sprinkled with sugar or drizzled with honey.

Adapted from Harris, Colin. *A Taste of West Africa,* New York: Thomson Learning, 1995.

In the south, people dress like Central Africans—colorful cotton print shirts and pants for men, and wraparound skirts and tailored shirts for women.

Many ethnic groups distinguish themselves with decorative facial and body tattoos.

12 ● FOOD

Despite the harsh climate, Chadians grow a large variety of food. The staples are sorghum and millet. The millet is pounded into flour. Dough, shaped into a ball, *boule* (bOOl), is made by combining boiling water

United Nations

The sun, heat, and blowing sand in the north require clothing that covers the entire body except for the face. Men often wear light cotton pants under white cotton robes.

and millet flour. Millet also makes a delicious porridge. It is sweetened and eaten to break the fast during Ramadan. Chadians in the Sahel are fond of okra and meat sauce. Travelers find grilled goat meat with dried hot pepper and freshly squeezed lime at "truck stop" eateries in Sahelian roadside villages.

13 ● EDUCATION

The effects of the war, limited financing, overcrowding, and the classical French curriculum have combined to make it difficult for Chadian children to excel in school. Primary school is compulsory, although only one in four children actually attends. There are far more elementary and high schools in the south than in the north. Students who make it to high school attend either a four-year program *(collége)* or a seven-year program *(lycée)*. To get a diploma, students must take a state exam, the *bac*, which is passed by only about a third of those who take it.

Ten years after independence, Chad opened its first university for the 1971–72 academic year.

14 ● CULTURAL HERITAGE

Many Chadians express their cultural heritage through ceremonial dress, music, and dance. The Chadian national folkloric ballet is particularly popular.

Among the principal musical instruments are tam-tams, pottery drums, goat-horn whistles and flutes, and gourd-calabash horns. Chadians also excel at making five-stringed harps and *balafons*, which are similar to xylophones.

15 ● EMPLOYMENT

More than 80 percent of Chadians are engaged in subsistence farming, herding, and fishing. Cotton is the biggest cash crop, providing more than 50 percent of the country's foreign earnings. Industries include textiles, meatpacking, beer brewing, and the manufacture of soap, cigarettes, and construction materials.

16 ● SPORTS

Children and young people play organized soccer, European handball, and basketball. In the cities, soccer club teams compete with one another. The game is played wherever space permits. Horse racing is practiced in the Sahel, northeast of N'Djamena.

17 ● RECREATION

With the exception of a small urban elite, Chad remains one of the few places in the world insulated from Western pop culture. In contrast to American teenagers, most Chadian young people have never seen a movie, either at the theater or on a video cassette recorder. Many have never seen television. Chadian entertainment consists of social and cultural events and ceremonies, which include dancing, drumming, and musical performance (*see* Cultural Heritage).

18 ● CRAFTS AND HOBBIES

Traditional folk art in Chad has a long history, dating to the iron age. Artists and craftsmen learn and master the techniques of their craft and pass on the traditions to their sons and daughters. Articles produced by Chadian artists include masks, jewelry, ceramic pots, and bronze statuettes and figurines. Craftspeople spin cotton fabrics and weave strips of cloth that are sewn together to make durable garments. They also fashion leather goods including sandals and amulets.

Chadian craftsmen produce musical instruments of extremely high quality using materials such as wood, animal guts and horns, and calabashes.

19 ● SOCIAL PROBLEMS

As Chad modernizes, traditional social networks have been disrupted. Its people must also cope with other problems that come from urbanization, such as crime and pollution. The political anarchy (disorder) of the 1970s and 1980s has led to lawlessness in parts of the country.

20 ● BIBLIOGRAPHY

Azavedo, Mario, ed. *Cameroon and Chad in Historical and Contemporary Perspectives.* Lewiston, N.Y.: E. Mellen Press, 1990.

Harris, Colin. *A Taste of West Africa.* New York: Thomson Learning, 1995.

Works, John Arthur. *Pilgrims in a Strange Land: Hausa Communities in Chad.* New York: Columbia Univ. Press, 1976.

WEBSITES

World Travel Guide. Chad. [Online] Available http://www.wtgonline.com/country/td/gen.html, 1998.

Chile

■ CHILEANS 119
■ ARAUCANIANS 126

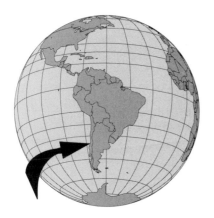

The people of Chile are called Chileans. The population is estimated to be about 75 percent mestizo (mixed white and Amerindian), almost 20 percent white, and about 5 percent Amerindian (native people, mainly Araucanians). The population of pure Araucanians numbers as many as 600,000.

Chileans

PRONUNCIATION: chill-LAY-ans
LOCATION: Chile
POPULATION: 12 million
LANGUAGE: Spanish
RELIGION: Roman Catholicism (official); some Protestantism; some indigenous religions

1 ● INTRODUCTION

Several Amerindian cultures thrived in Chile prior to the arrival of Inca invaders from Peru in the fifteenth century. From the sixteenth century to the beginning of the nineteenth, Chile was under Spanish colonial rule. Then Chilean military leader, Bernardo O'Higgins (1778–1842), joined forces with José de San Martín (1778–1850) from Argentina to liberate the Chileans from Spanish rule. O'Higgins became the first ruler of the independent republic of Chile in 1818.

Trade, first with the European powers, then with the United States, helped Chile's economy develop. First, there was a nitrate boom in the late nineteenth and early twentieth centuries. Copper and silver mining became important sources of income. Agriculture developed as well.

In the twentieth century Chile has experienced dramatic changes of government. In 1970, socialist Salvador Allende (1908–73) was freely elected to power. A military takeover by Augusto Pinochet (1915–) followed in 1973. Pinochet's rule ended in 1990, when Patricio Aylwin (1918–) took office as president and democratic rule resumed.

2 ● LOCATION

The Andes Mountains run the full length of the immensely long, narrow country of Chile. The nation's Pacific coastline is over 2,485 miles (4,000 kilometers) long. Its terrain ranges from the northern Atacama

The Chilean newspaper El Mercurio *was first published in 1827 and is still widely read.*

desert to the snow-clad Andean peaks. There are farmlands where grapes are grown, grain and cattle country, and fishing zones where snow-covered volcanoes and lakes abound.

3 ● LANGUAGE

The official language of Chile is Spanish. The Chilean accent is quite distinct from those of neighboring countries such Argentina and Uruguay. It has a softer sound, and a melodious lilt.

Many Chilean names are derived from the saints and apostles of the Catholic Church. Others have Roman, Spanish, Anglo-Saxon, or even German origins.

4 ● FOLKLORE

Many myths and legends survive in Chilean folklore. One legend from the islands of Chiloé tells of a lost city. It contains fabulous wealth: its streets are paved with gold and silver. A mist always hides it from sight. It is said that all who go there lose their memory. It will be seen only once: at the end of the world. Then all the nonbelievers will know of its existence.

One of the important folk heroes of Chile is a Mapuche Indian called *Lautaro* (?–1557). He served the Spanish conqueror Pedro de Valdivia (c. 1498–1553), learning the Spanish language and arts of war. Using his knowledge, he later led the resistance against the Spanish.

Susan D. Rock

A view of the town of Castro on Chiloe Island.

5 ● RELIGION

The official religion of Chile is Roman Catholicism, and the majority of Chileans are Catholic. There are also Protestants in Chile, and some Mapuche Indians practice their traditional religion. Their beliefs include worship of the creator Ngenechen and the destroyer Wakufu.

Many Chileans believe that the spirits of people who have died violently will linger in the area where they died. The living can appeal to them in their prayers, asking them to intercede on their behalf. *Animitas* (little shrines with flowers and candles) are often set up near where they died. Sometimes anamitas become places of prayer and pilgrimage.

The religious festival of La Tirana near the northern city of Iquique developed out of a mixture of Catholic and Amerindian beliefs. It includes dances representing good and evil forces in the form of maidens and devils.

6 ● MAJOR HOLIDAYS

Chileans celebrate the main Catholic holidays, including Christmas (December 25), the Immaculate Conception on December 8, Corpus Christi, and Easter. Their secular holidays include Labor Day on May 1, as

Recipe

Empanada de pino

Ingredients

For the pastry:
2 cups flour
½ teaspoon salt
1 cup shortening or lard
¼ cup ice water (approximate)

For the filling:
⅓ pound ground beef
3 or more jalapeño chilies, seeded and chopped
½ onion, finely chopped
1 Tablespoon ground cumin
2 Tablespoons chopped parsley
2 Tablespoons chopped cilantro
2 small tomatoes, peeled, seeded, and finely chopped
½ cup raisins
10 olives, stuffed with pimentos, cut in half
2 hard-boiled eggs, sliced

Directions

Prepare pastry.

1. Mix the flour, salt, and shortening together in a bowl. Using a pastry blender or two knives, combine the ingredients thoroughly until the mixture looks like coarse meal.
2. Add ice water slowly until the mixture forms a ball of dough.

Dough may be wrapped in plastic and chilled (for up to three days) until ready to use.

Prepare filling

1. Brown the meat in a pan, breaking up the pieces.
2. Add the onion, garlic, jalapeño chilies, cumin, and salt and pepper to taste. Cook until onion is soft.
3. Add the parsley, cilantro, tomatoes, and raisins, and cook until the mixture is dry.

Preheat oven to 375°F.

Assemble empanadas

1. Divide the dough into balls about the size of a golf ball.
2. Pat the ball into a circle about three inches in diameter.

(Note: Alternatively, the dough may be rolled out and cut into three-inch circles with a biscuit cutter.)

3. Place one-half an olive and one slice of hard-boiled egg in the center of each dough circle. Top with a spoonful of filling.
4. Fold the dough circle in half to form a half-moon. Seal the edges by pressing down with the tines of a fork.
5. Bake for 25 minutes, or until browned, at 375°F.

Adapted from Barbara Karoff, *South American Cooking: Foods and Feasts from the New World*. Reading, Mass.: Addison-Wesley, 1989.

well as two Independence holidays: Independence Day on September 18, and the controversial Liberation Day on September 11. Day of the Glory of the Armed Forces on September 19 is celebrated with a military parade. The discovery of America by Christopher Columbus is marked on October 12.

7 ● RITES OF PASSAGE

To Chilean Catholics, baptism and first communion are important milestones. Civil marriage is often accompanied by a church ceremony. Some very religious families observe nine days of prayers when a person dies. These are held in the home and attended by family and close friends.

8 ● RELATIONSHIPS

Chileans have a relaxed attitude toward time. On social occasions people are expected to be up to an hour late.

Formal greetings and introductions involve handshakes. However, the usual greeting among friends, both women and men, is a kiss on the cheek.

9 ● LIVING CONDITIONS

Many families in Chile's wealthy landowning class own ranches. Often they will also have a summer home in the Valparaíso-Viña del Mar coastal resort area.

Poor city dwellers (*pobladores)* live in crowded shantytowns, especially in Santiago. They often live in a type of squatter's home made from any material at hand, such as zinc and bits of wood and brick.

10 ● FAMILY LIFE

Until recently, most Chileans had large families. Today the average urban middle-class family has two or three children. Both middle-class professional women and low-income women work outside the home. However, they still assume most of the household responsibilities. In poorer households, women often rely on the older children to look after younger ones.

11 ● CLOTHING

Modern, middle-class city dwellers dress in Western-style clothes. Men wear suits. Women with office jobs are expected to wear suits or dresses, although trousers are also accepted.

In the countryside, *huasos* (cowboys) wear the *poncho,* a type of cloak, with colorful stripes for festivities. Regular, plain-colored ponchos are worn at other times. *Huasos* wear broad-rimmed straw hats in summer and felt hats in winter. They wear boots, and sometimes finely crafted spurs.

12 ● FOOD

Pastel de choclo (baked corn paste) is a typical Chilean dish. A favorite soup, and a hearty meal in itself, is *porotos granados* or white bean soup, which also includes pumpkin, peppers, and sweet corn. A delicious and popular Latin American snack is a type of turnover called an *empanada*. In Chile the most typical empanada, the *empanada de pino,* is filled with minced meat, onions, a slice of hard-boiled egg, and an olive. Other empanadas are fried and filled with cheese. Native stews called *cazuelas* are made from beef, chicken, or fish and include potatoes, pumpkin, corn and green beans.

13 ● EDUCATION

Education is highly valued in Chile, especially as a means of escaping poverty. Primary schooling has been free in Chile since 1860. The country has a current estimated 80 percent literacy rate. The national University of Chile was founded in 1843. Increasing numbers of Chileans attend university, forming a rapidly growing middle

Susan D. Rock

Chileans selling souvenirs of moai *(huge carved stone heads of unknown origin) on the Chilean territory of Easter Island. The strange sculptures attract tourists from both mainland Chile and around the world.*

class. The Catholic Church has also played an important role in developing education.

14 ● CULTURAL HERITAGE

Chile has a rich cultural heritage and a love of the arts. The New Song movement *(La Nueva Canción Chilena)* was an important political and artistic protest movement that arose during the 1960s. Its most famous figure was singer Violeta Parra. Her style blended folk, classical, and modern influences. Her children Isabel and Angel continued in her footsteps. Chile also has the distinction of having produced two Nobel

Prize-winning poets, Gabriela Mistral and Pablo Neruda.

The national dance of Chile is the *cueca*. It involves rapid, spirited steps similar to the Spanish *zapateado* (flamenco), in which the feet tap the beat on the floor

15 ● EMPLOYMENT

Since the 1980s, fruit growers have benefited from government programs. Copper mining continues to be very important. Working conditions vary sharply according to social class. The urban poor *(pobladores)*

in the shantytowns often have to make do with informal labor and odd jobs.

16 ● SPORTS

The most popular sport is soccer, which is played and followed enthusiastically by many Chileans.

Horse-racing is a popular spectator sport in Santiago. In rural areas, Chilean *huasos,* or cowboys, compete in unusual *medialunas* (corrals in the shape of a half moon).

Chile has fine beaches, and many people enjoy swimming at resort areas such as Valparaíso and Viña del Mar. Boating and fishing in Chile's beautiful lakes are both popular, and there are several ski resorts near Santiago and in the south.

17 ● RECREATION

The typical Chilean *asado,* or barbecue, is a favorite occasion for family and friends to gather. Large quantities of meat are grilled on open charcoal fires in private yards or in parks or other public places.

Chilean town-dwellers enjoy movies, and there is a lively theatrical tradition. Young people often meet in the evening in cafés or bars, and they enjoy dancing. People also enjoy shopping. Some of the better neighborhoods have elegant shopping districts and malls.

Chileans also enjoy trips to such seaside resort areas as Valparaíso and Viña del Mar.

18 ● CRAFTS AND HOBBIES

There are many musical groups or *peñas* in towns across Chile, playing a variety of music ranging from folk to *salsa* music from other Latin American countries as well as modern, Western-style pop music.

Chile's Amerindian communities practice crafts including weaving, basket-making, pottery, woodcarving, and jewelry-making. The potters of Pomaire are famous for miniature figures derived from folkloric or religious traditions. Their beautiful clay *pailas* (pots) of varying sizes and shapes are found in many Chilean gardens and kitchens.

19 ● SOCIAL PROBLEMS

The growth of a well-educated middle class in Chile is an important indicator of development. However, the gap between rich and poor is still quite wide. The *pobladores,* or urban poor, do not have enough work or can only find temporary work. Many Amerindians in rural areas also live in poverty.

20 ● BIBLIOGRAPHY

Dwyer, Christopher. *Chile,* Major World Nations. Philadelphia: Chelsea House, 1997.

Galvin, Irene Flum. *Chile: Journey to Freedom.* Parsippany, N.Y.: Dillon Press, 1997.

Hintz, Martin. *Chile.* Chicago: Childrens Press, 1993.

Pickering, Marianne. *Chile: Where the Land Ends.* New York: Benchmark Books, 1997.

Winter, Jane Kohen. *Chile.* New York: Marshall Cavendish, 1994.

WEBSITES

Interknowledge Corporation. Chile. [Online] Available http://www.interknowledge.com/chile/, 1998.

World Travel Guide. Chile. [Online] Available http://www.wtgonline.com/country/cl/gen.html, 1998.

Araucanians

PRONUNCIATION: arr-oww-KAH-nee-ens
LOCATION: Chile; Argentina
POPULATION: About 800,000
LANGUAGE: Araucanian
RELIGION: Roman Catholicism with indigenous religious beliefs

1 ● INTRODUCTION

Historically, the Araucanian Indians lived in southern, central, and northern areas of Chile and in present-day Argentina. They were divided into three main groups: the *Picunche* in the north, the *Mapuche* in the central area, and the *Huilliche* in the south. The Araucanians fought Inca invaders from Peru in the fifteenth century and Spanish conquerors in the seventeenth century.

The northern Picunche, who lived in the pleasant farming areas of Chile's Central Valley, were a relatively peaceful people. They were easily overcome by the Incas, and were later subdued and assimilated by the Spaniards. The Mapuche and the Hulliche, however, established a reputation as fierce warriors. Both groups bravely defended their lands and their way of life. They continued to resist the Spaniards for hundreds of years. The Mapuche finally lost their independence in the War of 1880–1882. After this defeat they were forced to settle further south on small reservations called *reducciones*. About half the Mapuche family groups still live there today,

2 ● LOCATION

The main group of Araucanians that still remain in Chile today are the Mapuche, numbering some 800,000 people. Initially they lived between the Itata and Toltén rivers. Today many live in the vicinity of towns such as Temuco, Villarica, Pucón, Valdivia, and Osorno, as well as in the southern island region of Chiloé. Some 400,000 Mapuche have had to migrate to the cities and now live the life of poor, urban workers

There are still a few Mapuche reservations in Argentina, particularly on the shores of Lake Rucachoroi and Lake Quillén. However, most Mapuche Araucanians today continue to live in Chile.

3 ● LANGUAGE

Most Mapuche in Chile and the small number living in Argentina speak the Araucanian language. Called *Mapudungu*, it also survives in many place names: *quen* means "place," as in the town of Vichiquen, while *che* means "people," and *mapu* means "land." (Mapuche, therefore, translates as "people of the land.")

The Mapuche leader in times of war was called a *Toqui*, while the peacetime leader was called an *Ulmen*. Messengers were called *huerquenes*.

4 ● FOLKLORE

Araucanian folklore survives today, perpetuated by the surviving Mapuche people.

One Mapuche legend involves the southern islands of the Chiloé region: The evil serpent *Cai Cai* rises furiously from the sea to flood the earth. Her good twin *Tren Tren*, slumbers in her fortress among mountain peaks. The Mapuche try unsuccessfully to wake Tren Tren. Cai Cai's friends, the pillars of Thunder, Wind, and Fire, pile up the

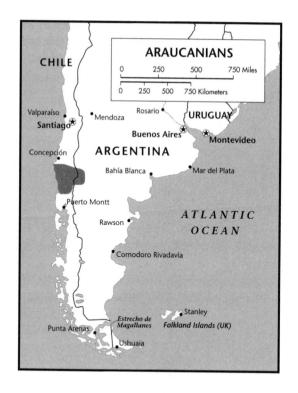

ARAUCANIANS

0   250   500   750 Miles

0   250   500   750 Kilometers

CHILE

Valparaíso
Santiago

Concepción

Puerto Montt

Rawson

Punta Arenas

Ushuaia

Mendoza   Rosario

URUGUAY

Buenos Aires

Montevideo

ARGENTINA

Bahía Blanca

Mar del Plata

ATLANTIC
OCEAN

Comodoro Rivadavia

Stanley

Estrecho de
Magallanes   Falkland Islands (UK)

5 ● RELIGION

The Mapuche believe in an ultimate balance between the forces of creation *(Ngenechen)* and destruction *(Wakufu)*. Reverence for nature and acknowledgment of the forces of good and evil are also part of their belief system. Traditional prayer meetings called *machitunes* invoke the help of the gods and goddesses for rain and good crops. Another type of meeting, called a *malón,* involves listening to dreams and prophecies.

Roman Catholicism has coexisted alongside the original religious beliefs of the Araucanians. In some cases the two have merged.

6 ● MAJOR HOLIDAYS

Mapuche who live in cities celebrate the major Chilean national holidays together with the rest of the population, including Independence Day and the discovery of America by Columbus on October 12, 1492.

The Mapuche who live on reservations have maintained some of their traditional celebrations. One of the best-known festivals is the *nquillatún,* which lasts for three days and dedicates the lands and the harvest to the gods and goddesses.

7 ● RITES OF PASSAGE

All major stages in the life cycle, such as birth, puberty, marriage, and death, are marked by special ceremonies. Important members of the tribe, such as *lonkos (*chieftains*),* play special roles. They are accompanied by music and also include elements of the Araucanians' oral tradition, such as poetry and legends.

clouds to make rain, thunder, and water. Finally, a little girl dances with her reflection in Tren Tren's eye and her laughter awakens Tren Tren, who also begins to laugh. Deeply insulted, the evil Cai Cai and her friends fall down the hill..

But Cai Cai is angry and shatters the earth, scattering islands all over the sea. The water climbs higher and higher, trying to flood the mountain peaks where Tren Tren lives. But Tren Tren manages to raise the mountain up toward the sky and the sun. Finally the evil serpent Cai Cai and the Pillars of Thunder, Wind, and Fire fall from the mountain peak into the deep pit below, where they are silenced.

8 ● RELATIONSHIPS

Greetings have well-defined levels of formality and informality. Strangers can only come into a traditional Mapuche environment with the utmost care. Those who are accompanied by a Mapuche may be welcomed with elaborate feasting and great hospitality. However, those who come alone could just as easily be met with hostility and silence.

9 ● LIVING CONDITIONS

Some Mapuche continue to live in a fairly traditional style, but many have migrated to towns where they share the lot of other poor urban workers as *pobladores* living in shantytowns with poor housing and health conditions. The housing in shantytowns is basic. Shelters can be of adobe and bits of other materials. In remote country areas the traditional thatched-roof huts known as *rucas* provide shelter.

10 ● FAMILY LIFE

The Mapuche group of Araucanians who still live on *reducciones,* or reservations, have tried to maintain the traditional family structures. These include the extended family unit and a clan-like structure with a clan head or chief.

Traditionally, each extended family was headed by a *lonko,* or chief, who had several wives and many children. The sense of family identity extended to grandparents, aunts and uncles, cousins, and relatives by marriage. This type of social structure is gradually being undermined by efforts to Christianize the Mapuche and by government attempts to assimilate them into mainstream society.

Because the male family members come into contact with white society through their work, it is they who are influenced by mainstream culture. Women often take the most active role in maintaining the group's traditions.

11 ● CLOTHING

Men in towns wear Western-style shirts and trousers. Women are sometimes dressed more traditionally, with long skirts and colorful, embroidered aprons. They may also wear head scarves, sometimes decorated with gold coins.

Younger Mapuche girls often wear Western-style clothing such as sweaters and skirts. Boys wear shirts or sweaters and trousers.

12 ● FOOD

Traditional hunting and fishing, as well as crops such as corn and various fruits, ensure a varied, traditional diet for the Araucanians. The distinctive *curanto* oven is still used by some Mapuche on the island of Chiloé. It allows meat and vegetables wrapped in leaves to steam for hours. A recipe for humitas, steamed corn wrapped in leaves, follows. Traditional feasting on special occasions can last for several days.

13 ● EDUCATION

The Mapuche who lost their lands and had to emigrate to the towns now try to offer their children opportunities to attend school. On the reservations many still try to educate their children about their traditional way of life.

Recipe

Humitas

Ingredients

24 to 30 ears of corn
¼ cup butter
1 medium onion, peeled and chopped
1 large tomato, seeded and finely chopped
1 Tablespoon kosher salt
1 cup corn meal
⅓ cup grated cheese (Parmesan or Jarlsberg), optional

Directions

1. Carefully peel back the husks from the corn. Using a sharp knife, cut the husks off the corn cob. Peel away the husks, one at a time, and save three or four husks of the inner husks without tears.

2. Using a grater set over a bowl, grate the corn kernels off the cobs. There should be about 7 cups of corn.

3. In a large skillet, melt the butter. Add the onion and cook over medium heat until the onion is soft.

4. Add the chopped tomato and cook for about 4 minutes more, stirring constantly with a wooden spoon.

5. Remove the pan from the heat and add the corn. Sprinkle the mixture with the corn flour and mix. Add the grated cheese, if desired, and mix thoroughly.

6. Allow the mixture to rest for about 30 minutes, but stir every few minutes.

7. Assemble the humitas: Place 2 corn husks, one overlapping the other, on the work surface. The pointed ends should be facing away from each other. Place a third husk in the center.

8. Place 1 generous tablespoon of the corn mixture in the center of the stack of husks. Wrap the corn mixture completely with the husks. (Fold the sides in first, and then fold up each pointed end. The result should be a neat rectangle.) Tie the package with strips of corn husk or kitchen string.

9. Place a steamer rack in a large saucepan with about an inch of water. Stack the humitas in the steamer, cover the pan tightly, and steam for about 45 minutes.

Cool until the humitas can be handled. Cut and discard the tie, open the package, and serve the contents warm. Cooked humitas may be refrigerated for up to one week. To serve, steam for about 10 minutes to heat through.

Adapted from Rojas-Lombardi, Felipe. *The Art of South American Cooking.* New-York: HarperCollins, 1991.

14 ● CULTURAL HERITAGE

The music of the Araucanians is played on special instruments. There are whistles made of wood, a type of flute called the *trutruca,* and various percussion instruments such as the *cultrun.* Music and dancing traditionally accompany important rituals. A type of poetic singing (*mapudungu)* in the Araucanian language includes the reciting of legends, special invocations and prayers, and stories associated with the forces of life and death.

15 ● EMPLOYMENT

The Mapuche who still live on reservations engage in farming and fishing. They also produce handicrafts. A majority of Mapuche town dwellers live as urban workers. Since the 1930s, the Mapuche in towns have been active in trade union movements. During the period of military rule in the 1970s and 1980s, employment opportunities and working conditions were closely linked to the Mapuches' struggle to preserve their ethnic identity.

Women often contribute to the family's earnings by selling their wares at markets and fairs.

16 ● SPORTS

Many of the younger Mapuche are enthusiastic soccer fans. Some Mapuche from the island of Chiloé are skilled boaters.

17 ● RECREATION

Mapuche who live in or near towns enjoy the many *fiestas* (celebrations) loved by Chileans. Some of these are religious feast days. Others are linked to the agricultural cycle or to cultural events.

18 ● CRAFTS AND HOBBIES

The Mapuche are skilled jewelry-makers, potters, and weavers of cloth and baskets.

The ethnic Mapuche who live on the island of Chiloé still use a traditional loom to weave sweaters and ponchos from sheep wool. The women prepare dyes made from herbs.

There are several important craft fairs in Chile that display Araucanian arts and crafts.

19 ● SOCIAL PROBLEMS

The social problems of the Mapuche are related to economic hardship as well as to the struggle to preserve their traditions and identity. Many inhabitants of the reservations (*reducciones*) are primarily concerned with preserving the traditions and beliefs of their culture. On the other hand, those who have emigrated to the towns often see the struggle for workers' rights as their primary cause.

20 ● BIBLIOGRAPHY

Dwyer, Christopher. *Chile,* Major World Nations. Philadelphia: Chelsea House, 1997.

Gavin, Irene Flum. *Chile: Journey to Freedom.* Parsippany, N.Y.: Dillon Press, 1997.

Hintz, Martin. *Chile,* Enchantment of the World. Chicago: Children's Press, 1993.

Rojas-Lombardi, Felipe. *The Art of South American Cooking.* New York: HarperCollins, 1991.

WEBSITES

Interknowledge Corporation. Chile. [Online] Available http://www.interknowledge.com/chile/, 1998.

World Travel Guide. Chile. [Online] Available http://www.wtgonline.com/country/cl/gen.html, 1998.

China

■ **CHINESE** **132**

■ **DONG** **141**

■ **HAN** **148**

■ **MAN (MANCHUS)** **153**

■ **MIAO** **157**

■ **TIBETANS** **163**

■ **UIGHURS** **168**

■ **ZHUANG** **173**

China is the most populous nation on Earth. The largest ethnic group in the world is the Han, who alone account for over 1 billion of China's total population of 1.1 billion. In comparison, the population of the United States (the world's third most populous country) is only 265 million people, less than one-fourth the size of China's population. In addition to the Han, China recognizes fifty-five ethnic minorities with a total population of 91.2 million. The largest minority, with a population exceeding 15 million, is the Zhuang, a Buddhist people related to the Thai. The lands occupied by China's minorities have great size and importance compared to their small population. All together, two-thirds of China's territory is inhabited by minorities.

This chapter begins with an overview article on the Chinese people as a nationality. Separate articles are devoted to a number of representative ethnic groups, including the Han. Other large minorities in China profiled elsewhere include the Mongolians (see the chapter on Mongolia in Volume 6), the Koreans (see Korea in Volume 5) and the Kazaks (see Kazakstan in Volume 5).

Chinese

PRONUNCIATION: chy-NEEZ
ALTERNATE NAMES: Han (Chinese); Manchus; Mongols; Hui; Tibetans
LOCATION: China
POPULATION: 1.1 billion
LANGUAGE: Austronasian; Gan; Hakka; Iranian; Korean; Mandarin; Miao-Yao; Min; Mongolian; Russian; Tibeto-Burman; Tungus; Turkish; Wu; Xiang; Yue; Zhuang
RELIGION: Taoism; Confucianism; Buddhism

1 ● INTRODUCTION

Many people think of the Chinese population as uniform. However, it is really a mosaic made up of many different parts. The land that today is the People's Republic of China has been home to many nationalities. Often they ruled over their own lands and were treated as kingdoms by the Chinese. There have been centuries of intermarriage between the different groups, so there are no longer any "pure" ethnic groups in China.

Sun Yatsen founded the Republic of China in 1912 and called it "The Republic of the Five Nationalities": the Han (or ethnic Chinese), Manchus, Mongols, Hui, and Tibetans. Mao Zedong, the first leader of the People's Republic of China, described it as a multi-ethnic state. China's ethnic groups were recognized and granted equal rights. By 1955, more than 400 groups had come forward and won official status. Later, this number was cut to fifty-six. The Han form the "national majority." They now number more than 1 billion people, by far the largest ethnic group on earth. The other fifty-five ethnic groups form the "national minorities." They now account for 90 million people, or 8 percent of the total Chinese population.

All nationalities are equal under the law. National minorities were granted the right to self-government (*zizhi*) by the Chinese state. To increase their populations, national minorities were excused from the "one child per family" rule. Their share of the total Chinese population rose from 5.7 percent in 1964 to 8 percent in 1990.

2 ● LOCATION

Five large homelands, called "autonomous regions," have been created for China's major national minorities (Tibetans, Mongols, Uighur, Hui, and Zhuang). In addition, twenty-nine self-governing districts and seventy-two counties have been set up for the other national minorities.

The lands occupied by China's national minorities have great size and importance compared to their small population. All together, two-thirds of China's territory is inhabited by national minorities. China's northern frontier is formed by the Inner Mongolia Autonomous Region (500,000 square miles or 1,295,000 square kilometers); the northwestern frontier is formed by the Uighur Autonomous Region (617,000 square miles or 1,598,030 square kilometers); the southwestern frontier consists of the Tibet Autonomous Region (471,000 square miles or 1,219,890 square kilometers) and Yunnan Province (168,000 square miles or 435,120 square kilometers).

3 ● LANGUAGE

One of the main ways to identify China's ethnic groups is by language. The following is a list of China's languages (grouped by language family) and the groups that speak them. Population figures are from the 1990 census.

HAN DIALECTS (SPOKEN BY 1.04 BILLION HAN)
Mandarin (over 750 million)

Wu (90 million)

Gan (25 million)

Xiang (48 million)

Hakka (37 million)

Yue (50 million)

Min (40 million)

ALTAIC DIALECTS
Turkish (Uighur, Kazakh, Salar, Tatar, Uzbek, Yugur, Kirghiz: 8.6 million)

Mongolian (Mongols, Bao'an, Dagur, Santa, Tu: 5.6 million)

Tungus (Manchus, Ewenki, Hezhen, Oroqen, Xibo: 10 million)

Korean (1.9 million)

SOUTHWEST DIALECTS
Zhuang (Zhuang, Buyi, Dai, Dong, Gelao, Li, Maonan, Shui, Tai: 22.4 million)

Tibeto-Burman (Tibetans, Achang, Bai, Derong, Hani, Jingpo, Jino, Lahu, Lhopa, Lolo, Menba, Naxi, Nu, Pumi, Qiang: 13 million)

Miao-Yao (Miao, Yao, Mulao, She, Tujia: 16 million)

Austronasian (Benlong, Gaoshan [excluding Taiwanese], Bulang, Wa: 452,000)

INDO-EUROPEAN
Russian (13,000)

Iranian (Tajik: 34,000)

Some dialects vary widely. For example, Mandarin can be divided into four regions: northern, western, southwestern, and eastern.

Mandarin Chinese is increasingly spoken as a second language by the national minorities.

EPD Photos

A Chinese newspaper. The press in China is closely controlled by the government.

4 ● FOLKLORE

Each ethnic group in China has its own myths, but many myths are shared by groups in the same language family. Many different Chinese groups share an ancient creation myth that explains from where human beings came. According to this tale, humans and gods lived in peace long ago. Then the gods began fighting. They flooded the earth and destroyed all the people. But a brother and sister escaped by hiding in a huge pumpkin and floating on the water. When they came out of the pumpkin, they were alone in the world. If they did not marry, no more people would ever be born. But brothers and sisters were not supposed to marry each other.

The brother and sister decided to each roll a big stone down a hill. If one stone landed on top of the other, it meant Heaven wanted them to marry. If the stones rolled away from each other, Heaven did not approve. But the brother secretly hid one

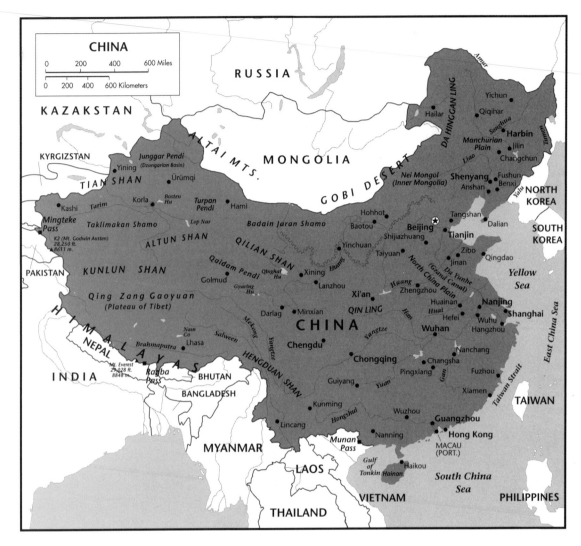

CHINA

RUSSIA

KAZAKSTAN

KYRGIZSTAN

MONGOLIA

Junggar Pendi (*Dzungarian Basin*)

Yining

ALTAI MTS.

GOBI DESERT

DA HINGGAN LING

Amur

Yichun

Qiqihar

Hailar

Harbin

Jilin

Manchurian Plain

Songhua

Changchun

Tumen

TIAN SHAN

Ürümqi

Nei Mongol (Inner Mongolia)

Shenyang

Fushun

Benxi

NORTH KOREA

Korla

Bosten Hu

Turpan Pendi

Hami

Hohhot

Baotou

Anshan

Tangshan

Dalian

SOUTH KOREA

Kashi

Tarim

Mingteke Pass

Taklimakan Shamo

Lop Nur

Badain Jaran Shamo

Yinchuan

Beijing

Tianjin

K2 (Mt. Godwin Austen) 28,250 ft. 8611 m.

ALTUN SHAN

QILIAN SHAN

Shijiazhuang

Zibo

Qingdao

PAKISTAN

KUNLUN SHAN

Qaidam Pendi

Qinghai Hu

Golmud

Gyaring Hu

Xining

Lanzhou

Taiyuan

Huang

Da Yunhe (Grand Canal)

Jinan

Yellow Sea

Huang

North China Plain

Zhengzhou

Xi'an

QIN LING

Huainan

Nanjing

Shanghai

Qing Zang Gaoyuan (Plateau of Tibet)

Darlag

Minxian

Han

Huai

Hefei

Wuhu

HIMALAYAS

Nam Co

Lhasa

Salween

Mekong

CHINA

Yangtze

Wuhan

Hangzhou

Brahmaputra

Chengdu

Nanchang

Mt. Everest 29,028 ft. 8848 m.

Ragba Pass

NEPAL

BHUTAN

HENGDUAN SHAN

Yangtze

Chongqing

Changsha

Fuzhou

East China Sea

INDIA

BANGLADESH

Guiyang

Pingxiang

Gan

Yuan

Xiamen

Taiwan Strait

TAIWAN

Kunming

Wuzhou

Guangzhou

Hongshui

Lincang

Nanning

Hong Kong

MYANMAR

Munan Pass

Gulf of Tonkin

Haikou

MACAU (PORT.)

South China Sea

PHILIPPINES

LAOS

VIETNAM

Hainan

THAILAND

stone on top of another at the bottom of the hill. He and his sister rolled their two stones. Then he led her to the ones he had hidden. After they got married, the sister gave birth to a lump of flesh. The brother cut it into twelve pieces, and he threw them in different directions. They became the twelve peoples of ancient China.

This myth was begun by the Miao, but it spread widely. It was retold by the Chinese and by the national minorities of southern and southwest China.

5 ● RELIGION

Many national minorities have preserved their native religions. However, they have also been influenced by the three major religions of China: Taoism, Confucianism, and Buddhism.

Taoism may be called the national religion of the Chinese people. It is based on ancient religions involving magic and nature worship. Around the sixth century BC, the main ideas of Taoism were collected in a book called the *Daode jing*. It is thought to have been written by the sage Lao-tzu. Taoism is based on a belief in *Dao* (or Tao), a spirit of harmony that drives the universe.

In contrast to Taoism, Confucianism is based on the teachings of a human being, Confucius (551–479 BC). He believed it is natural for human beings to be good to each other. Confucius was called the "father of Chinese philosophy." He tried to establish a system of moral values based on reason and human nature. Confucius was not considered a divine being in his lifetime. Later, some people came to regard him as a god. However, this belief never gained many followers.

Unlike Taoism and Confucianism, Buddhism did not originate in China. It was brought to China from India. It was begun by an Indian prince, Siddhartha Gautama (c.563-c.483 BC), in the sixth century BC. In Buddhism, a person's state of mind matters more than rituals. Mahayana Buddhism, one of the two main branches of Buddhism, came to China in the first century AD. It taught the Four Holy Truths discovered by the Buddha: 1) life consists of suffering; 2) suffering comes from desire; 3) to overcome suffering, one must overcome desire; 4) to overcome desire, one must follow the "Eightfold Path" and reach a state of perfect happiness (*nirvana*). Buddhism has had a deep influence on all classes and nationalities in China.

6 ● MAJOR HOLIDAYS

Most of the many holidays celebrated in China were begun by the ethnic Chinese. However, many are shared by the groups. The dates are usually on the lunar calendar (which is based on the moon rather than the sun). The following are among the most important:

The Spring Festival (or Chinese New Year) lasts about a week, from January 21 to February 20. It begins with a midnight meal on New Year's Eve. At dawn, the house is lighted and gifts are offered to the ancestors and the gods. Friends and relatives visit each other and share delicious feasts, where the main dish is Chinese dumplings (*jiaozi*). Children receive gifts—usually money in a red envelope (*hongbao*).

The Lantern Festival (*Dengjie*), held around March 5, is a holiday for children. Houses are lighted and large paper lanterns of every shape and color are hung in public places. A special cake (*yanxiao*) made of sticky rice is eaten.

The Qingming is a feast of the dead at the beginning of April. On this day, families visit the tombs of their ancestors and clean the burial ground. They offer flowers, fruits, and cakes to those who have died.

The Mid-Autumn Festival (or Moon Festival) is a harvest celebration at the beginning of October. The main dish is "moon cakes." The Dragon-Boat Festival is usually held at the same time.

The National Day of China on October 1 marks the founding of the People's Republic of China. It is celebrated in grand style. All the main buildings and city streets are lit up.

7 ● RITES OF PASSAGE

The birth of a child, especially a boy, is considered an important and joyous event. The older marriage customs have given way to freer ways of choosing partners. Under

Susan D. Rock

Although most of the numerous feasts and festivals celebrated in China originated with the Chinese, many are shared by the other groups. Practically every month there is at least one major celebration. The celebrations are usually held in accordance with the lunar calendar and are based on the yearly solstices and equinoxes.

China's communist government, the marriage ceremony has become a sober occasion involving only the bride and groom, some witnesses, and government officials. However, private celebrations are held with friends and relatives. In major cities such as Shanghai, Beijing, and Guangzhou, wealthy families enjoy Western-style marriages. However, the traditional rituals are still alive in the rural areas.

Because of China's large population, cremation has become common. Following a death, family and close friends attend private ceremonies.

8 ● RELATIONSHIPS

Close interpersonal relations (*guanxi*) characterize Chinese society, not only within the family, but also among friends and peers. Numerous feasts and festivals throughout the year strengthen individual and community ties. Visiting friends and relatives is an important social ritual. Guests bring gifts such as fruits, candies, cigarettes, or wine. The host usually offers a specially prepared meal.

Most young people like to choose a husband or wife on their own. But many still get help from their parents, relatives, or friends. The role of the "go-between" is still important.

9 ● LIVING CONDITIONS

From the 1950s to the late 1970s, many ancient structures were torn down and replaced by newer buildings. The isolation of China's national minorities has kept their traditional buildings from being destroyed. In the country, many apartment buildings built after 1949 have been replaced by modern two-story houses. There are still housing shortages in growing cities such as Beijing, Shanghai, Tianjin, and Guangzhou.

10 ● FAMILY LIFE

In most of China's ethnic groups, the man has always been the head of the family. The lives of women have improved greatly since the communist revolution in 1949. They have made progress in the family, in education, and in the work place. But they are still not equal politically.

Communist China's first leader, Mao Zedong (1893–1976), wanted people to have large families. From 1949 to 1980, the population of China grew from about 500 million to over 800 million. Since the 1980s, China has had a strict birth control policy of one child per family. It has greatly slowed population growth, especially in cities. National minorities, which make up only 8 percent of the population, are excused from the policy. Thus, their demographic growth is double that of the Han (or majority) Chinese.

11 ● CLOTHING

Until recently, all Chinese—men and women, young and old—wore the same plain clothing. Today brightly colored down jackets, woolens, and fur overcoats liven the bleak winter scene in the frozen north. In the milder climate of the south, people wear stylish Western suits, jeans, jackets, and sweaters year-round. Famous brand names are a common sight in large cities. The national minorities living near the Han Chinese dress in a similar way. However, those in isolated rural areas continue to wear their traditional styles of clothing.

12 ● FOOD

There are important differences in the diets and cooking methods of China's national minorities. The most common foods in China are rice, flour, vegetables, pork, eggs, and freshwater fish. The Han, or majority Chinese, have always valued cooking skills, and Chinese cuisine is well known all over the world. Traditional Chinese food includes dumplings, wonton, spring rolls, rice, noodles, and roasted Peking duck.

13 ● EDUCATION

The Han Chinese have always cared about education. They opened the first university over 2,000 years ago. China has more than 1,000 universities and colleges and 800,000 primary and middle schools. Their total enrollment is 180 million. Still, about 5 million school-age children do not enter school or have dropped out. Among China's national minorities, education varies greatly. It depends on local traditions, the nearness of cities, and other factors.

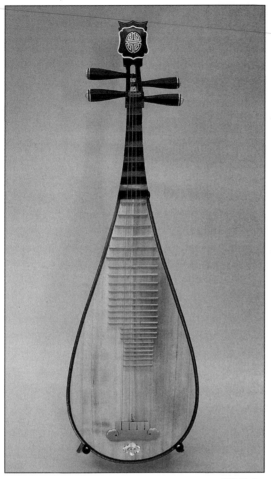

The pipa, *a traditional Chinese musical instrument.*

14 ● CULTURAL HERITAGE

There are enough traditional musical instruments in China to form a complete orchestra. The most popular include the two-stringed violin (*er hu*) and the *pipa*. Organizations that promote traditional Chinese music have preserved the rich musical heritage of many national minorities.

Most nationalities in China only have oral literary works (recited out loud). However, the Tibetans, Mongols, Manchus, Koreans, and Uighur have written literature as well. Some of it has been translated into English and other Western languages. The Han Chinese have produced one of the world's oldest and richest written traditions. Extending over more than 3,000 years, it includes poems, plays, novels, short stories, and other works. Renowned Chinese poets include Li Bai and Du Fu, who lived during the Tang Dynasty (AD 618–907). Great Chinese novels include the fourteenth-century *Water Margin*, *Pilgrim to the West*, and *Golden Lotus*.

15 ● EMPLOYMENT

Economic development in China varies by region. Most lands inhabited by the national minorities are less developed than the Han Chinese regions. A growing number of poor farmers have migrated to cities and to the eastern coast to improve their lives. However, migration has led to unemployment in urban areas. About 70 percent of China's population is still rural, and almost all rural dwellers are farmers.

16 ● SPORTS

Many sports in China are played only during seasonal festivals or in certain regions. China's national sport is ping-pong. Other common sports include shadow boxing (*wushu* or *taijiquan*). Western sports have been gaining popularity in China. These include soccer, swimming, badminton, basketball, tennis, and baseball. They are

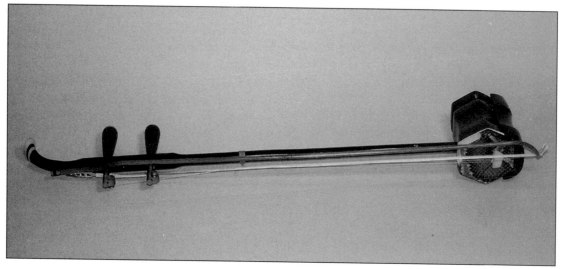

The two-stringed violin (er hu) *is one of the most popular traditional musical instruments in China.*

played mainly in schools, colleges, and universities.

17 ● RECREATION

Watching television has become a popular evening pastime for a majority of Chinese families. Video cassette recorders are also very common in urban areas. Movies are popular, but theaters are scarce and therefore are attended by only a small portion of the population. Young people enjoy karaoke (singing for others in public) and rock music. The elderly spend their free time attending the Peking Opera, listening to classical music, or playing cards or mahjongg (a tile game). Travel has become popular since the five-day work week was adopted in 1995.

18 ● CRAFTS AND HOBBIES

China's fifty-six nationalities all have their own folk art and craft traditions. However, the rich tradition of the Han Chinese is shared by many of China's nationalities.

Calligraphy (artistic lettering) and traditional painting are the most popular folk arts of the Han Chinese. Chinese paper-cutting, embroidery, brocade, colored glaze, jade jewelry, clay sculpture, and dough figurines are famous around the world.

Chess, kite flying, gardening, and landscaping are popular hobbies.

19 ● SOCIAL PROBLEMS

There is a growing gap in China between the rich and the poor. Other social problems include inflation, bribery, gambling, drugs, and the kidnapping of women. Because of the difference between rural and urban standards of living, more than 100 million people have moved to cities in the coastal areas to find better jobs.

Susan D. Rock

Since the 1980s, China has adopted a strict birth control policy, called the "one child per family" policy. It has succeeded (mainly in urban areas) in drastically slowing population growth, but at a great human cost, including forced abortions, female infanticide, and international adoption.

20 ● BIBLIOGRAPHY

Feinstein, Steve. *China in Pictures.* Minneapolis, Minn.: Lerner Publications Co., 1989.

Harrell, Stevan. *Cultural Encounters on China's Ethnic Frontiers.* Seattle: University of Washington Press, 1994.

Heberer, Thomas. *China and Its National Minorities: Autonomy or Assimilation?* Armonk, N.Y.: M. E. Sharpe, 1989.

McLenighan, V. *People's Republic of China.* Chicago: Children's Press, 1984.

O'Neill, Thomas. "Mekong River." *National Geographic* (February 1993), 2–35.

Terrill, Ross. "China's Youth Wait for Tomorrow." *National Geographic* (July 1991), 110–136.

Terrill, Ross. "Hong Kong Countdown to 1997." *National Geographic* (February 1991), 103–132.

WEBSITES

Embassy of the People's Republic of China, Washington, D.C. [Online] Available http://www.china-embassy.org/, 1998.

World Travel Guide. China. [Online] Available http://www.wtgonline.com/country/cn/gen.html, 1998.

Dong

PRONUNCIATION: dAWNg
ALTERNATE NAMES: Liao; Geling
LOCATION: China
POPULATION: 2.5 million
LANGUAGE: Dong; Chinese
RELIGION: Polytheism

1 ● INTRODUCTION

The Dong are a nationality whose origin can be traced through a branch of the Xiou tribe during the Qin (221–206 BC) and Han (206 BC–AD 220) dynasties more than 2,000 years ago. They were also called Liao, Geling, and other names in ancient Chinese works. It was said that some of the Dong ancestors went upstream through the Xun River and the Duliu River and arrived in the area now inhabited by the Dong. The Dong have lived in areas surrounded by the Miao, Zhuang, and Yao; these were ruled by the central government of successive Chinese dynasties. The Dong had their own social and administrative organization. The families of a given Dong village all bore the same surname. Public order was maintained by customary laws, which were decided through consultation among the heads of the villages. As a member of the village organization, every adult male participated in the general membership meeting to discuss matters of concern. This organization has been markedly weakened since the 1950s, but some of the customary laws are still effective to a certain extent.

2 ● LOCATION

The Dong are mainly concentrated in a mountainous area at the junction of three provinces, Guizhou, Guangxi, and Hunan, with warm a climate and abundant rainfall, and criss-crossed by rivers running in all directions. The villages, located at the foot of hills and bordered by streams, are adorned by a drum-tower of exquisite beauty at the center with an ancient banyan tree on the side. Dong population was 2.5 million in 1990.

3 ● LANGUAGE

Dong language belongs to the Sino-Tibetan family, Zhuang-Dong group, Dong-Shui branch. There are southern and northern dialects, each having three regional idioms. Most of the Dong know the Chinese language, both spoken and written. An alphabetic system of writing based on Latin was created in 1958, and proved very helpful to those who did not know the Chinese language.

4 ● FOLKLORE

The rich mythology of Dong has been transmitted orally from one generation to the next without written records. An epic described the achievements of the Goddess Sasui and her offspring including the creation, the flood, and the marriage of the brother and sister. This myth of origins is common (with many variants) to many national minorities of southwest China.

Another story described four tortoises incubating four eggs. Three eggs went bad. Only one egg hatched a boy. They tried again. This time, also only one egg hatched, giving birth to a girl. The offspring married and gave birth to twelve sons and daughters. Among them were a brother, Jiangliang, and his sister, Jiangmei, who were naughty. The

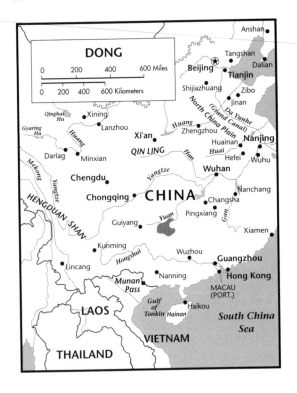

DONG

0   200   400   600 Miles

0   200   400   600 Kilometers

Qinghai Hu
Gyaring Hu
Xining
Lanzhou
Darlag
Minxian
HENGDUAN SHAN
Chengdu
Chongqing
Guiyang
Kunming
Lincang
Hongshui
Munan Pass
Nanning
LAOS
Gulf of Tonkin
THAILAND
VIETNAM
Anshan
Tangshan
Beijing
Tianjin
Dalian
Shijiazhuang
Zibo
Jinan
Huang
Zhengzhou
Xi'an
QIN LING
Huainan
Huai
Hefei
Wuhu
Nanjing
Han
Wuhan
Yangtze
CHINA
Nanchang
Changsha
Pingxiang
Yuan
Gan
Xiamen
Wuzhou
Guangzhou
Hong Kong
MACAU (PORT.)
Haikou
Hainan
South China Sea
Da Yunhe (Grand Canal)
North China Plain
Huang
Mekong
Yangtze

5 ● RELIGION

The Dong are polytheistic (they worship more than one god). They regard the almighty Goddess Sasui, the most lofty of all gods, as their protector. Each village has a temple in which there is a round altar made of stone, 4 (1.2 meters) feet in height, more than 10 feet (3 meters) in diameter, surrounded by banana trees and brambles. On February 7 or 8 (lunar calendar; Western calendar, between February 28 and March 27) the Dong will bring chicken, duck, fish, and a gruel of sweetened fried flour, as offerings to the goddess. They also revere huge stones, large trees, wells, and bridges. Divination by means of chicken, grass, eggs, snails, rice, or divinatory symbols is prevalent among the Dong.

6 ● MAJOR HOLIDAYS

The Spring Festival (lunar New Year; Western calendar, between January 21 and February 20) is the most important holiday of the year. In some districts, however, they choose one day in October or November (lunar calendar; Western calendar, between October 24 and January 18) as the Dong's New Year. Before the feast, every family member will take a bowl of rice gruel symbolizing a watery field to be ploughed in the future.

On the first of January (lunar calendar; Western calendar, between January 21 and February 20), right after the first cockcrow appears, girls will scramble to draw water from the well. The luckiest sign is to draw a bucket of water with white bubbles. Festival activities include buffalo fighting, mountain climbing, and bronze drum percussions. April 8 (lunar calendar; Western calendar,

boy cut a tree with a saw, leading to a fire that hurt the Thunder Goddess. She got angry, so it rained continuously for nine months. Fortunately, Jiangliang and Jiangmei hid in a huge melon when the flood came. The Thunder Goddess raised twelve suns to dry up the flood, but they scorched the earth and the trees. Helped by bees, Jiangliang and Jiangmei shot down ten suns out of twelve. They left one sun for the daytime and the other for the night. An eagle tried to persuade them to marry. They rolled two millstones from the mountain top, which laid one on top of the other, a Heaven-given sign that they should marry. They married and their progeny formed various peoples, including the Han, Miao, Yao, and Dong.

Cynthia Bassett

Young Dong maidens in their traditional festival dress.

between May 1 and May 30) is the Festival of the Birth of the Buffalo God. Every household will clean the buffalo pen, feed it with black glutinous rice, give the animal a day off, and kill a chicken or duck as a sacrificial offering. In addition, this is also the day when a heroine boldly delivered a meal of black glutinous rice to her brother (imprisoned for having led an insurrectionary army to occupy Liuzhou City) and rescued him from jail. Commemorating that day, married women gather to sing and dance, and to make black glutinous rice cakes that are carried to their parents' homes and offered as gifts to their relatives.

7 ● RITES OF PASSAGE

Three days (or one week) after childbirth, relatives bring glutinous rice, eggs, and chickens, as well as a hat, for congratulations. Gifts also include 3 to 5 feet (0.9 to 1.5 meters) of yellow cloth for the baby's clothing. According to Dong custom, one is not allowed to make baby clothes before childbirth. The infant should be draped with used pieces of cloth right after birth. The new clothing should be made of the yellow cloth given by relatives. The maternal grandmother chooses a name for the baby while sewing the baby's clothes. Girls gather to sing blessing songs until late in the evening. When the baby is one month old,

Cynthia Bassett

Terraced rice fields with a Dong village in the distance.

the mother paints the baby's brow with a little tang oil and soot from the bottom of a pan. Accompanied by her mother-in-law, the new mother will bring gifts to her own mother's house, where she will be received warmly. The next day, her mother will send a large glutinous rice cake to her house, indicating that the mother is allowed to call on relatives to present the baby.

The Dong bury the dead underground after shaving the hair and washing the body. It is taboo to have any copper or iron touch the body.

8 ● RELATIONSHIPS

The Dong are hospitable. Bowls of gruel of sweetened fried flour will be repeatedly offered to the guest. Each bowl is offered with different refreshments. This ritual usually takes one hour or more. The wine before meal is sweet, but bitter wine is offered during the meal. All dishes taste sour: pork, fish, chicken, duck, cucumber, and hot pepper; it is a "sour feast." There is a Dong custom in Guizhou to receive a guest from each family. A man, representing his family, will bring his family's dishes to the dinner party. Thus, a great variety of dishes will be offered to the guests. A grand occasion of Dong celebration is when all the members of a village call on a neighboring village, usually after autumn harvest: there is a deafening sound of gongs and drums, reinforced by songs and reed-pipe wind music. Dating is common, lasting often late into the night.

9 ● LIVING CONDITIONS

Most Dong houses have two or three stories, sometimes more, made of wood. The roof is covered with tiles or bark of China fir. Houses occupied by branches of the same family are sometimes connected by verandas and open into each other. Buildings at the foot of a hill or beside a river are built on stilts, sometimes 20 to 30 feet (6 to 9 meters) high. The family lives upstairs. Firewood and livestock are placed on the ground. A shrine for idols or ancestral tablets is set up in the central room. The "wind-swept rooms" on both sides are used as bedrooms and firepools. A Dong village is usually made up of row upon row of wooden houses. The pathways are paved with flagstones or crushed stones. The Dong live on self-sufficient agriculture. City dwellers have a standard of living similar to that of other residents.

10 ● FAMILY LIFE

Dong families are patrilineal. The position of women is much lower than that of men. They are not allowed to touch the bronze drum or to go upstairs if the men stay downstairs. They have a limited right of succession from their parents ("girl's field") only after their marriage—while the man inherits the property. Women participate in heavy labor in the fields and bear the responsibility of all household chores.

The Dong are monogamous. They have freedom to choose their spouse. Arranged marriages are very rare. The bride, holding an umbrella, accompanied by six women, walks directly to the bridegroom's house. They are received by boys of the bridegroom's branch, who see the bride to her family's door right after the wedding ceremony. She will return to live with her husband, for a few days only, during festivals or after the busy season.

If she gets pregnant, she will then move to her husband's house. If she does not get pregnant, she is expected to move three to five years after the wedding.

11 ● CLOTHING

Rural people make the yarn, dye it, and then knit their traditional clothes. Colors are dark navy, purple, white, and blue. Men wear cotton shirts and pants and always wrap their heads. Most women wear short tops and pleated skirts. They use dark navy cotton fabric to wrap their legs from knee to ankle and wear sandals. They usually wear

Cynthia Bassett

Wooden towers such as this are found in every Dong village. They are made without nails in a pagoda-like architectural style.

their hair in a bun, decorated with colorful flowers. Some women like to use a floral cotton scarf to cover their shoulders, and sew large silver buttons on their costumes for decoration. Others wear knee-length shirts and loose pants, with the cuffs of the sleeves and pants trimmed with piping and lace. Some embroider dragons on their clothes.

Dong people living in urban areas usually wear the same basic clothes as the Chinese.

Cynthia Bassett

A Dong woman harvesting glutinous rice.

12 ● FOOD

The staple food is rice. The Dong like hot and sour dishes. One of their traditional meals is salted fish or meat. Raw fish or meat is salted for three days, seasoned with spicy pepper powder, ginger, and glutinous rice, and then put in hermetically sealed pots or wooden barrels. The preparation may be served after three months, but only reaches full flavor after many years. The salted fish or meat can be steamed, but the Dong prefer to eat it raw. A gruel of sweetened, fried flour is a favorite dish. Rice is stir-fried with tea leaves, then cooked in water; when it is done, the tea leaves are discarded. To serve, one puts fried glutinous rice, peanuts, walnuts, soybeans, sausages, or pork liver selectively in a bowl, then adds the hot gruel, sweetened or salted.

13 ● EDUCATION

Primary schools have been established in every village, and middle schools in every district. The number of college students is increasing. More and more teachers, engineers, scholars, and medical doctors are being trained.

However, illiteracy (not being able to read and write) is still present in remote mountainous areas, especially among women. Parents support the education of their children, but boys form the majority of middle school and, especially, university students.

14 ● CULTURAL HERITAGE

The Dong have created the Great Song of Dong, a women's chorus unaccompanied by musical instruments. It is led by a woman, and is known for a unique style, with a free tempo, full of power and grandeur.

The Pipa Song is also typical of the Dong musical tradition. The *pipa* is a plucked string instrument with a fretted fingerboard. The song borrows the name of the accompanying instrument.

Dong plays were developed in the last century from a genre of popular entertainment consisting of talking and thinking. The gait and movement are rather simple, but the music for voices is manifold. The actors wear Dong dress, but use no makeup. Songs

Cynthia Bassett

The magnificent "Wind and Rain Bridge" is a wooden bridge built on stone piers.
Pavilions are raised on each of the the piers.

are accompanied by a two-stringed bowed instrument, the *huqin*.

The Dong practice group dancing in a circle, boys and girls holding hands and singing while dancing. A musician-dancer blows the reed-pipe wind instrument (*lüshen*) while going through various dance movements.

The Dong area is the "land of poems and sea of songs." The rhyme scheme of their poems is rather loose. The Dong Song is a chanted rhymed poem, marked by an abundance of striking metaphors. The content includes themes of creation, flood, the ori-gin of human beings, the migration of the Dong, customary law, as well as the exploits and the loves of heroes. Chinese stories also appear in Dong songs and plays.

15 ● EMPLOYMENT

In addition to farming, men are adept at carpentry and in building Dong-style wooden structures. Today there is a trend among young people to move to coastal areas and to engage in trade.

16 ● SPORTS

Wrestling is a favorite sport among the youth, while spinning tops is a popular game with children. Other sports widely practiced are basketball, table tennis, volleyball, and chess.

17 ● RECREATION

Some movies have been dubbed into the Dong language. Many Dong families now have black-and-white television. Recreation for youngsters is almost always related to dating. Singing is one of the favorite pastimes in Dong areas; the aged teach songs, the youth sing songs, and the children learn songs. Singers take much pleasure in performing. The Lion Dance and the Dragon Dance are performed on the Spring Festival.

18 ● CRAFTS AND HOBBIES

Dong crafts include embroidery, cross-stitching, rattan artifacts, bamboo articles, silver ornaments, brocade, and Dong garments. The Dong's wooden buildings are renowned for their exquisite architecture. The Drum Tower (interconnecting wood) is held together by tenon and mortise, without a single iron nail; numbering three to fifteen stories, it may reach 40 to 50 feet (12 to 15 meters) in height. It is the symbol of the family branch and a place of rally. The magnificent "Wind and Rain Bridge" is a wooden bridge built on stone piers, with pavilions raised on top of the piers.

19 ● SOCIAL PROBLEMS

Poverty and slow development are still the most important social problems. Changes are slow and the way to modernization and wealth is long and difficult.

20 ● BIBLIOGRAPHY

Dreyer, June Teufel. *China's Forty Millions.* Cambridge, Mass.: Harvard University Press, 1976.

Eberhard, Wolfram. *China's Minorities: Yesterday and Today.* Belmont, Calif.: Wadsworth Publishing Company, 1982.

Heberer, Thomas. *China and Its National Minorities: Autonomy or Assimilation?* Armonk, N.Y.: M. E. Sharpe, 1989.

Lebar, Frank, et al. *Ethnic Groups of Mainland Southeast Asia.* New Haven, Conn.: Human Relations Area Files Press, 1964.

Miller, Lucien, ed. *South of the Clouds: Tales from Yunnan.* Seattle: University of Washington Press, 1994.

Ramsey, S. Robert. *The Languages of China.* Princeton, N.J.: Princeton University Press, 1987.

WEBSITES

Embassy of the People's Republic of China, Washington, D.C. [Online] Available http://www.china-embassy.org/, 1998.

World Travel Guide. China. [Online] Available http://www.wtgonline.com/country/cn/gen.html, 1998.

Han

PRONUNCIATION: hAHn

LOCATION: China; Taiwan; (overseas: Southeast Asia, Japan, North America, Oceania, and Europe)

POPULATION: 1 billion in mainland China

LANGUAGE: Mandarin Chinese

RELIGION: Taoism; Confucianism; Buddhism

1 ● INTRODUCTION

The Han are the largest ethnic group in China. In ancient times, the ancestors of the Han lived in the Yellow River basin. Over the centuries they met, fought, and merged with neighboring tribes. Later the Han founded Huaxia, which slowly expanded along the Yangtze River.

The Chinese became a unified nation with their center in Huaxia during the Han Dynasty (206 BC–AD 220). They are known to this day as the "people of Han" or simply "Han." Many Han Chinese migrated to south China (south of the Yangzi River). The Han population eventually exceeded that of the north.

After 2,000 years, the Chinese empire was overthrown in 1911. Since 1949, there have been two Chinese governments, one in mainland China and one in Taiwan.

2 ● LOCATION

Based on the 1990 census, there are more than 1 billion Han in mainland China. They live mainly in cities and in the river valleys, which are farming areas. The great majority of people in Taiwan are also Han. In addition, many Han have emigrated to Southeast Asia, Japan, North America, Oceania, and Europe.

3 ● LANGUAGE

The Han language is usually called Chinese. The United Nations has named it an official international language. There are seven dialects. The written language, invented over 3,000 years ago, can be used with all of them. The northern dialect (Mandarin Chinese) is the common spoken language (*putonghua*) of China.

4 ● FOLKLORE

The Han people have recorded thousands of myths, as well as popular folktales. In Han folklore, the god Pangu created the world; the goddess Nüwa formed human beings. Ji is the god of all crops, and Shennong is the god of herbs. Huang Di was the first ancestor of the Han people. The *Sanhaijing*, written 2,000 years ago, recorded Han legends and folk customs.

5 ● RELIGION

The Han have historically accommodated religions of diverse origin. Popular oral traditions reflect early beliefs in nature gods and deified heroes. Historical writings dating from the fourteenth century BC testify to the ruling class belief in the deified ancestor and ancestor worship. During the Han Dynasty (206 BC–AD 220) three religions grew: Taoism, Confucianism, and Buddhism. They were based on the respective teachings of three men: Lao-tzu, Confucius, and the Buddha. Buddhism had the most followers.

6 ● MAJOR HOLIDAYS

The Han celebrate many holidays. The most important is the Spring Festival, or Chinese New Year, between January 21 and February 20. Almost everybody returns home, even from distant places. Family members share a dinner party on the eve of the New Year. Fireworks and firecrackers are lit. People dress up and celebrate for days in the city and for weeks in the country.

The mid-autumn or moon festival (October 15 on the lunar calendar) is the second most important day of the year. Han people watch the full moon and eat moon cakes, which are a symbol of family unity. The Lion Dance, Dragon Dance, and Dragon Boat Regatta (boat race) are part of this festival.

HAN

0 200 400 600 Miles
0 200 400 600 Kilometers

7 ● RITES OF PASSAGE

Han couples in mainland China are supposed to have no more than one child. More than ever before, childbirth is a major event in a family. Eggs cooked and dyed red are often sent to relatives and friends. Couples often have a dinner party when their baby is one month old.

In the past, the dead were usually buried. Today, cremation is common in cities. The Qingming Festival is a day to honor dead relatives and visit their tombs. It is held on April 4, 5, or 6.

8 ● RELATIONSHIPS

New Year visits are very popular during the Spring Festival. Guests usually bring gifts such as fruits, candies, cigarettes, or a bottle of wine. They always get a warm welcome. Holiday greetings by telephone are popular in large cities these days. So are Christmas and New Year greeting cards.

Most young people like to choose the person they will marry. However, parents, relatives, or friends often help out.

9 ● LIVING CONDITIONS

Housing styles vary by region. From the 1950s to the late 1970s, newer buildings replaced many ancient dwellings. In the country, many apartment buildings have been replaced by modern two-story single homes. Housing shortages are a problem in big cities such as Beijing, Shanghai, Tianjin, and Guangzhou.

Today many Han live in comfort, both in the city and the country. In addition to meeting their basic needs, many own such items as household electrical appliances.

10 ● FAMILY LIFE

Men dominate the Han family, and the family name is carried on by male children.

The Han are monogamous (they marry one person). They are free to choose the person they will marry. Most couples stay together, but the rate of divorce has been rising. An average urban Han family consists of a man, his wife, and their only child. In rural areas, it is common for three or more generations to live in the same household.

11 ● CLOTHING

Just two decades ago, Han Chinese—young and old, men and women—wore clothes of the same plain style and color. Their city streets all looked grey and dull. Today, colorful down and woolen jackets and fur overcoats are worn in the frozen north. In the south, where the climate is milder, people wear suits, jeans, jackets, sweaters, and other stylish clothing all year. Famous brand names are often seen in large cities. In some rural areas, Han peasants still wear their "Mao suits" (the plain two-piece outfit named after the former Chinese leader).

12 ● FOOD

The main foods of the Han are rice, flour, vegetables, pork, eggs, and freshwater fish. The Han have always valued cooking skills, and Chinese (Han) cuisine is well known all over the world. Dumplings, wanton, spring rolls, rice, noodles, and roasted Peking duck are some examples of Han food.

13 ● EDUCATION

The Han Chinese created the first university over 2,000 years ago. They have always valued education. China has over 1,000 universities and colleges and 800,000 primary and middle schools. They have a total of 180 million students. Still, about five million school-age children do not enter school or have dropped out. About 98 percent of children enroll in school when they reach school age. Only about 10 percent of Han cannot read or write.

14 ● CULTURAL HERITAGE

There are enough Han musical instruments to form an orchestra. Three of the most popular instruments are the two-string violin *(erhu),* the lute *(zheng),* and the *pipa.* There are also many percussion instruments, including *gu* (drums), *ban* (clappers), *muyu* (a wooden "fish" played by striking with a stick), *xiao luo* (gong), and *bo* (cymbals). Han cultural treasures include poems, dramas, novels, and works of history and philosophy. Many works have been translated into other languages. The great poets include Li Bai and Du Fu, who lived in the age of great Chinese poetry (Tang Dynasty, AD 618–907). The great Chinese novels began in the fourteenth century with the epic *Water Margin*. They also include *Pilgrim to the West* and *Golden Lotus*.

The Han invented paper, ceramics, gunpowder, and the compass.

15 ● EMPLOYMENT

Economic contrasts in Han society are dramatic. Scientists work in nuclear power plants while peasants farm using primitive methods. Two kinds of work that go back thousands of years are porcelain making (from which we get the name "china") and producing raw silk.

16 ● SPORTS

As China's main ethnic group, the Han have competed in almost every Olympic sport and in many other sporting events. Soccer, volleyball, basketball, table tennis, badminton, jogging, and swimming are popular sports played by children and adults. *Wushu* and *Taijiquan* are two kinds of shadow-boxing that are methods of gymnastics and meditation.

17 ● RECREATION

Watching television in the evening is a common pastime for Han families. Video cassette recorders are also very popular in urban areas. Movies are another form of

EPD Photos

Percussion instruments used in Han musical performances include (clockwise from large drum) the tang gu *(large drum),* ban *(clappers),* muyu *(wooden "fish" with stick),* xiao luo *(gong with stick), and* bo *(cymbals). Courtesy of the Center for the Study of World Musics, Kent State University.*

recreation. Many young people enjoy dancing and rock music. The elderly like Chinese opera, drama, classical music, and playing mah-jongg (a tile game). Travel has become popular since the five-day work week took effect in 1995.

18 ● CRAFTS AND HOBBIES

Calligraphy (fancy lettering) and traditional Chinese painting are the most popular folk arts of the Han. They are also famous for embroidery, brocade, colored glaze, jade products, clay sculpture, and figures made out of dough. Chess, kite flying, and gardening in pots are hobbies among people of all ages.

19 ● SOCIAL PROBLEMS

China's current social problems include a growing gap between the rich and the poor, rising inflation, and bribery, as well as gambling, drugs, prostitution, and the kidnapping of women. There is also a growing difference in the way people live in rural and urban areas. More than 100 million people have moved to the coastal areas to look for jobs.

20 ● BIBLIOGRAPHY

Harrell, Stevan, ed. *Cultural Encounters on China's Ethnic Frontiers.* Seattle: University of Washington Press, 1995.

Heberer, Thomas. *China and Its National Minorities: Autonomy or Assimilation?* Armonk, N.Y.: M. E. Sharpe, 1989.

Moser, Leo J. The Chinese Moustaches *Peoples and Provinces of China.* Boulder, Colo.:Westview Press, 1984.

WEBSITES

Embassy of China, Washington, D.C. [Online] Available http://www.china-embassy.org/.

World Travel Guide. China. [Online] Available http://travelguide.attistel.co.uk/country/cn/gen.html.

Man (Manchus)

PRONUNCIATION: man-CHOOZ
ALTERNATE NAMES: Jurchens; Manzhou
LOCATION: China
POPULATION: 9.85 million
LANGUAGE: Chinese
RELIGION: Shamanism

1 ● INTRODUCTION

The Man, better known as the Manchus, dwell mainly in northeast China. They are descended from the Jurchens of the Central Plains. The Jurchens were conquered by the Yuan Dynasty (1271–1368) and later ruled by the Ming (1368–1644). Starting in the fifteenth century, the Jurchens' tribal leaders were appointed by the central government. In the sixteenth century, a Jurchen hero, Nurhachi (1559–1626), unified all the tribes by military force. His leadership combined military operations, government administration, and economic management. He was the founder of Qing Dynasty (1644–1911). His eighth son succeeded him on the throne. In 1635, he changed the name of his nationality to Manzhou (origin of the Western term "Manchu"). It was shortened to Man in 1911 when China's last dynasty ended.

2 ● LOCATION

The Manchus live all over China. Most live in Liaoning Province. Smaller numbers are found in the regions of Jilin, Heilongjiang, Hebei, Inner Mongolia, Xinjiang, Gansu, and Shandong, as well as the cities of Beijing, Tianjin, Chengdu, Xi'an, and Guangzhou. The Manchu population was

9.85 million in 1990, second in size only to the Zhuang among the national minorities.

3 ● LANGUAGE

The Man language belongs to the Altaic family. It has been spoken less and less since the end of the eighteenth century. Today it is used only by a small number of Manchus. Almost all of the Manchus speak Chinese.

4 ● FOLKLORE

A large portion of Manchu mythology is about ancestors. According to one myth, three fairy maidens took a bath in Tianchi (Heavenly Lake) in the Changbai Mountains. The youngest ate a small red fruit that a golden bird carried in its bill. She got pregnant and bore a boy who could speak as soon as he was born. She named him Aixin-jueluo (the last name of Qing Dynasty emperors). When he had grown up, she told him the story of his birth and then rose up to heaven.

5 ● RELIGION

The traditional beliefs of the Manchus are rooted in shamanism, which revolves around magical healers. Shamans help women bear children, and they cure illness and shield people from harm. The shaman dances in a trance to cure the sick. There is only one real shaman in each village. When he performs, the shaman wears a long skirt and a special hat. Many long strips of colored cloth hang from it and cover his face and head. Shamanism still exists in Manchu villages, but it disappeared from cities long ago.

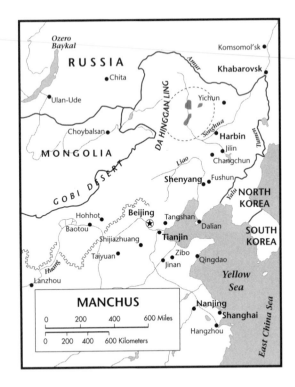

6 ● MAJOR HOLIDAYS

The Chinese Spring Festival, or New Year, occurs between January 21 and February 20 on the Western calendar. It is a major holiday for the Manchus. They decorate their doors with red, yellow, blue, or white banners.

Some Manchu festivals are related to sacrificial rites. For example, every family offers a sacrifice (usually a black male pig) to its ancestors in autumn.

7 ● RITES OF PASSAGE

In order to obtain the gods' blessings, a small bow and arrow are hung at a family's gate when a boy is born. A strip of cloth is hung when a girl is born. Girls are made to lie on their backs with a special pillow under their heads because it is considered pretty for the back of the head to be flattened.

When a person dies, the coffin is brought in and carried out through a window instead of through the door. The funeral must be held on an odd-numbered day. Before the funeral, a post is erected in the courtyard. A long, narrow flag made of red and black pieces of cloth is hung on it. During the funeral, relatives and friends take pieces of the flag. They then use the pieces to make clothes for their children. They believe this will protect the children from harm. After the funeral ceremony, the dead person is buried.

8 ● RELATIONSHIPS

Guests are warmly welcomed in a Manchu home. However, they must avoid sitting in the part of the house reserved for ancestors.

When the bride-to-be visits her future husband's family for the first time, she is given a small heart-shaped bag. It is used for carrying money and other objects and actually consists of two smaller bags. The girl keeps one and gives the other to her future husband.

9 ● LIVING CONDITIONS

Inside a Manchu courtyard, there is usually a post for sacrificial offerings. The house is made of wood and adobe. Its central room opens to the south. The room in the west part of the house is usually the bedroom. The parents and older family members sleep on the north side, the children on the south side.

10 ● FAMILY LIFE

The Manchu family name is carried on by males. Three or more generations often live in one household. The Manchus have great respect for their elders. Men and women hold equal power in the family. Men engage in farming. Women work in the fields, but they usually spend most of their time doing household chores. The Manchu are monogamous (they marry only one person). Arranged marriages are common. Young people become engaged at sixteen or seventeen.

11 ● CLOTHING

The traditional Manchu costumes included long robes. These robes were still worn in the first part of this century. Then they slowly disappeared. However, women's robes (*cheongsam*) are still worn on special occasions, but their style has changed. Women wear wooden blocks about 2.5 inches (6.2 centimeters) high under the middle part of their shoe soles. Their hair is worn in a flat bun behind the neck.

12 ● FOOD

The Manchus like to eat millet, including sticky millet. "Cooked mutton held in the hand" is a required part of the Spring Festival. Mutton (the meat of a sheep) is chopped into pieces and partly cooked with a little salt. Each piece is held in the hand while it is eaten. Sometimes a knife is needed. The most popular snack is *saqima*, a candied fritter. It is made by mixing flour with eggs, cutting the mixture into noodles, and frying it. It is then taken out, covered with syrup, and stirred. Finally, it is put into a wooden frame, pressed, cut into squares, and served.

13 ● EDUCATION

The Manchus have always had a high level of literacy (ability to read and write). Many young people (mainly men) needed an education in order to work for the emperor during the Manchu Qing Dynasty. More recently, the growth of cities has furthered education among the Manchu.

14 ● CULTURAL HERITAGE

One of the main Manchu art forms is dancing. In the Hunting Dance, the dancers wear leopard and tiger costumes. Some ride on horseback as they hunt "animals" wearing costumes. Manchu songs are accompanied by a bamboo flute and a drum.

The Octagon Drum Opera is the Manchu version of the famous Chinese Peking Opera.

Famous Manchu figures in the arts include writer Lao She (1899–1966), comic writer Hou Baolin, and actor Cheng Yanqiu.

15 ● EMPLOYMENT

Metals, coal, hydroelectric power production, agriculture, and forestry are the main sources of income among the Manchu. Since the end of the nineteenth century, the Manchu homeland has become the center of Chinese heavy industry. Many Manchu are workers and managers in large factories.

16 ● SPORTS

The Manchu have a long tradition of ice skating. During the long, cold winters in northeast China they skate on rivers and lakes or in skating rinks. Some Manchu skaters have won international fame.

17 ● RECREATION

Urban Manchus watch television in the evening. They go to the movies about once or twice a month. Adults enjoy Peking opera, chess, gardening, keeping pet birds, and storytelling. Young people like dancing, listening to popular songs, and karaoke (singing for others in public). Recreation is similar in rural areas. However, people see fewer television programs and movies.

18 ● CRAFTS AND HOBBIES

The Manchus are experts at jade sculpture, bone carving, making small clay and dough figures, and painting the insides of small bottles. They are also known around the world for their ice carving and sculptures.

19 ● SOCIAL PROBLEMS

Urban Manchus have one of the highest standards of living in China. However, they have lost much of their cultural identity. In contrast, the rural Manchu remain poor because of their long, cold winters, but they have preserved their traditions.

20 ● BIBLIOGRAPHY

Harrell, Stevan, ed. *Cultural Encounters on China's Ethnic Frontiers.* Seattle: University of Washington Press, 1995.

Heberer, Thomas. *China and Its National Minorities: Autonomy or Assimilation?* Armonk, N.Y.: M. E. Sharpe, 1989.

Ma Yin, ed. *China's Minority Nationalities.* Beijing: Foreign Languages Press, 1989.

WEBSITES

Embassy of the People's Republic of China, Washington, D.C. [Online] Available http://www.china-embassy.org/, 1998.

World Travel Guide. China. [Online] Available http://www.wtgonline.com/country/cn/gen.html, 1998.

Miao

PRONUNCIATION: mee-OW
ALTERNATE NAMES: Hmong; Hmu; Meo
LOCATION: China (also Vietnam, Laos, Kampuchea, Thailand, Myanmar and about 1 million migrants to the West)
POPULATION: 7 million
LANGUAGE: Miao
RELIGION: Shamanism; ancestor worship; Roman Catholicism; Protestantism

1 ● INTRODUCTION

The Miao have a very long history. Their legends claim that they lived along the Yellow River and Yangtze River valleys as early as 5,000 years ago. Later they migrated to the forests and mountains of southwest China. There they mostly lived in Guizhou Province. Military attacks in the eighteenth and nineteenth centuries forced them into the nearby provinces of Guangxi, Hunan, Hubei, and Yunnan. Some Miao even migrated across the Chinese border into Vietnam, Laos, Kampuchea, Thailand, and Burma (Myanmar).

From their earliest days, the Miao practiced primitive farming using slash-and-burn methods. Families never lived in the same house more than five years. As the soil in one area became depleted, they would move away. The Miao became known for always being on the move. However, most of the Miao have settled down since the middle of the twentieth century.

2 ● LOCATION

The Miao live in over 700 cities and counties in the seven provinces of south China. They number over seven million, based on the 1990 census. They are widely scattered and live in very small settlements. The Wuling and Miaoling mountain range in Guangxi Autonomous Region is home to nearly one-third of China's Miao people. An old Miao saying goes: "Birds nest in trees, fish swim in rivers, Miao live in mountains."

3 ● LANGUAGE

Miao is a Sino-Tibetan language of the Miao-Yao family. It is similar to the Thai language, and it has three dialects. Today, it is written using the Chinese *pinyin* system, which is based on the Western alphabet. Language is an important way to recognize the many different Miao groups.

4 ● FOLKLORE

Miao myths describe the creation of the world, the birth of the Miao people, and their battles and migrations. A typical Miao creation myth is the ancient "Maple Song": White Maple was an immortal tree that gave birth to Butterfly Mama. She married a water bubble and then laid twelve eggs. The treetop changed into a big bird that hatched the eggs over a period of twelve years. When the eggs hatched, they gave birth to a thunder god, a dragon, a buffalo, a tiger, an elephant, a snake, a centipede, a boy called Jiangyang, and his sister. So Butterfly Mama was the mother of God, animals, and human beings

5 ● RELIGION

The Miao believe that a supernatural power in everything around them decides their fate. They also believe that everything that moves or grows has its own spirit. They worship the sun, moon, lightning, thunder,

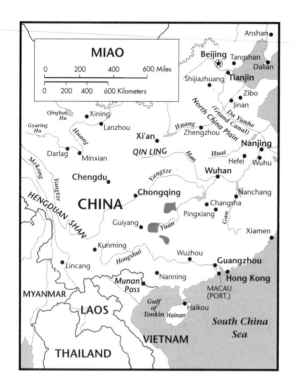

The Miao New Year is a joyful holiday. The Spring Festival occurs between January 21 and February 20 on the Western calendar. It is now a major holiday for all of China's nationalities. There are songs, dances, horse races, and music.

7 ● RITES OF PASSAGE

To the Miao, a sturdy stone stands for a strong child. When a child is three years old, parents will take gifts to a huge stone. Bowing down, they will burn joss sticks (incense) and pray for blessings and protection. This rite is repeated three times a year. If the child is not healthy, the parents go to a large tree or cavern instead.

Miao boys and girls may date from the age of thirteen or fourteen. In some districts, girls may begin dating at twelve.

The Miao bury their dead underground. A shaman (healer) sings mournful songs. He leads the soul of the dead person back to the family, blesses the children, and tells the dead person how to join his or her ancestors.

8 ● RELATIONSHIPS

The Miao are a very generous people. They always keep their house open for guests and greet them with wine and song. Guests are greeted outdoors. Then they are invited to drink, eat, and sing.

The Miao have a group dating custom called *youfang (yaomalang), tianyue, zuoyue,* or *caiyueliang.* Boys and girls meet and fall in love by singing and dancing. Group dating is held on many occasions, such as the Sisters' Feast Festival in February or March. For about three days, the girls

fire, rivers, caverns, large trees, huge stones, and some animals. They also believe the spirits of the dead become ghosts that may haunt their families and animals, make them sick, or even kill them. Shamans (healers) allow people to communicate with ghosts. The Miao also worship their ancestors. Since the nineteenth century, many Miao have become Roman Catholics and Protestants.

6 ● MAJOR HOLIDAYS

There are dozens of Miao festivals. Among the most important are those honoring ancestors. Other holidays celebrate the end of the busy farming and hunting season. Chiguzhang is a ritual held every thirteen years. A buffalo is killed and offered as a sacrifice in honor of the Miao ancestors.

Cynthia Bassett

Three generations of a Miao family in front of their home.

of a village are courted by young men. The parents prepare meals that their daughters offer to the boys. Each girl offers food to the boy of her choice, who sings for his meal.

9 ● LIVING CONDITIONS

The Miao live in houses one or two stories high. The back of the house is built on the mountain slope and the front rests on stilts. The roof is made of straw. Grain is stored in the ceiling. The first floor of the house is for the livestock and poultry. There are three to five rooms in the living quarters. Sons and daughters live separately and infants live

with their parents. Furniture includes a bed, cupboard, table, and stool, all made of wood. There are big bamboo baskets for storing food and clay pots for water and wine. The living conditions of the Miao in urban areas are like those of their neighbors of other ethnic groups.

10 ● FAMILY LIFE

The Miao are monogamous (they marry one person). The family consists of parents and their children. Property is passed down to men, but women have the most power in the family. Young people may choose who they will marry by dating and falling in love. For

Cynthia Bassett

Older Miao women in the traditional dress of their village.

Miao from another. Brilliant embroidery and silver ornaments are distinctive national features, as is the accordion-pleated women's skirt.

12 ● FOOD

The Miao's main food is rice. Other foods are yams, millet, corn, wheat, buckwheat, and sorghum. All of them are cooked in a rice steamer. Sticky rice is eaten on holidays. The Miao like hot pepper, and all their food is spicy. They also like sour flavorings. Their diet is mainly vegetables. However, they also eat poultry, eggs, beef, veal, pork, frogs, fish, snails, eels, snakes, crabs, and shrimp. Wine is made at home with rice.

13 ● EDUCATION

All children can have a formal education. Some parents, however, do not believe in educating girls. Many girls drop out of school when they are teenagers. As many as 95 percent of Miao women cannot read or write.

14 ● CULTURAL HERITAGE

Song and dance are an important part of Miao life. There are many special songs, including love songs, funeral songs, and wedding songs. The Miao also sing as part of the group dating custom.

The dances of the Miao culture express both grief and joy. Sometimes the dancer also blows on a reed pipe.

15 ● EMPLOYMENT

The Miao are subsistence farmers (they grow food only to feed their families). Rice is their main crop. They also grow corn, yams, millet, sorghum, beans, wheat, buck-

the first three years of marriage, the bride goes back to live with her own family. She lives with her husband only during holidays and at certain other times. If she gets pregnant, she moves to her husband's house sooner. The Miao, like China's other national minorities, are not governed by China's policy of one child per family.

11 ● CLOTHING

The many Miao branches have their own costumes. These costumes and their hairstyles are the best way to tell one branch of

Cynthia Bassett

A typical village festival with dancers wearing traditional dress. Silver jewelry and headdresses are handed down through the centuries. If you look closely in the upper left corner of the photograph you will see a basketball backboard and hoop. Miao teenagers love basketball.

wheat, fruit, cotton, tobacco, peanuts, sunflowers, and other crops. They grow a large number of hot peppers.

In the past, weeding was thought to be a woman's job and plowing was left to men. Today, women plow and do other farm work.

16 ● SPORTS

The Miao like horse races, which are often held on holidays. Teenagers love basketball, table tennis, and Chinese chess. The dragon boat regatta is a traditional 1.2-mile (2-kilometer) race. The members of a team usually come from the same village. Other popular sports are kicking the shuttlecock and Chinese shadowboxing *(wushu).*

17 ● RECREATION

In rural areas people enjoy dining together, chatting, and visiting relatives. Married women like to visit their parents' homes. At festivals, weddings, and funerals, the Miao sometimes dance and sing for several days and nights. Movies, television, videos, libraries, and cultural centers also provide recreation.

Cynthia Bassett

Miao women planting rice.

18 ● CRAFTS AND HOBBIES

Embroidery, wax printing, brocade, and paper-cutting are four famous crafts of the Miao. Craftspeople also create silver ornaments.

19 ● SOCIAL PROBLEMS

The Miao face the problems of poverty and isolation. Many Miao young people migrate from their villages to cities and coastal areas. When they return, they can bring new knowledge and skills back to their hometowns. However, their absence removes talents and skills needed in the present.

20 ● BIBLIOGRAPHY

Heberer, Thomas. *China and Its National Minorities: Autonomy or Assimilation?* Armonk, N.Y.: M. E. Sharpe, 1989.

Ma Yin, ed. *China's Minority Nationalities.* Beijing: Foreign Languages Press, 1989.

Miller, Lucien, ed. *South of the Clouds: Tales from Yunnan.* Seattle: University of Washington Press, 1994.

WEBSITES

Embassy of the People's Republic of China, Washington, D.C. [Online] Available http://www.china-embassy.org/, 1998.

World Travel Guide. China. [Online] Available http://www.wtgonline.com/cn/gen.html, 1998.

Tibetans

PRONUNCIATION: tuh-BET-uhns
ALTERNATE NAMES: Bod Qiang
LOCATION: China (Tibet Autonomous Region); India
POPULATION: 4.6 million
LANGUAGE: Tibetan; Chinese
RELIGION: Lamaism

1 ● INTRODUCTION

Tibetan civilization began near the Yarlung Zanbo River in present-day Tibet. A Tibetan kingdom was created in the sixth century AD. In the seventh century, the ruler Songtsen Gampo made Lhasa the capital of Tibet. While he ruled, the Tibetan laws, calendar, alphabet, and system of weights and measures were created. Princess Wenchen, his Chinese bride, came to Tibet in 641. She had a great effect on Tibetan culture.

Warfare and political strife weakened the Tibetan dynasty and it collapsed in 877. Tibet was conquered by the Mongolians in the thirteenth and fourteenth centuries. Later it came under Chinese control. The Qing Dynasty (1644–1911) recognized Tibet's spiritual leaders, the Dalai Lama and the Panchen Lama. A local government was set up in Tibet, with its own minister from the emperor. This system continued under the Republic of China until 1949, when the communist revolution created the People's Republic of China. The new government created the Tibetan Autonomous Region, covering all of Tibet. The political power of the lamas was taken away and given to Tibetan leaders nominated by the central government in Beijing.

2 ● LOCATION

The Tibetans live on the Qinghai-Tibetan Plateau. It extends to the Himalayas, the highest mountain range in the world. Most Tibetans are found in the Tibet Autonomous Region. However, many live in Qinghai, Gansu, Sichuan, and Yunnan provinces. China's total Tibetan population was 4.6 million in 1990. There are about 100,000 Tibetans in India, and tens of thousands live in North America and Europe. Southwest Tibet has a damp, mild climate. Northwest Tibet is quite barren, but its river valleys provide land for nomads to raise their cattle.

3 ● LANGUAGE

The Tibetan language belongs to the Sino-Tibetan family. It has three dialects. Tibetan is written from left to right. Tibetan writing was developed in the seventh century. In urban Tibet, many Tibetans also speak Chinese.

4 ● FOLKLORE

According to a Tibetan myth, a divine monkey married a female monster in Yarlung Valley long ago. They gave birth to six children whose descendants spread over the earth but had a hard life. They lived off of wild fruits of the forest. Then the monkey gave them seven kinds of grain, and they learned how to farm and began to speak.

5 ● RELIGION

Mahayana Buddhism combined with the native Tibetan religion (Bon) to create a new form of Buddhism, called Lamaism. Many different lamaist sects arose. The Gelupa, or Yellow Sect, which came to

Cynthia Bassett

A family strolling in the central market in the city of Lhasa.

gods, spirits, and nature. Its practices include ritual dance.

6 ● MAJOR HOLIDAYS

The Tibetan New Year takes place the first week of January and lasts three to five days. Tibetans all dress in their finest clothes. Relatives and friends pay New Year calls and visit monasteries to pray for a good year. Tibetan operas are performed. People wear masks and pretend to be gods. They sing and dance to drive away the ghosts.

The Lantern Festival is held on January 15. Huge sculptures of birds, animals, and humans made from colored yak butter are paraded in the streets of Lhasa. Festive lanterns, also made of yak butter, are hung on fences. People dance under the lanterns all night.

April 15 marks both the Buddha's enlightenment and the Chinese Princess Wenchen's arrival in Tibet. The streets overflow with people on pilgrimages, and the monks pray. People walk around the Potala Palace, go boating on the lake, and then pitch tents to rest.

7 ● RITES OF PASSAGE

Three or four days after a baby is born, a tiny piece of *zamba* (the Tibetans' main food) is stuck to the infant's forehead. This is a rite to make the baby pure. When the baby is one month old, the parents paint the tip of its nose with soot from the bottom of a pan to keep away ghosts. With their relatives, the child's parents go to the monastery and pray to the Buddha for protection.

Girls' hair is combed into two braids when they are under twelve years of age.

dominate Tibet, was founded by Tsong Khapa (1357–1419).

Reincarnation (the belief in rebirth) was an established Buddhist doctrine. When an important lama died, his successor (the divine child) was sought among male children who were born at about the time he died.

Bon, the native Tibetan religion, is still practiced in western Tibet and in parts of Qinghai and Sichuan. It calls for worship of

TIBETANS

0   200   400   600 Miles
0   200   400   600 Kilometers

RUSSIA

KAZAKSTAN

KYRGIZSTAN

Yining

TIAN SHAN

Ürümqi

ALTAI MTS.

MONGOLIA

GOBI DESERT

DA HINGGAN LING

Amur

Yichun

Hailar   Qiqihar

Songhua

Manchurian Plain   Harbin   Jilin

Changchun

Nei Mongol (Inner Mongolia)   Shenyang   Fushun   Benxi

Anshan

NORTH KOREA

Kashi   Tarim   Korla   Bosten Hu   Turpan Pendi   Hami

Mingteke Pass

Lop Nur

Taklimakan Shamo

Badain Jaran Shamo

Hohhot

Baotou

Yinchuan   Shijiazhuang

Beijing   Tangshan   Dalian

Tianjin

SOUTH KOREA

K2 (Mt. Godwin Austen) 28,250 ft. 8611 m.

ALTUN SHAN

QILIAN SHAN

PAKISTAN

KUNLUN SHAN

Qaidam Pendi

Golmud

Qinghai Hu

Xining

Huang

Taiyuan

Zibo

Jinan   Qingdao

North China Plain

Da Yunhe (Grand Canal)

Yellow Sea

Qing Zang Gaoyuan (Plateau of Tibet)

Gyaring Hu

Lanzhou

Xi'an

Huang   Zhengzhou

QIN LING

Han

Huainan

Huai   Hefei

Nanjing   Shanghai

Wuhu   Hangzhou

Darlag   Minxian

Mekong

Chengdu

Wuhan

Nam Co

Brahmaputra   Lhasa   Salween

HENGDUAN SHAN

Yangtze

Yangtze

Chongqing   Changsha

Pingxiang

Gan

Fuzhou

Nanchang

HIMALAYAS

NEPAL

Mt. Everest 29,028 ft. 8848 m.

Ragba Pass

BHUTAN

BANGLADESH

INDIA

Guiyang

Yuan

Xiamen

TAIWAN

Kunming

Hongshui

Wuzhou

Guangzhou

Lincang

Nanning   Hong Kong

MACAU (PORT.)

MYANMAR

Munan Pass

LAOS

Gulf of Tonkin   Haikou   Hainan

South China Sea

VIETNAM

THAILAND

PHILIPPINES

East China Sea

Taiwan Strait

They wear three braids when they are thirteen or fourteen, and five braids at the age of fifteen or sixteen. When a girl reaches seventeen, her hair is combed into dozens of braids to show that she is an adult.

There are several types of Tibetan funerals, depending on the social status of the person who has died. In a "sky burial," friends burn piles of pine tree branches and scatter food over them. The smoke is supposed to draw vultures. The body is chopped up and the bones are pounded together with zamba. Vultures eat what remains of the body. The rest of the remains are burned and the ashes are scattered over the ground. "Water burial" is for widows, widowers, and poor people. "Fire burial" is for lamas, and "ground burial" is for people who died of infection or were executed as criminals.

8 ● RELATIONSHIPS

Tibetans are polite. When they meet, they stretch out their arms with their palms turned up, and bow to each other. To show respect, one person nods his head and sticks his tongue out. The other nods and smiles. When two people meet for the first time, one gives the other a *hada*. This is a long, narrow strip of white or light blue silk that is a sign of respect. It is held in both palms while bowing.

Today, young boys and girls mingle freely but still have some traditional restrictions.

9 ● LIVING CONDITIONS

Tibetans build their houses on high ground, facing south, and close to water. The walls are made from earth or piled up stones. Houses are two or three stories high. They have flat roofs, many windows, and court-yards. The living room and bedrooms are on the second floor, and the first floor is for storage or to house livestock. Herdsmen dwell in large tents made of canvas or woven yak wool.

10 ● FAMILY LIFE

The Tibetan family centers around males. The man inherits property. A woman must obey her husband, even when he lives with her parents. Today, most Tibetans are monogamous (married to only one person). Nomads and peasants still have arranged marriages. Lamas and shamans (spiritual leaders) are usually consulted.

Cynthia Bassett

A young woman wearing a jacket made from yak wool.

11 ● CLOTHING

Men in urban areas wear a felt or fur-trimmed hat, a short vest with sleeves, trousers, and a robe. Those in rural areas wear a very long robe with long sleeves and a loose collar. The robe is tied around the waist with a long band. Herdsmen wear the fur of a sheep year-round, and a pair of long trousers. Tibetan men all wear boots. Women usually wear a sleeveless robe with a shirt under it and a beautiful apron around the waist. A long robe with sleeves is worn during the winter. Women living in rural areas wear a sheep fur over a long skirt.

Cynthia Bassett
A Tibetan women in the countryside harvesting barley.

13 ● EDUCATION

Education was once reserved for monks in monasteries. Since 1949, a complete educational system from primary school to university has been created in Tibet and Qinghai. It includes medical and technical schools. However, Tibet's small population is scattered over such a wide geographic area that it is difficult for many students to travel to a school. A growing number of young Tibetans go to the cities to study.

14 ● CULTURAL HERITAGE

Tibetan dances differ strongly from those of China's other minorities. The dancers' long sleeves add to their charm. They sing on high pitches and mostly in minor keys. Tibetan opera is performed in the street without any stage. There is a band, and performers sing while they dance.

Tibetan literature includes novels, poems, stories, fables, and dramas. Many works have been translated and published in other countries. The Tibetan religion has effected every part of Tibet's culture.

12 ● FOOD

In rural areas, Tibetans eat barley, wheat, corn, and peas. They stir and fry barley and peas and grind them into flour. Then they mix it with yak butter and tea. This is called *zamba*. They press it with their fingers in a wooden bowl and make it into a ball before eating it. They may also cook zamba into a porridge with meat, wild herbs, and water. Their favorite drinks are barley wine and tea with butter. The main foods of Tibetan herdsmen are beef, mutton, and milk products.

15 ● EMPLOYMENT

Tibetan herdsmen raise sheep, goats, yaks, horses, mules, and oxen bred from cattle and yaks.

16 ● SPORTS

Yak racing is one of the favorite Tibetan sports. It is similar to horse racing. It takes a highly trained expert to ride a racing yak. Tibetans are also excellent mountain climbers.

17 ● RECREATION

The Tibetans have their own theater company, opera, music and ballet performers, broadcasting stations, and film studio. Many Tibetan newspapers, magazines, and books are published each year.

18 ● CRAFTS AND HOBBIES

Tibetan folk art includes figures of the Buddha found in monasteries and figures made of yak butter. Goldsmiths and silversmiths craft items for daily use. These include spoons, chopsticks, bowls, plates, and dishes. They also make bracelets, rings, and necklaces. *Tangka* is a painted Tibetan wall-hanging depicting Buddhist themes.

19 ● SOCIAL PROBLEMS

Lack of formal education is one of the major social problems facing Tibet today. It is hard to educate Tibet's small population because the Tibetans are scattered over huge stretches of land.

20 ● BIBLIOGRAPHY

Kendra, Judith. *Tibetans*. Threatened Cultures. New York: Thomson Learning, 1994.

Snellgrove, David L., and Hugh Richardson. *A Cultural History of Tibet*. New York: F. A. Praeger, 1968.

Stein, R. A. *Tibetan Civilization*. Trans. by J. E. Stapleton Driver. Stanford: Stanford University Press, 1972.

WEBSITES

Embassy of the People's Republic of China, Washington, D.C. [Online] Available http://www.china-embassy.org/, 1998.

World Travel Guide. China. [Online] Available http://www.wtgonline.com/country/cn/gen.html, 1998.

Uighurs

PRONUNCIATION: wee-GURS
LOCATION: China (Xinjiang Uighur Autonomous Region)
POPULATION: 7.2 million
LANGUAGE: Uighur
RELIGION: Islam

1 ● INTRODUCTION

The Uighurs form the ethnic majority of Xinjiang Uighur Autonomous Region. Their ancestors can be traced back 2,000 years. After the fifth century, many moved to Xiyu (present-day Xinjiang). Three centuries later, the Uighurs formed their own government under the control of the Tang Dynasty (AD 618–907). Chinese culture spread throughout their lands. Little by little, the Uighurs abandoned their nomadic life and settled down about 1,000 years ago.

After the fourteenth century, there were long periods of conflict in Xinjiang. Order was finally restored by the Manchu government of the Qing Dynasty (1644–1911). Many Mongols and Chinese were assimilated into Uighur society. However, the Uighurs had no lasting peace until the mid-1940s.

2 ● LOCATION

The Uighurs live in the autonomous (self-governing) region of Xinjiang. It is the largest government district of China. The Uighurs live mainly in oases south of the Tianshan Mountains. They are also found in some counties of Hunan Province, in south China. The Tianshan Mountains divide Xinjiang into two parts. South Xinjiang has a huge basin (Tarim) and desert (Taklimakan) at its center. The Uighur population numbered 7.2 million in 1990.

3 ● LANGUAGE

The Uighur language belongs to the Turkic group of the Altaic family. There are three dialects. The written language uses Arabic characters. It has existed since the eleventh century. The name Uighur means "to unite" and "to help."

4 ● FOLKLORE

According to a Uighur tale, the Queen of Kala Khan gave birth to a son with a blue face and a hairy body. His mother breast-fed the infant only once. He then lived on raw meat and wine. He was able to talk right after birth and to walk forty days later. He grew up to be a hero and was called Wugusi. He killed a wild animal, saving many lives. One night, after hunting, he saw a beautiful girl after a flash of blue light. They got married. She gave birth to three sons called Sun, Moon, and Stars. Wugusi married a second wife who also gave birth to three sons. They were called Heaven, Mountain, and Sea. Wugusi's six sons had a total of twenty-four children, who founded twenty-four tribes. Wugusi became a Khan (leader) and united the nearby territories to form a large nation.

5 ● RELIGION

In the past, the Uighurs believed in Buddhism, Zoroastrianism, and Nestorian Christianity. Since the eleventh century, they have turned to Islam.

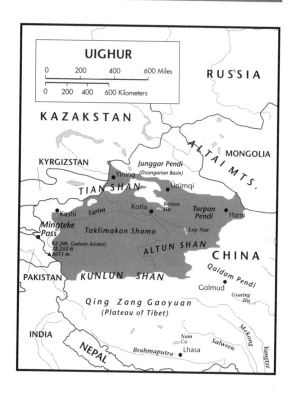

6 ● MAJOR HOLIDAYS

The Uighurs celebrate the two major holidays of Islam. (They call them the Corban Festival and the Lesser Bairam.) They also have their own traditional holiday, the Naoluzi Festival.

The annual Corban Festival is the biggest celebration. Each family fries twisted noodles and kills a sheep or an ox. Everyone dresses up and goes visiting. The Lesser Bairam (Festival of Fast-Breaking) marks the end of the fast month of Ramadan. After bathing, Muslims (followers of Islam) go to the mosque to pray, take part in rituals, and socialize. The Uighurs visit each other's homes, where guests are offered fried twisted noodles and other special foods.

Jeannine Davis-Kimball

Uighur women sit and talk.

The Naoluzi Festival is similar to the Chinese Spring Festival. Sports and other activities take place during this month-long holiday.

7 ● RITES OF PASSAGE

Uighur families celebrate the birth of a child. Because the Uighur revere wolves, a mother-to-be lies on a mat of wolf fur. If the child is a boy, the Uighurs say the mother has "given birth to a wolf." The ankle bone of a wolf is hung around an infant's neck or over its cradle. This is believed to protect the baby and ensure that he grows up to be a brave man.

Funeral rites follow Islamic law. The body is cleansed with water, wrapped with white cloth, then buried underground three days after death. After the funeral, sacrificial rites are performed.

8 ● RELATIONSHIPS

Uighur friends often embrace each other when they meet after a long time apart. Normally, they bow slightly or shake hands when they meet. The Uighurs are generous. Guests are served a meal of roast lamb and milk tea.

9 ● LIVING CONDITIONS

The Uighurs live in small, low, square houses made of adobe. Most are one story high. The door often opens to the north. There are no windows in the walls, only a skylight window in the ceiling. The Uighurs sit and sleep on a solid adobe platform one foot (thirty centimeters) high inside the house. A fireplace is used to cook food and to keep the house warm. Tapestries decorate the walls. Almost every house has a court-yard where trees, flowers, and grapes grow.

10 ● FAMILY LIFE

Uighurs are monogamous (they marry only one person). Sons and daughters leave their parents when they marry. The man is the head of the family, and children take their father's name. The Uighurs follow the west-ern naming convention: the given name comes first and the family name second, unlike the practice followed by the majority of Chinese.

11 ● CLOTHING

Men usually wear a cotton robe with no but-tons, two colored stripes, and a belt. The women usually wear a dress with a skirt underneath it and a black velvet vest on top. A small four-cornered hat embroidered with silk threads is worn by girls. Both men and women wear boots.

12 ● FOOD

The main foods of the Uighurs include flour, corn, and rice. They eat a *nang*, flat bread shaped like a bagel or pancake and made with wheat or corn flour. A popular food at festivals is "rice taken by hand." Raisins are boiled with sliced onions, car-rots, and small cubes of fried beef. Then they are put on soaked rice and boiled again. The ingredients are steamed for twenty min-utes, then served. Before eating, one washes one's hands three times and dries them with handkerchiefs. Sitting cross-legged on cush-ions, people serve the rice on plates and eat

Jeannine Davis-Kimball

Most Uighurs cultivate gardens. They are also known for their method of growing cotton.

it with their hands. Roast lamb is a special treat usually saved for guests.

13 ● EDUCATION

There are thirteen universities and colleges and 2,300 secondary schools in the Uighur districts. About 90 percent of children enter school when they reach school age.

14 ● CULTURAL HERITAGE

"The Twelve Great Songs" is an epic story performed with classical and folk songs, music, and dance. The Uighurs have dozens of musical instruments, including string and wind instruments and tambourines. The Uighur violin is played on one knee. Uighur

Jeannine Davis-Kimball

A busy city street.

dance is famous for its spinning. The many traditional dances include both solo and group dances.

Uighur literature includes folktales, fables, jokes, poems, and proverbs. A long poem titled "Fortune, Happiness and Wisdom" dates back to the eleventh century.

15 ● EMPLOYMENT

Most Uighurs garden and grow cotton. Their cotton growing methods have been copied in other Chinese provinces. The Uighurs are also known for their skill in commerce. They are active in the restaurant, grocery, and clothing businesses in Xinjiang and in many other provinces.

16 ● SPORTS

Ball games like basketball and volleyball are very popular. Rope walking is the Uighurs' favorite spectator sport. A pole 120 feet (36 meters) high is hammered into the ground. Then a long rope is connected to the top of the pole at one end and attached to the ground at the other. The athlete climbs up the rope while jumping, rolling, and performing other dangerous acts.

17 ● RECREATION

The Uighurs love to sing and dance. Everybody joins in the lively dancing at festivals. Hundreds of people may end up dancing on these occasions. Movies and television are also popular forms of entertainment, and the

Uighurs have a number of local musical and theater groups.

18 ● CRAFTS AND HOBBIES

The Uighurs are skilled in crafts. Hotan jade sculpture is a fine art. Ingisa (Yengisar) knives are famous for their sharp blades and precious stones. Other Uighur crafts include carpets, tapestries, silk embroidered hats, copper teapots, and musical instruments.

19 ● SOCIAL PROBLEMS

Because they lack natural resources and industry, the Uighurs have little income. They are leaving their homeland in growing numbers for work in other Chinese provinces. However, those who leave often return, bringing wealth and skills back to their communities.

20 ● BIBLIOGRAPHY

Heberer, Thomas. *China and Its National Minorities: Autonomy or Assimilation?* Armonk, NY: M. E. Sharpe, 1989.

Ma Yin, ed. *China's Minority Nationalities.* Beijing: Foreign Languages Press, 1989.

Miller, Lucien, ed. *South of the Clouds: Tales from Yunnan.* Seattle: University of Washington Press, 1994.

WEBSITES

Embassy of the People's Republic of China, Washington, D.C. [Online] Available http://www.china-embassy.org/, 1998.

World Travel Guide. China. [Online] Available http://www.wtgonline.com/country/cn/gen.html, 1998.

Zhuang

PRONUNCIATION: zhew-ANG
ALTERNATE NAMES: Buzhuang; Bunong; Buyang; Butu; Buyue; Buman; Gaolan
LOCATION: China
POPULATION: 15.6 million
LANGUAGE: Zhuang
RELIGION: Polytheistic; ancestor worship; Christianity

1 ● INTRODUCTION

The Zhuang were once a branch of the ancient Baiyue people. They descended from clans in present-day Guangxi province after the fall of the Han Dynasty in AD 220. Each clan had many slaves, much property, and great political power. The Tang Dynasty (AD 618–907) appointed local clan chieftains to govern for them. From then on, the Zhuang submitted to the rule of China's central government.

2 ● LOCATION

The Zhuang are the largest national minority of China. Their population was 15.6 million in 1990. More than 90 percent live in Guangxi Zhuang Autonomous Region. There are smaller numbers of Zhuang in Wenshan Zhuang, Miao Autonomous Prefecture (in southeast Yunnan), and other provinces. The hilly Guangxi landscape is like much of southern China. It has more than sixty gorges stretching over some 125 miles (201 kilometers).

3 ● LANGUAGE

Zhuang belongs to the Sino-Tibetan language family. A new alphabet based on

Latin was adopted in 1955. The Zhuang call themselves Buzhuang. "Bu" means "man."

4 ● FOLKLORE

The Zhuang have a rich mythology, much of it concerned with their origins. One story claims that there were no grains long ago and people had to eat wild plants. In fact, there were grain seeds in heaven but no one on Earth could get any of them. A dog was sent to hunt for seeds in heaven. In those days, dogs had nine tails. When the dog got to where the seeds were, it put its tails on the floor. Many seeds stuck in the hairs. Then the dog was discovered by a guard, who chopped off eight of its nine tails. But the dog ran away, and the seeds stuck to the one tail that was left. These seeds brought great benefits to humanity. For this reason, dogs are kept at home and fed with rice.

5 ● RELIGION

The Zhuang are polytheistic (they believe in more than one god). They worship their ancestors and also pray to large stones and trees, snakes, birds, and the earth. They offer sacrifices to the Mountain God, the Water God, the Kitchen God, the Sun God, and others. Their many sacrifices are supposed to protect their livestock, their crops, and their families.

6 ● MAJOR HOLIDAYS

The Zhuang observe dozens of holidays. New Year's Eve is celebrated with a family dinner and firecrackers. Women boil water with brown sugar, bamboo leaves, onions, and ginger to brew a special holiday drink. Sports and other activities are held in small towns. The Zhuang observe the same cus-

toms for the Late New Year at the end of the month.

The eighth of April is the birthday of the Buffalo God. People brush the buffalo, feed them colored sticky rice, and let them rest all day.

7 ● RITES OF PASSAGE

Huapo (flower woman) is the goddess of childbirth and also the patron saint of babies. Right after a child is born, a holy plaque in honor of Huapo and a bunch of wildflowers are placed by the wall near the baby's bed. If the baby gets sick, the mother offers gifts to Huapo and waters the wild-flowers.

The Zhuang's funeral rites are unusual. The dead person is buried in a coffin about two feet below ground level. Three or five years later, the coffin is opened. Any flesh that is left is cleaned off the bones. The skeleton is then placed sitting up inside a clay jar and sprinkled with cinnabar (a red powder). The dead person's name and dates of birth and death are written inside the lid. The sealed jar is then buried in the clan graveyard.

8 ● RELATIONSHIPS

Young people may date freely. Singing parties are a popular way to meet people. They are held on all holidays.

A straw hat hung on a door means that there is a woman giving birth inside.

9 ● LIVING CONDITIONS

Most Zhuang houses are now similar to those of their Chinese neighbors. Some areas, though, still have traditional "stilt

ZHUANG

However, she will move to her husband's house if she gets pregnant.

11 ● CLOTHING

In some rural areas, the Zhuang preserve their ancient traditions. Women wear a garment with no collar and buttons down the left side, loose trousers, and embroidered aprons. Some wear navy printed straight skirts with embroidered shoes and embroidered scarves on their heads. However, most Zhuang wear two-piece plain clothing in muted, dark colors.

12 ● FOOD

The main foods of the Zhuang are rice and corn. They like salted and sour dishes. Raw boneless fish are considered a special treat. On holidays, they make dishes from sticky rice. These include cakes, noodles, and dumplings wrapped in leaves.

13 ● EDUCATION

About 95 percent of school-age children attend school. There are seventeen universities in Guangxi province. One-quarter of the college students in the province belong to China's national minorities. The great majority of these are Zhuang.

14 ● CULTURAL HERITAGE

Singing is an important part of Zhuang popular culture. It is the main activity at festivals. A singing event at a major festival may draw more than 10,000 people. Dance is also important. Zhuang dances include the Bronze Drum Dance, the Tea-Leaves Collecting Dance, the Shoulder Pole Dance, and the Buffalo Dance.

dwellings." The house is built on stilts to keep the family above the damp earth and away from animals. In Guangxi the houses and stilts are made of bamboo and wood. The size of the house may vary from three to seven rooms. Livestock and stored goods are placed on the ground floor.

10 ● FAMILY LIFE

The Zhuang family is small and the family name is carried on by males. The Zhuang are monogamous (they marry only one person). The women's position is somewhat lower than that of men. Right after the wedding, the bride, together with her bridesmaids, goes back to her own family. For the first three to five years of marriage, she will return to her husband only on holidays.

15 ● EMPLOYMENT

The Zhuang's traditional employment is farming and forestry. The Zhuang of Guangxi grow rice and other grains. They also produce sugarcane, bananas, pineapples, and mangoes for the food industry.

16 ● SPORTS

The Zhuang are known as top gymnasts. Intensive training for young boys and girls is provided on a voluntary basis after school hours.

A traditional ball-tossing game is played with a padded cloth bag weighing about one pound (half a kilogram). A colored string is tied to the bag. Boys and girls are divided into two teams. Members toss the ball to the opposing team by holding the string in one hand, swinging it in circles, and letting it go. If the other side misses the ball, one of its members is captured. When the last team member is captured, the game is over.

17 ● RECREATION

Television is a very popular pastime for the urban Zhuang. Most small towns now have television stations, and families can watch many kinds of television programs.

There are many festivals during the year, and a large fair is held every spring. Biannual commemorative feasts for the ancestors feature many recreational elements, such as singing parties, dance performances, and Zhuang opera.

18 ● CRAFTS AND HOBBIES

The Zhuang are famous for their bronze drums. The drums are hollow and bottomless with a flat surface. They vary in size and are decorated with pictures and designs.

Brocade is another well-known art form of the Zhuang. It is woven from cotton and colored silk to form beautiful and lasting designs. Zhuang brocade is used in wall hangings, table cloths, cushions, and curtains. Zhuang girls like to wear brocaded knapsacks.

19 ● SOCIAL PROBLEMS

Guangxi has fertile soil, a warm climate, and a plentiful rainfall, but the Zhuang are not wealthy. The rich mineral resources and tourist sites of the region have not been fully tapped. Many rural workers, including the Zhuang, have migrated from Guangxi to the nearby province of Guangdong because its economy is more developed. This migration poses serious problems for both provinces.

20 ● BIBLIOGRAPHY

Eberhard, Wolfram. *China's Minorities: Yesterday and Today.* Belmont, Calif.: Wadsworth Publishing Company, 1982.

Heberer, Thomas. *China and Its National Minorities: Autonomy or Assimilation?* Armonk, N.Y.: M. E. Sharpe, 1989.

Miller, Lucien, ed. *South of the Clouds: Tales from Yunnan.* Seattle: University of Washington Press, 1994.

WEBSITES

Embassy of the People's Republic of China, Washington, D.C. [Online] Available http://www.china-embassy.org/, 1998.

World Travel Guide. China. [Online] Available http:// www.wtgonline.com/country/cn/gen.html, 1998.

Colombia

■ COLOMBIANS 177
■ PÁEZ 183

The people of Colombia are called Colombians. About 50 percent of the population is mestizo (mixed white and Amerindian or native people). An estimated 25 percent of are white, 20 percent are mulatto (mixed black and white) or zambo (mixed black and Amerindian), 4 percent are black, and 1.5 percent are pure Amerindian (native people). Among the Amerindians in Colombia are the Páez, profiled in this chapter after the article on the Columbians.

Colombians

PRONUNCIATION: koh-LUHM-bee-ens
LOCATION: Colombia
POPULATION: 36 million
LANGUAGE: Spanish (official); various Amerindian languages
RELIGION: Roman Catholicism; native Amerindian religions

1 ● INTRODUCTION

Amerindian tribes, including the Páez, inhabited the area of modern-day Colombia before the Spanish arrived in the sixteenth century. By the late 1700s, the Amerindians grew tired of paying high taxes to the Spanish, and decided to fight for independence. On July 20, 1810, they successfully revolted against Spanish officials in the capital, Bogotá. This day is still commemorated as Independence Day.

However, the struggle for independence continued for nine more years. In 1819, Colombia, Venezuela, and Ecuador together became the Republic of Gran Colombia. Before long, though, each became an independent nation.

Colombia has had a democratically elected government since the 1950s. By the late 1990s, illegal activity in drug trafficking threatened the survival of democracy.

2 ● LOCATION

Colombia occupies the northwestern corner of South America. It has coastlines on both the Pacific Ocean on the west and the Caribbean Sea on the east. The mighty Andes Mountains divide into three long ranges—called *cordilleras*—that run the length of the country. To the east, there are extensive plains. To the south, a thick jungle extends toward the Amazon River.

COLOMBIANS

Colombia has a population of over 36 million people. The majority of its inhabitants are *mestizo*—of mixed Amerindian and white heritage.

3 ● LANGUAGE

Spanish is the official language of Colombia. It is spoken with an accent that varies considerably according to region. In addition, various Amerindian groups speak their own languages.

People usually use both their father's and their mother's surnames, in that order. The strong influence of the Catholic Church has made names like María very popular, usually in combination with another name, such as María Cristina or María Teresa. Even men are often named María, in combination with masculine names, such as José María or Pedro María.

4 ● FOLKLORE

Amerindian, black African, and Spanish folk customs have combined to create a rich culture that expresses itself in festivals throughout the year. According to one legend, a mythical hero named Bochica introduced culture and civilization to the people living around Bogotá. He taught them how to build dwellings and introduced laws to govern daily life. Problems started when his wife, Chia the moon goddess, kept leading people astray, encouraging them to break the laws. The couple fought, and Chia used magic powers to make the rivers flood the home the people had built.

Bochica led the people who survived the floods to the top of a mountain. To make sure that Chia would not cause any more trouble, he sent her away to be exiled in the night sky forever.

Barranquilla and other coastal towns celebrate a yearly Carnival. Celebrants wear colorful costumes and masks, and play flutes and African drums.

5 ● RELIGION

Roman Catholicism is the religion of Colombia. Amerindians in remote areas practice beliefs that include forms of shamanism (belief in good and evil spirits).

6 ● MAJOR HOLIDAYS

Colombia celebrates Independence Day on July 20 and the discovery of America on October 12. The main Roman Catholic holidays are also observed. Easter (late March or early April) is marked by major religious events. One is the Holy Week procession in the town of Popayán. Statues of Jesus, the Virgin Mary, and saints are paraded by groups of *cargueros* (carriers) along the streets. Others walk alongside them carrying candles called *alumbrantes*.

7 ● RITES OF PASSAGE

All the main Catholic rituals that mark important phases in a person's life are observed by a majority of the population. Among these are baptism and first communion, as well as Catholic marriage and burial rites. Some practices have included a mixture of either Amerindian or black African customs.

8 ● RELATIONSHIPS

Women usually greet each other with a kiss; men shake hands. Good friends shake hands and pat each other on the back several times as well.

It is considered essential to offer any visitor a small cup of black coffee called a *tinto*. This is the custom on both business and social occasions. Colombians consider it rude to launch directly into a discussion without first asking about the other person's welfare and that of his or her family.

9 ● LIVING CONDITIONS

Living conditions vary greatly according to social class. The wealthy suburbs have modern houses and apartment blocks. In poorer neighborhoods there are often large areas with poorly constructed or rundown shacks. These are called shantytowns.

AP/Wide World Photos

A man and his son prepare to deliver fresh-baked cookies to a small shop in Cartagena.

In mountain villages some houses have adobe walls and thatched roofs. Others have plaster walls and tiled roofs. In hotter climates along the Pacific and Caribbean coasts, housing is built from local cane, reeds, and palm branches. In such areas it is not unusual for people to use hammocks rather than beds.

10 ● FAMILY LIFE

Colombians keep in touch with large extended families through weddings, baptisms, and other special occasions. Close ties with immediate and extended families are an important aspect of Colombian life, providing support in many aspects of life. The family network extends to second and third cousins. Godparents, or *padrinos,* may also play an important role, helping with tuition or assisting the family in other ways. Family members are also depended upon to provide jobs whenever possible.

11 ● CLOTHING

Western-style clothing is worn throughout Colombia. However, it varies according to climate. In warm coastal areas, men wear cotton shirts with bright, colorful patterns. In the cooler climate of the Andes mountains, both men and women wear woolen *ruanas* (capes). Middle- and upper-class women wear stylish versions of the ruana. The most primitive ruanas are made from undyed wool in shades of brown. More stylish versions may be striped or plain, using a wide range of colors. Traditional peasant women in mountain areas wear large, fringed shawls called *pañolones.* The traditional women's folk costume, seen mostly at festivals, consists of a round-necked, lace-edged blouse and a wide, flowery skirt.

12 ● FOOD

Colombia has a great variety of fruits and vegetables. *Cocido,* a traditional stew served in Bogotá, can include twenty different kinds of vegetables. *Ajiaco,* another local dish, includes a bright yellow potato (*papa criolla),* chicken, and corn, served with a slice of avocado and cream. A typical dessert is made with sweet, stewed figs called *brevas.* They are served with *arequipe,* milk cooked with sugar until it resembles toffee. On the coast a variety of

Recipe

Ajiaco Bogotano (Potato and Chicken Soup)

Ingredients

2 cups cooked chicken, cut into bite-size pieces
8 cups (4 cans) chicken broth
1 onion, cut in half
1 bay leaf
½ teaspoon ground cumin
¼ teaspoon thyme
2 pounds potatoes (Colombian cooks use several kinds of potatoes, including yellow potatoes), peeled and coarsely chopped
2 cups frozen corn
1 cup heavy cream, brought to room temperature
1 avocado, cut into slices

Directions

1. Put chicken broth, onion, bay leaf, cumin, and thyme into soup pot and bring to a boil.
2. Lower heat and simmer about 20 minutes. Remove onion and bay leaf.
3. Add potatoes. Simmer until potatoes are very soft (about 20 minutes).
4. Add corn and cooked chicken and simmer about 5 minutes more.
5. Pour about 1 Tablespoon of cream into each soup bowl and ladle the hot soup over it.
6. Garnish with one slice of avocado and serve immediately.

Adapted from Karoff, Barbara, *South American Cooking.* Berkeley, Calif.: Aris Books, 1989.

fish are served fried or sometimes grilled, often with rice flavored with coconut milk.

13 ● EDUCATION

Primary education is free in Colombia, but it is not compulsory. About 20 percent of children in cities and 40 percent in rural areas do not go to school.

College and university education has expanded since the 1960s. There are dozens of universities, and technical and commercial institutes. Technical training schools have helped Colombia improve the skills of factory workers.

14 ● CULTURAL HERITAGE

Colombia has a rich musical heritage that blends Amerindian, African, and Spanish elements. In the Andes region, twelve-string guitars called *tiples* are often used to sing courtly and romantic songs called *bambucos*. On the coast, the style of music is the *cumbia,* played with flutes and drums.

Colombia's main cities, especially Bogotá, have symphony orchestras, theaters, art galleries, bookshops, and many movie theaters. Colombia's most famous novelist is Nobel Prize-winner Gabriel García Márquez (1928–), author of *One Hundred Years of Solitude.*

15 ● EMPLOYMENT

Small commercial traders and shopkeepers form an important part of the economy. There is also a growing educated class that finds employment in trade, manufacturing, or finance. In addition, jobs are increasing in the fields of engineering, communications, and computers. In rural areas people usually work in the fields. In many parts of Colombia children must work to help the family make ends meet.

16 ● SPORTS

The most popular sport is soccer, but many other sports are played in Colombia. These include basketball, volleyball, golf, tennis, and swimming. In cattle-ranching areas there are rodeos. People in river or coastal areas enjoy boating and fishing. Cycling has developed as a competitive sport. A game called *tejo,* similar to horseshoe pitching, is played in the small towns in the mountainous Andes region. Players try to land a horseshoe over an upright stick fixed some distance away from the thrower.

17 ● RECREATION

Colombians participate enthusiastically in the many secular and religious *fiestas* (festivals) around the country. Many people enjoy festivals that revolve around beauty pageants. Some towns, such as Manizales and Bogotá, have bullfighting seasons that draw large crowds. Movie-going is also popular with Colombians.

Another favorite pastime is the *paseo,* or outing to the countryside by a group of friends or family members. Some town-dwellers own land or a small farm in the country, or have relatives they can visit in rural areas. Others simply choose a small town or village with beautiful scenery. They and their friends travel there by bus to relax, have a picnic, and spend the day.

18 ● CRAFTS AND HOBBIES

Colombians are very fine craftspeople, known for beautiful woodwork, metalwork, and weaving.

The Quimbaya Indians of northwestern Colombia have been skilled gold- and silversmiths since the 1500s. Pottery has also been made in Colombia for centuries, both by the Amerindians and by mestizo (mixed Amerindian and white ancestry) craftspeople.

The *tiple,* or twelve-string guitar, is still produced by hand. On the coast, an African drum-making tradition was brought to Colombia through the slave trade and continues to this day. Craftspersons also make reed flutes and rattles.

A number of Amerindian tribes weave beautiful bags called *mochilas* that are hung loosely over the shoulder. Amerindian hammocks in various styles are also produced. In the tropical (hot-weather) zones of Colombia, people often hang hammocks on their front porches.

19 ● SOCIAL PROBLEMS

One of Colombia's most serious problems is the wide difference in the living standards of the rich and poor.

The activities of drug traffickers cause many problems. Drug lords resort to violence to settle scores with rivals and use bribes to obstruct the course of justice.

There are also ongoing conflicts between government army units and guerrilla armies. Both guerrilla armies and drug traffickers often resort to kidnapping in order to obtain ransom money. Sometimes they do it to threaten people they think are interfering with their activities. The resulting atmosphere of insecurity has led to the increased use of security guards. They guard individual citizens who feel threatened and are also used to protect private homes and public buildings.

20 ● BIBLIOGRAPHY

DuBois, Jill. *Colombia, Cultures of the World.* New York: Marshall Cavendish, 1991.

Hanratty, Dennis M., and Sandra W. Meditz, eds. *Colombia: A Country Study.* Washington, D.C.: Federal Research Division, Library of Congress, 1990.

Karoff, Barbara. *South American Cooking.* Berkeley, Calif.: Aris Books, 1989.

Markham, Lois. *Colombia: The Gateway to South America.* New York: Benchmark Books, 1997.

WEBSITES

Embassy of Colombia, Washington, D.C. [Online] Available http://www.colombiaemb.org/, 1998.

Ruiz-Garcia, Pedro. The Latino Connection. [Online] Available http://www.ascinsa.com/LATINOCONNECTION/colombi.html, 1998.

World Travel Guide. Colombia. [Online] Available http://www.wtgonline.com/country/co/gen.html, 1998.

Páez

PRONUNCIATION: PA-es
ALTERNATE NAMES: Nasa (people)
LOCATION: Colombia
POPULATION: 68,487 (1980)
LANGUAGE: Páez
RELIGION: Roman Catholicism; evangelical Protestantism

1 ● INTRODUCTION

The Páez Indians of Colombia resisted the Spanish conquerors who arrived in the sixteenth century. One of the first Spanish explorers to enter southwestern Colombia, where the Páez live, was Sebastián de Belalcázar. He found many Amerindian peoples there. The Pasto Indians in the Nariño region were peace-loving. In contrast, the Pijao fought many bloody battles with the Spaniards. Eventually, they were completely killed off. The Páez of southwestern Colombia, in the present-day state of Cauca, also resisted the Spanish. They were badly beaten, but their rugged mountain homeland saved them. They were able to avoid being destroyed by the Spanish or assimilated (mixed) into the general population by retreating into the mountains.

2 ● LOCATION

The Páez Indians have lived for centuries in southwestern Colombia, in the present-day state of Cauca. They make their home amid the rugged mountain ranges and high plateaus of the Andes Mountains. The eastern portion of this region is called *Tierradentro*. It is an extended reservation with widely scattered settlements. The main centers are Inzá and Belalcázar.

3 ● LANGUAGE

The Páez language is related to many other Amerindian languages. Most of those languages had died out by the late 1990s, but the Páez still speak their own language.

One of the traditional Páez names still in use is *Calambás*. It is the family name of a famous Páez hero and chieftain.

The Spaniards found that the Páez had not only male chiefs, but also female chiefs. A famous female chief was *Taravira*. Today, her name is still in use, along with those of her brothers, *Avirama* and *Esmisa*. Names like these are often used alongside Spanish names.

4 ● FOLKLORE

Juan Tama, called the "Son of the Star," is an important figure in Páez folklore. According to legend, when he was a baby, he was found in a gorge one day when the Morning Star was shining. He was nursed by several women and grew up to be very strong. Eventually, he married a female chief named Doña María Mendiguagua. He became the Indians' chief and teacher. He showed them how to guard their land and advised them to avoid white people.

Juan Tama appointed Calambás as his assistant, but Calambás turned out to be rebellious. Juan Tama defeated Calambás, but he later forgave him because Calambás was so brave. When he knew that his death was near, Juan Tama went to the lake on the high, cold plateau of Moras and disappeared into the water.

5 ● RELIGION

Members of a Roman Catholic religious order, the Jesuits, were sent by leaders in Spain to convert the Amerindians of southwestern Colombia to Roman Catholicism. Much later, this task was taken up by other missionaries, who arrived in 1905. They learned the Páez language, and they still run missions among the Páez. Modern Páez religious customs and beliefs combine with aspects of Catholicism. The Páez still have their own shamans (holy men).

6 ● MAJOR HOLIDAYS

The Páez celebrate Roman Catholic holidays, including Christmas and Holy Week (the week before Easter, in late March or early April). They also have their own music and include some of their own traditional rites. Although they observe many Roman Catholic rituals, they do not allow the Roman Catholic priest to attend their own traditional celebrations.

7 ● RITES OF PASSAGE

When a woman is about to give birth, she stays in a special hut. She gives birth either alone or with the help of a female relative.

From very early childhood, both girls and boys learn adult skills by imitating their parents. Adults form their own households and live in family units at a distance from the homes of other families.

The discovery of funeral urns and elaborate burial caves suggests that in earlier times the Páez were cremated. Important people were given elaborate funerals. Páez burial customs, like other aspects of Páez culture, include both traditional and Christian elements. Before returning home from a burial, both men and women traditionally bathed, fully dressed, in a stream. This was done to wash out the spirit of death.

8 ● RELATIONSHIPS

The Páez are a reserved people. Some occasions require very formal greetings. A boy has to approach his godfather in a respectful manner when greeting him. A visitor or guest is given a formal "gift of affection." This is usually food, such as a chicken or an egg, and also includes some vegetables and coffee beans.

The Páez do not engage in Western-style dating. However, their traditions include one-year trial marriages. This year is called the *amaño* or adaptation period. During this time, the young man observes the qualities of the young woman, and she also observes him. If either partner turns out to be unsuitable, the trial marriage can be ended.

9 ● LIVING CONDITIONS

The Páez live in poor farming communities. They make do with the basic necessities required for survival. Their lifestyle is simple.

Traditional houses are rectangular with thatched roofs and walls of cane and sticks. Newer houses have walls made of adobe blocks or bricks, with roofs of corrugated zinc or cement. Houses are usually divided into two rooms. One is for sleeping and storage. The other is for eating and sitting around the fire to talk and keep warm. The more modern houses have one or two open windows. These are covered with wooden shutters during bad weather and at night.

An eight-year-old Páez girl shells corn as she sits on a pile of corncobs at a ranch in southwestern Colombia.

10 ● FAMILY LIFE

The father has nearly absolute authority or power in a Páez family. Families often have more than three children. (This is true of all Colombian families.) Small children are given affection and much freedom. However, after the age of six or seven, they are expected to behave more quietly and obediently.

Marriage customs blend both Spanish and Páez cultures. Either the boy or his parents select a prospective bride. The boy and his parents and godparents, or *compadres,* visit the girl's family at their home to ask for her hand in marriage. If the girl's parents consent, her father is offered a half-bottle of *aguardiente* (a local drink). Her mother is then offered another half-bottle. The boy and his family then take the girl to their home to begin a year of trial marriage. If all goes well, the couple is usually married in the Catholic Church.

11 ● CLOTHING

A woman's traditional clothing consists of two pieces. A heavy woolen skirt pleated at the back is held in place by a woven sash. A blouse made from a single rectangular piece of woolen cloth is fastened at one shoulder, but it is more common for women to wear cotton blouses.

Many women buy ready-made clothing. Women may sew their own blouses or skirts if they have a sewing machine powered by a foot pedal or hand crank to use, since electricity is usually not available. Women wear necklaces with eight to ten strands of tiny white beads.

Young girls wear a simple one-piece dress. Young boys wear a long shirt and short pants. Older men and women wear a plastic, straw, or felt hat—even indoors. Younger people are less apt to wear hats, although baseball caps are popular.

A practical garment for the cool weather of the Andes Mountains is the *ruana*. This is a type of woolen cloak or poncho worn in many parts of the highlands. Ready-made sweaters and jackets are now common as well. Women wear tennis shoes, plastic sandals, or low shoes. Men often wear rubber or plastic boots. Children often go barefoot until they go to school.

12 ● FOOD

The basic diet of the Páez includes potatoes, corn, and other vegetables that grow in the Andes. A traditional, hearty Páez breakfast begins the day; the only other large meal is dinner. A typical breakfast dish, called *mute* (MOO-the), is a stew of boiled cabbage, corn, potatoes, and squash. During the day,

the Páez drink fresh fruit juices or juice that has been fermented to make *guarapo*. For special occasions, there are rich stews of vegetables, potatoes, and chicken or roasted meats.

Food is cooked either over a wood fire or on a dried mud or brick stove. The food for large gatherings is cooked in heavy, shallow metal pots large enough to hold food for up to one hundred people.

13 ● EDUCATION

Children attend primary school from the first through third grades, and sometimes through the sixth grade. When farm activities require their help, children often skip school. Young people who hope to go to high school often must live with family friends or relatives in order to be near a school. Some earn high-school diplomas by taking courses broadcast on the radio. The teacher dictates the lessons over the radio. Students travel to a central location in their region when it is time to take examinations. Either way, a high-school education involves expense.

Members of the Páez community want to preserve their native language, so some schools have agreed to teach classes both in Spanish and in the native language.

14 ● CULTURAL HERITAGE

The Páez play traditional music for all special occasions, including religious celebrations. Their musical instruments include both short and long flutes (*chirimías*). They also play drums made from hollowed-out tree trunks and animal skins. Some of their music has absorbed elements of Colombian folk tunes, such as the *bambuco*. Guitars are popular with young men. Dance is another important traditional form of expression for the Páez.

15 ● EMPLOYMENT

The Páez today live mainly in farming communities. Each Páez farmer must donate work days for collective (group) projects. These include planting, road-building, and bridge-building, and working in the villages. Men and women cultivate plots of land together.

Weaving is done only by women. Husbands must obtain permission to sell any of the goods their wives have made.

16 ● SPORTS

Soccer is a very popular sport among young men, and teams compete on Sunday afternoons.

The main traditional sport among the Páez was a type of war game. It was performed as a rite to honor the dead after a community feast. There were two teams, each led by a chief. The teams attacked each other with bows and arrows. Sometimes there were deaths, but they were accepted as part of the ceremonial game.

17 ● RECREATION

The Páez sometimes make market day into a special occasion. After the buying and selling have taken place, people enjoy drinking and chatting with their friends.

On feast days, the church is decorated with candles and flowers. Members of the community, carrying offerings of food, form a kind of parade to lead the priest to the church. The priest is greeted with much

fanfare, sometimes even with fireworks and rockets. There may also be a *chirimía* orchestra of flutes and drums. After vespers (an evening service), the celebration continues outside the church. There is music and dancing all night.

Small transistor radios and cassette players, or boom boxes, are carried everywhere for entertainment and as status symbols.

18 ● CRAFTS AND HOBBIES

Páez crafts once included pottery, weaving, and basketmaking. Older women continue to weave long, colorful sashes with red wool yarn on a white cotton background. The sashes are decorated with geometric designs and human or animal figures.

The Páez make jewelry, such as beaded necklaces. Metalworking is a traditional craft in southwestern Colombia. Inexpensive earrings are popular among Páez women, as well as barrettes for holding their long hair in place.

19 ● SOCIAL PROBLEMS

Guerrillas (private armies) have waged war for many years in Colombia, and the Páez have sometimes suffered at their hands. In addition, they have been hurt in raids by drug barons and by the actions of some police forces. In December 1991, a group of Páez Indians, including women and children, were massacred as they sat down to their evening meal.

The Páez are active in the council of Indian communities of the Cauca region. The Amerindian groups in Colombia have representation in the national congress.

However, the struggle for a decent life with sufficient autonomy (self-rule) continues.

20 ● BIBLIOGRAPHY

DuBois, Jill. *Colombia, Cultures of the World.* New York: Marshall Cavendish, 1991.

Hanratty, Dennis M., and Sandra W. Meditz, eds. *Colombia: A Country Study.* Washington, D.C.: Federal Research Division, Library of Congress, 1990.

Rappaport, Joanne. *The Politics of Memory: Native Historical Interpretation in the Colombian Andes.* New York: Cambridge Univ. Press, 1990.

WEBSITES

Embassy of Colombia, Washington, D.C. [Online] Available http://www.colombiaemb.org/, 1998.

Ruiz-Garcia, Pedro. The Latino Connection. [Online] Available http://www.ascinsa.com/LATINOCONNECTION/colombi.html, 1998.

World Travel Guide. Colombia. [Online] Available http://www.wtgonline.com/country/co/gen.html, 1998.

Congo,
Democratic Republic of the

■ **CONGOLESE** **189**

■ **AZANDE** **197**

■ **EFE AND MBUTI** **201**

The Democratic Republic of the Congo (DROC) was formerly known as Zaire. This chapter begins with an overview article on the people of the DROC (the Congolese). Six ethnic groups account for more than 69 percent of the population. One of these groups, the Azande, is profiled in this chapter. Other African groups living in the DROC and profiled elsewhere include the Tutsi (see the chapter on Burundi in this volume) and the Hutu (see the chapter on Uganda in Volume 9). Another group, the Bakongo, is profiled in the chapter on Republic of Congo in this volume. In the densely forested center of the country (the cuvette) are about 80,000–100,000 Pygmies, including the Efe and Mbuti profiled in this chapter. Non-Africans living in the DROC number around 200,000 and include Belgians, Greeks, Lebanese, and Asian Indians.

Congolese

PRONUNCIATION: kahn-go-LEEZ
ALTERNATE NAMES: Congo-Kinshasans
LOCATION: Democratic Republic of the Congo (formerly Zaire)
POPULATION: 45 million
LANGUAGE: Lingala; Swahili; Ciluba; Kikongo; French (language of government)
RELIGION: Christianity (Catholicism, Protestantism, African Christianity)

1 ● INTRODUCTION

The Democratic Republic of the Congo (DROC—the former Zaire) is Africa's third-largest country. Its boundaries were drawn arbitrarily at the Conference of Berlin in 1884–85. More than 300 ethnic groups speakng between 300 and 600 dialects and languages live within those boundaries. In 1997, Zaire returned to using the name by which it had been known from 1960 to 1970, the Democratic Republic of the Congo. (The DROC was earlier known by the names "The Independent State of the Congo" and "The Belgian Congo.")

Archeological evidence indicates that this part of the world is one of the oldest places inhabited by humans. Prior to European colonization, the peoples of the DROC were part of empires, kingdoms, and small forest village communities.

At the Berlin Conference, the European powers gave King Leopold II (1965–1909) of Belgium sole control of the territory. Leopold ruled it ruthlessly, and forced labor killed some 10 million Congolese between 1880 and 1910. When these horrible realities gained international attention, the Belgian state took over the colony. However, oppression and exploitation continued through Belgian mining companies.

The possibility of revolt forced the Belgians to grant what is now the DROC its independence in 1960. Prime Minister Patrice Lumumba (1925–61), who had socialist leanings (advocating collective rather than private economic ownership), was killed in February 1961. The U.S. Central Intelligence Agency (CIA) allegedly was involved, and brought Mobutu Sese Seko (1930–97) to power in 1965. Mobutu stole the country's resources and impoverished his fellow Congolese. His fortune, estimated at over $8 billion, made him possibly the richest man in the world. He was ousted in May 1997 and died in exile later that year. Laurent Désiré Kabila (1939–) then became president.

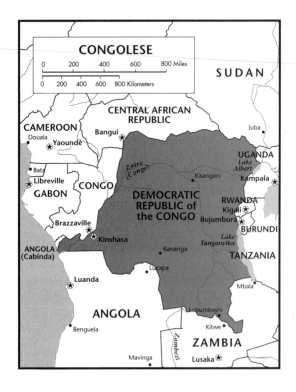

2 ● LOCATION

The DROC is roughly equal in size to the United States east of the Mississippi River. Geographically, it extends from the Atlantic Ocean to the snow-capped Ruwenzori Mountains—the fabled "Mountains of the Moon." The mostly highland plateau is broken up by hilly and mountainous terrain, and a vast central basin drains into the Congo River.

Population density varies greatly from extremely dense urban centers to the sparsely populated central basin. Six ethnic groups account for more than 69 percent of the population. These include the Luba, Kongo, Mongo, Rwandese, Azande, and Bangi and Ngale.

The DROC claims the second-largest remaining rainforests in the world. However, deforestation from commercial logging threatens the fragile ecosystem.

3 ● LANGUAGE

In spite of the many dialects or languages spoken throughout the DROC, four national languages predominate. These are Lingala, Swahili, Ciluba, and Kikongo. French is officially used in the government, and in education at university and high school levels. In public elementary schools, French is often taught as a second language. It is common to find people speaking a national language at the market, French in school, and their native language at home.

4 ● FOLKLORE

Folklore is communicated in many ways, including literature, art, music, and dance. It is a means of carrying on tradition from generation to generation. Each ethnic group has its own legends and folktales, though similarities exist. Animals figure importantly. For example, the rabbit is identified with intelligence and cunning, while the crocodile is associated with something bad, such as an unforgiving traffic cop.

On television, a popular figure, *Grandpère* (grandfather), tells folktales in a village setting. This is a modern version of an older tradition where storytelling took place around an evening fire. The purpose of the tales is to teach while entertaining. Grandpère frequently explains the morals of these stories and their application to daily life.

5 ● RELIGION

Nearly half of all Congolese practice Catholicism, and another third are Protestant. However, Christian and traditional forms of religion are often combined. For example, at holy Mass, ancestors are begged for protection. People dance in the liturgy and offer in-kind gifts, including goat, cassava, fish, fruits, and vegetables. In 1921, Simon Kimbangu (1889?–1951), claiming to be a prophet of Jesus Christ, led a religious revival against colonialism. Some 17 percent of the population now profess a form of African Christianity.

Traditional belief holds that all things have life and deserve respect. This even includes inanimate objects such as rocks. Life never ends, and no separation exists between the living and the dead. Offering the ancestors a drink by pouring some beer on the ground is symbolic of this belief. Nzambe, assisted by the spirits of ancestors, is the supreme being from whom all things come.

6 ● MAJOR HOLIDAYS

The increasingly difficult political and economic climate in the DROC has dampened popular celebrations of secular holidays. Until recently, May 20, the day Mobutu's Popular Revolutionary Movement Party (MPR) was founded, was marked by parades and huge celebrations highlighting regional folkloric troupes wearing the party colors. Independence Day celebrations seemed small in comparison. Christmas (December 25), New Year's Day (January 1), and Easter (late March or early April) are festive occasions. Those who can afford it celebrate with a meal of roasted goat or cow.

Parent's Day, August 1, is a unique holiday. In the morning Congolese celebrate the dead, and in the afternoon, the living. Residents of Kinshasa, for example, go to the cemeteries early to clear and spruce up family graves. Adults then return home to eat again together with the children.

7 ● RITES OF PASSAGE

In the DROC, children are a symbol of wealth, and all births are celebrated with joy. However, boys are more desired because they continue the family name.

Prior to colonization, boys and girls passed to adulthood through initiation rites.

Boys were circumcised and were taught the elders' wisdom and the values of their culture. Girls were never circumcised, but they were taken to a secret place and taught how to succeed in marriage and how to raise a family. Nowadays, male circumcision occurs soon after birth. Because of social changes in the cities, young men and women are usually taught about life and their culture by a family member such as an uncle or aunt.

8 ● RELATIONSHIPS

Congolese are extremely friendly. They commonly stop to greet friends, and even strangers, on the street. It is customary to shake hands when meeting people and when taking leave of them. There are several ways to greet people depending on time of day, the nature of the relationship, and so forth. In the morning a Lingala-speaker greets by asking, "Hello, is that you? *(Mbote, Yo wana?)*, Are you awake? *(Olamuki?)*, How did you sleep? *(Olalaki malamu?)*." Asking someone how they are consists of literally asking, "What news? *(Sango nini?)*." The typical reply would be, "No news! *(Sango te)*" meaning, "Fine."

Congolese place great importance on family and social relations. A grandparent affectionately refers to his or her grandchild as "little husband or wife," and the grandchild refers to the grandparent in the same way. A woman lightheartedly addresses a neighbor as "father-in-law" *(bokilo)* because she likes his young son, whom she calls her "little husband." Many people call friends and even strangers "brother-in law" or "sister-in-law." This serves to build friendships and avoid conflict.

9 ● LIVING CONDITIONS

For the majority of Congolese, living standards are low. Political instability and rising inflation increase the cost of basic goods practically by the hour. Consequently, goods in the market are priced in U.S. dollars. A typical good-humored response to the question "How's it going?" has become, *Au taux du jour!* meaning, "According to the daily rate!"

Homes in the village are often made from mud brick, and thatch or galvanized-iron roofing. They are clean but not mosquito-proof. In the towns, some houses have electricity, running water, and flush toilets.

10 ● FAMILY LIFE

Families tend to be large, with as many as ten or more children. Parents invest what they can in their children. In return, children are expected to take care of their parents when they reach old age. The number of children per family is shrinking, especially in urban centers. Polygyny (more than one wife) is practiced, but second wives are not recognized by the state or by the Church.

A couple often participates in three marriage ceremonies: traditional, civil, and religious. The traditional ceremony consists of exchanging gifts between the two families. The civil ceremony consists of exchanging wedding vows before a government representative. Finally, at the church, the bride might wear a Western-style wedding dress for the religious ceremony. In rural areas, wedding celebrations can last weeks, punctuated with singing, dancing, and feasting.

Richard Peterson

Women working together to make kwanga *or manioc bread. The loaves are wrapped in banana leaves and tied with strips of bark cut from a forest plant.*

11 ● CLOTHING

In the DROC, people dress up, even when going to work. If they lack the means to buy fancy clothes, they wear washed and neatly pressed clothing bought second-hand. In the 1970s, the government banned Westernized business suits for men. They were replaced with collarless suits, or *abacost,* meaning "down with suits." Neckties and bow ties were replaced with scarves and matching handkerchiefs in the front pockets.

Traditionally, women were not permitted to wear wigs, Western pants, jeans, or mini-skirts. Even today as these rules are over-turned, women prefer African wraparounds

(pagnes), tailored in creative styles with bright African patterns. Women with the means wear made-to-order jewelry of ivory, malachite, gold, silver, copper, and dia-monds.

12 ● FOOD

Congolese love to eat. Staples in their diet include cassava, rice, potatoes, plantains, and sweet potatoes or yams, accompanied by a sauce of greens, fish, or meat, depend-ing on the region. The DROC is perhaps best known for *mwamba,* a sauce made of palm-nut paste, in which chicken, meat, and fish are cooked. Mwamba is eaten with rice, *fufu* (similar to a dumpling), or *chikwange* (cassava prepared in banana leaves). Other traditional foods include pounded sesame seeds *(wangila)*, squash seeds *(mbika)*, steamed chicken or fish *(maboke)*, shiska-bobs *(kamundele)*, and plantain dough *(lituma)*. In some regions, people consider caterpillars, grubs, roasted crickets, and termites to be delicacies. Near the equator, wild game such as elephant, monkey, hippopotamus, and crocodile are enjoyed. The Congolese fondness for beer is legendary. However, in the villages, palm-wine is the favorite.

13 ● EDUCATION

About 72 percent of Congolese are able to read and write, due to a strong elementary school system. Education is not required by law, but 90 percent of all Congolese children attend primary school for at least a few years. Many children drop out at times to work when parents are unable to pay admission fees and other expenses. A unique Congolese tradition is *salongo*, which brings all the students together on Saturday afternoons to clean up the school yard and remove weeds and brush.

Secondary school begins with a two-year middle school program. A high school diploma must be earned by passing a rigorous state exam. Public university, plagued by political and social problems, closes frequently. Currently, Congolese are trying to solve their problems by creating privately funded and administered universities.

14 ● CULTURAL HERITAGE

Congolese modern dance music has been popular throughout sub-Saharan Africa since the 1950s. Referred to as "Sukus" in the United States, it continues to gain international popularity. The dance is to music that combines jazz, traditional tunes, and Latin-influenced rhythms. The instrumentation consists of electric guitars, keyboards, trumpets, saxophones, conga drums, and Western-style drum sets. Lyrics in Lingala comment on society, give advice, make political statements, criticize behavior, or simply relate love stories.

Congolese are imaginative dancers, constantly inventing new dances that come and go almost monthly. Drumming and dancing are part of any festive occasion. The national folkloric ballet has gained an international reputation.

From ancient times, Congolese peoples have used their oral literature to carry on traditions, customs, and social values. Modern written literature has been built on this oral foundation. It varies widely from classical to popular forms, and is written in French as well as in national languages. Drama is one of the most popular forms of literature today.

15 ● EMPLOYMENT

Among the greatest challenges facing the DROC are the rebuilding of its crumbling factories and mining operations, and creating jobs for its citizens. At least 75 percent of the people still work in subsistence agriculture; they produce only a little more than what is needed for personal use.

Industry employs only 13 percent of the work force, mainly in copper smelting, metal production, timber extraction, oil palm processing, textiles, chemicals, and

Richard Peterson

Pit-sawing is a way of preparing lumber for market without the destruction caused by mechanized logging.

food processing. Services employ about 12 percent of the labor force.

16 ● SPORTS

Soccer is the national pastime, played or watched virtually throughout the country. Competition with African national teams is intense. When the DROC national team defeated the Moroccans for the Africa Cup in the 1970s, the returning players were welcomed like royalty and given houses, cars, and large sums of money by the gov-

ernment. Congolese were treated to a national holiday.

People love playing cards, chess, checkers, and board games. A traditional board game called *Mangula* is played mainly in rural areas by men.

Mangula

Equipment

A carved wooden board with two rows of shallow pockets separated by a divider, or an empty egg carton

About 36 small stones

Directions

1. Place a few small stones in each shallow pocket in the board.

2. Player One moves and continues according to the number of stones he picks up. Each time he lands, he picks up his opponent's stones in the pocket opposite him across the divider, and uses these stones to continue his play.

3. When he fails to pick up any stones, his opponent takes his turn. The first person to move all his opponent's stones to his side of the board wins.

17 ● RECREATION

Besides playing and watching soccer, people in towns love watching television dramas. Cinemas are also popular and are found in most towns, as are satellite dishes and videos. Although American and world cultures are becoming more popular, people still love Congolese music and dance. Young people and adults enjoy going out on Saturday night to socialize, listen to music at outdoor pubs, dance at nightclubs, and watch theatrical events.

Richard Peterson

A man weaves a basket made from the bark of a forest vine.

18 ● CRAFTS AND HOBBIES

The DROC is famous for its traditional folk art and crafts. Artists and craftspeople produce ceramic pots, reed mats, woven baskets, woodcarvings, chess games, sand paintings, handmade clothing, and jewelry. In general, African art is functional, but increasingly art produced for tourists generates income. Masks were traditionally assigned power to communicate with the divine. Some are still only brought out on very specific occasions for initiations and for solving community problems. The Bakuba people from the Kasai regions still produce wood sculptures, masks, and statuettes that may be used to increase fertility and to chase away evil spirits. In recent times, a distinct style of oil painting has emerged that reflects the magnitude of contemporary social challenges. In these paintings, snakes or lions within striking distance of unsuspecting human prey depict impending doom.

19 ● SOCIAL PROBLEMS

Congolese must conquer hunger, political repression, and political and economic instability, and meet their basic daily needs. People work hard for very little. Many people resort to *debrouillez-vous,* which means "make do in whatever way possible." Children leave school early, girls prostitute themselves, civil servants steal, police officers take bribes, and military personnel loot and pillage. Enormous human losses caused by human immunodeficiency virus/acquired immune deiciency syndrome (HIV/AIDS) and the Ebola virus challenge Congolese to care for the sick and orphaned. A hidden tragedy is that generations of Congolese children may be growing up undernourished on a basic diet of cassava, which is extremely poor in nutrition.

20 ● BIBLIOGRAPHY

Africa on File. New York: Facts on File, Inc., 1995.
Kelly, Sean. *America's Tyrant: The CIA and Mobutu of Zaire.* Washington, D.C.: The American University Press, 1993.
Nzongola-Ntalaja, Georges, ed. *The Crisis in Zaire: Myths and Realities.* Trenton, N.J.: Africa World Press, 1986.

WEBSITES
World Travel Guide. [Online] http://www.wtgonline.com/country/zr/gen.html, 1998.

Azande

PRONUNCIATION: uh-ZAHN-day

LOCATION: Southern Sudan; Democratic Republic of the Congo (formerly Zaire)

POPULATION: 1 million (estimate)

LANGUAGE: Azande (Niger-Congo group)

RELIGION: *Mangu* (witchcraft)

1 ● INTRODUCTION

The ethnic term *Azande* refers to a culturally diverse group of peoples who, over the past two hundred years, have been brought together under the governments of a number of distinct kingdoms. Little is known of their history prior to this period. Reliable first-hand accounts of the Azande only began to appear toward the middle of the nineteenth century. By the 1950s, however, the Azande had become well known to anthropologists through the work of British anthropologist Sir Edward Evan Evans-Pritchard (1902–73).

It is widely accepted that the ancestors of Azande society migrated from the west into the Democratic Republic of the Congo and the southern Sudan beginning in the 1600s. Because of their relative isolation from Westerners, the Azande practiced many traditional beliefs and customs well into the twentieth century. Azande now live across the borders of three modern nation-states. In recent decades they have been more exposed to the effects of market economies, missionary education, and related cultural influences.

2 ● LOCATION

Reliable estimates of population figures for the Azande are not available. In the 1950s, it was estimated that some one million people considered themselves ethnically Azande. Azande territory covers a vast expanse of land from the fringes of the upper Nile basin in the southern Sudan to the borders of semitropical rain forests in the Democratic Republic of the Congo. Most of Azande country is marked by the open savanna (grassland) forest laced with streams that comprise the Nile/Congo divide. Throughout this region of Africa, there is a season of occasional rain (roughly from April to October), followed by a dry season (from November to March) when rain seldom falls.

3 ● LANGUAGE

Azande belongs to the Niger-Congo group of languages. Approximately five dialects of Azande are spoken throughout the area they occupy. Some groups speak languages unrelated to Azande. Most Azande also speak rural dialects of Arabic, French, or English. The Azande language is tonal, so that identical words have different meanings according to the tone of pronunciation.

4 ● FOLKLORE

Traditional Azande culture is rich and highly developed. The anthropologist E. E. Evans-Pritchard collected hundreds of Azande folktales and legends and published as many as he could in the Azande language with English translations. The most famous Azande tales center on the imagined activities of the trickster Ture. The character of a trickster is common to folklore throughout

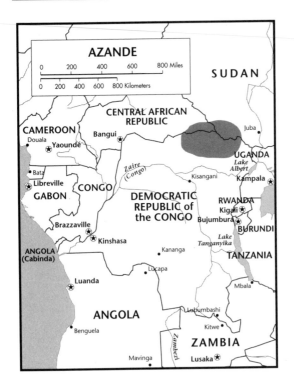

AZANDE

0   200   400   600   800 Miles

0   200   400   600   800 Kilometers

SUDAN

CENTRAL AFRICAN
REPUBLIC

CAMEROON   Bangui
Douala
Yaoundé

Bata
Libreville   CONGO
GABON

Brazzaville
Kinshasa

ANGOLA
(Cabinda)

Luanda

ANGOLA
Benguela

Juba

Zaire
(*Congo*)
Kisangani

DEMOCRATIC
REPUBLIC of
the CONGO   Kigali
Bujumbura

Kananga

Lucapa

Lubumbashi

Kitwe

Zambezi

ZAMBIA
Mavinga   Lusaka

UGANDA
Lake
Albert
Kampala

RWANDA

BURUNDI

Lake
Tanganyika

TANZANIA

Mbala

Azande culture, it is most likely the result of contact with outsiders and the result of Islamic and Christian influences. During the period of British colonial rule in this part of Africa, policy dictated that formal education was to be provided by practitioners of various Christian faiths. Thus, becoming Christian was often a consequence of becoming literate (able to read and write). By the 1990s, some Azande practiced Islam or Christianity, but beliefs about causation, death, and misfortune still revolve around *mangu.*

6 ● MAJOR HOLIDAYS

The Azande clans consist of several families with a common ancestor or ancestors. They gather for important occasions, including weddings and funerals.

7 ● RITES OF PASSAGE

Before colonization, boys were often initiated into manhood by serving the Azande nobility. Later, a ritual circumcision, held in the forest, became common, although this practice has also been discontinued. Girls are initiated into their gender role by observing and assisting their mothers. Traditionally, in order to marry, an Azande male had to present the bride's family with a payment (called bridewealth), normally consisting of a certain number of iron spears. Today, the bride-wealth is usually paid in cash or in the form of material goods such as cloth, cassava, or goats.

the world. Typically, the trickster is an animal or human hero who disobeys and makes fun of the accepted order of things by doing the opposite of the expected behavior. The Azande character of Ture is also closely related to an important element of traditional Azande folklore known as *sanza,* or double-speak. Sanza includes ambiguous remarks or actions intended to have double meanings. Azande use sanza in conversations between princes and commoners, husbands and wives, at beer parties, and in the language of love.

5 ● RELIGION

Azande typically believe that misfortune, death, and the complications of life are the result of *mangu,* or witchcraft. Where the Western notion of divinity appears in

8 ● RELATIONSHIPS

Social identity was largely established by membership in a specific kinship group, by the division of labor, by the larger patriarchal social order (with men in authority), and by the hierarchical order of Azande political life. Thus, one was born a commoner or a member of the royalty, or was incorporated into this order through warfare or slavery.

One of the central aspects of life among the Azande is their belief in witchcraft. It is used to explain and cope with all kinds of difficulties. Rather than singling out particular individuals as witches, the Azande believe that anyone is capable of causing the misfortunes of another person by ill will toward that person—even if he is unaware of doing so. (Women are excluded from the tradition surrounding witchcraft.) When something bad happens to an Azande, he must first find out who caused it. For minor problems, an Azande consults an oracle (something or someone in communication with the spirit world) that he reaches by rubbing two pieces of wood together as he tries out the names of different suspects. The guilty one is identified when the pieces stick together instead of rubbing smoothly against each other.

For major misfortunes, the "chicken oracle" is consulted. In one version of this procedure, poison is placed on the beak of a chicken. The guilty party is the individual whose name is spoken at the moment when the chicken dies. Once the guilty one has been pinpointed, the victim confronts him and asks him to stop his witchcraft. On hearing of his misdeeds, the "witch" has no trouble believing that he is indeed the cause of his tribesman's misfortunes. He makes amends by expressing his goodwill toward the victim and spitting on the wing of the dead chicken.

9 ● LIVING CONDITIONS

In precolonial times, Azande homesteads were typically widely scattered. A common pattern was for men who shared patrilineal ancestry (tracing descent through the father's line) to live in the same general area. Traditionally, huts were made of wood and mud. Each homestead was surrounded by gardens where a man and one or more of his wives grew staple crops, from sorghum to cassava. Homesteads of closely related relatives were interconnected by footpaths through the savanna. During the colonial period, in a supposed effort to eradicate sleeping sickness, many Azande were forced to move from this type of settlement. As a result, many Azande found themselves living in European-style villages of parallel straight streets, often living next to people who were strangers rather than relatives or kin. This change had a significant impact on Azande culture.

10 ● FAMILY LIFE

Traditional Azande society was highly patriarchal. Men held all positions of public authority, and women were subservient (in a lesser, obedient, position) to their husbands. Marriages were contracted through the exchange of bridewealth. Commoner men were usually able to marry only one woman. However, nobles, and in particular kings, had many women as wives. Children were reared by their birth mothers and by a host of patrilineal kin living in nearby homesteads. Children were socialized early on about cultivating domesticated plants. Boys in particular were taught about hunting and fishing.

11 ● CLOTHING

Azande women wear cloth skirts. Infants and children wear necklaces made from chains of metal rings. Some Azande also have their heads wrapped in cord, which is thought to protect their brains from evil spirits. In the past, Azande musicians wore costumes consisting of a cloth skirt, an elaborate headdress, and beads and bangles on the arms and around the ankles.

12 ● FOOD

The traditional dietary staple of the Azande is a type of grain called *eleusine*. In the western portion of the group's territory, this has been replaced by cassava. Other crops include rice, maize (corn), sorghum, squash, peas, beans, okra, peanuts, greens, and bananas. To supplement their diet, the men hunt game and the women catch fish. Chicken and eggs are considered delicacies, as are termites during the dry season. Beverages include palm wine and alcoholic drinks made from cassava.

13 ● EDUCATION

Some Azande live in towns with modern educational facilities. Access to Western-style education has had social and political effects. In some areas, power traditionally held by the royal nobility has passed to better-educated commoners.

14 ● CULTURAL HERITAGE

Both vocal and instrumental music, as well as dance, play a significant role in Azande culture. The most common traditional musical instrument is a small, bow-shaped, harplike instrument. It is often decorated with a small carved human head at one end. The Azande also make a variety of other instruments, many with designs that include human or animal forms. One is a mandolin-like stringed instrument modeled on the human figure. Another is the *sanza,* made of wood or hollowed gourds. It is similar to a xylophone but in the shape of a dancing woman, with arms and legs jutting out from the body of the instrument. Other typical instruments include a bell in the shape of a stylized human figure with the arms used as handles, and drums shaped like cattle.

In addition to a variety of functional items, Azande artwork includes carved wooden sculptures thought to have been given as gifts by tribal chiefs.

15 ● EMPLOYMENT

With the introduction of cash and growing crops for sale, many Azande now supplement their labor with small subsistence gardens. This is common in sub-Saharan Africa.

16 ● SPORTS

Typical sports among the Azande include sparring, which serves as a way for males to practice their combat skills.

17 ● RECREATION

Singing and dancing are major forms of entertainment among the Azande, especially at feasts and other celebrations. Storytelling is another popular form of recreation.

18 ● CRAFTS AND HOBBIES

Functional artwork includes wood, bark, and pottery storage boxes. Another item is the distinctive Azande throwing knife, the multibladed *shongo*, which is used in combat. It is made of copper or steel and adorned with elaborate patterns. Some of these knives are also used as bridewealth. Other folk art includes pots, wooden utensils, and woven mats and baskets.

19 ● SOCIAL PROBLEMS

At the time of this writing, the Azande, along with hundreds of thousands of the people living in the southern Sudan, are in the midst of a second civil war following the end of colonial rule. Many Azande have fled the Sudan to live in neighboring Democratic Republic of the Congo, Uganda, and the Central African Republic. As a result, much of traditional Azande culture and custom has ceased to exist.

20 ● BIBLIOGRAPHY

Evans-Pritchard, E. E. *The Azande: History and Political Institutions.* Oxford, England: Clarendon Press, 1971.

Evans-Pritchard, E. E. *Witchcraft, Oracles and Magic among the Azande.* Oxford, England: Clarendon Press, 1937.

Schildkrout, Enid. *African Reflections: Art from Northeastern Zaire.* Seattle: University of Washington Press, 1990.

WEBSITES

World Travel Guide. [Online] http://www.wtgonline.com/country/zr/gen.html, 1998.

Efe and Mbuti

PRONUNCIATION: AY-fay and mm-BOO-tee

ALTERNATE NAMES: Bambuti

LOCATION: Ituri forest in northeast Democratic Republic of the Congo (formerly Zaire)

POPULATION: 20,000

LANGUAGE: Bambuti languages

RELIGION: Traditional tribal beliefs

1 ● INTRODUCTION

Researchers believe that pygmy peoples have lived in the rainforests of central Africa for more than 6000 years. The term "pygmy" refers to a person of short stature (typically under 5 feet, or 1.5 meters, tall) who hunts and gathers and has a strong identity with the tropical forest. It is generally a disrespectful term that emphasizes physical characteristics. Anthropologists suggest replacing the term with "tropical forest forager." These forest dwellers have a unique culture, set of values, and lifestyle that are all undergoing great change. Their adaptation to change may teach other cultures how to cope with radical disruptions to their societies.

In many respects, tropical forest foragers represent the opposite of modernity. In the 1960s, they possessed only the bare essentials for their livelihoods. They did not seek to create extra in goods for profit and they had no use for money. Government was simple; decisions were made by common consent, and those who disagreed were free to leave and join another community if they wished. The forest, their "mother," had the capacity to supply their every need.

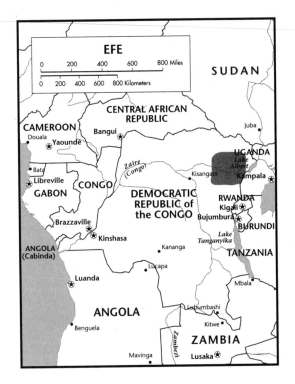

EFE

Although they have certain differences in language and hunting strategies, all of these peoples share a core culture. Collectively, the groups of the Ituri are called the Bambuti. Researchers estimate that no more than twenty thousand pure-blooded Bambuti remain in the world.

The terrain of northeast DROC is rolling, covered by rainforest. In areas where the forest has been cleared and allowed to grow back, thick, tangled underbrush makes movement difficult. Rain falls nearly every afternoon except during the "dry" season of January and February.

3 ● LANGUAGE

Sustained contact with African groups over long periods has all but led to the extinction of Bambuti languages. Nevertheless, researchers distinguish three linguistic groups who speak dialects of three major African languages. Some tonal patterns remain as well. The Efe have retained their language to a recognizable extent.

4 ● FOLKLORE

Tropical forest foragers believe that animals have the characteristics of people. Certain animals represent clans, sexes, and individuals, and they become very real people. Both forest dwellers and their village hosts have invented stories about these animals. They assign special characteristics to Mr. Turtle, Mr. Gray Antelope, or Mr. Chimpanzee. For example, Mr. Turtle is a wise and tricky individual, whereas the smallest antelope is king of the beasts. Animal stories thus serve to teach about human behavior and relationships.

Traditional values of interdependence and communality (good of the whole group) are being replaced by independence and individuality. Today, under environmental challenges and pressures to acculturate (fit in to the dominant culture), their society is changing rapidly. In spite of political and natural threats to their survival, tropical forest foragers have not given in to outside pressures yet.

2 ● LOCATION

Tropical forest foragers live in scattered groups throughout the equatorial band of Africa. This discussion focuses on the groups of the Ituri forest in northeast Democratic Republic of the Congo (DROC, formerly Zaire), including the Efe and their close relations to the south, the Mbuti.

Richard Peterson

Boys' initiation rites, known as Nkumbi *in the Ituri Forest, include masked dancers representing various ancestors and mythical figures.*

5 ● RELIGION

Religion in the lives of tropical forest foragers increasingly reflects borrowings from neighboring African groups. The Bambuti believe the wealth and goodness of the forest comes from *Muungu,* a high deity, the greatest of forest gods, who fills all their needs. Tropical forest foragers believe in totemic spirits *(sitana)*—animals whose spirits and characteristics represent the group's unity. They also believe in a water animal, called *nyama ya mai* in Swahili,

who is responsible for any serious water accidents.

Tropical forest foragers also practice magical rituals called *anjo* to help control the weather and improve hunting. Their main concern is to delay rain and storms until the hunt is over. The most important ritual ceremony is the *molimo.* It is held whenever hunting becomes unproductive or a special problem demands a solution.

6 ● MAJOR HOLIDAYS

Holidays hold little meaning for the Bambuti other than as opportunities for parties. The end of *Nkumbi,* the honey feast dance, and other ceremonial activities may be thought of as traditional holidays for tropical forest foragers.

7 ● RITES OF PASSAGE

In former times, girls went through initiation, the *elima,* but this practice has fallen away. Boys increasingly attend a village circumcision school *(nkumbi),* which is held every three or four years. The boys leave their parents for several months and live in close association with the village boys, who are their hosts. They are circumcised together. Thus, each group of boys belongs to an age-grade, much as American high school students identify with their graduating class. When strangers meet, they ask, "What class do you belong to?" Because each class acquires a name from a significant event during its initiation, they reply, "I'm a hurricane," or "I'm a great army worm," or something similar.

Marriage takes place soon after puberty, leaving little time for courtship. Nevertheless, at puberty, youthful deeds at the hunt

National Museum of African Art

Forest dwellers, including the Mbuti family pictured here, trust the forest to provide their needs, which are extremely minimal. Among their possessions are Bambuti reed spears, bows and arrows, and nets for hunting; pots to cook in; huts to sleep under; and loincloths to wear.

get publicized, and much flirtation occurs back in the camps.

8 ● RELATIONSHIPS

Tropical forest foragers place great importance on respect for each other, and children learn this early. In principle, children of the same age group remain on equal footing throughout their lives and call each other *apua'i*. Their games teach them to be social and interdependent in solving problems.

Evening campfires offer adults daily opportunities to discuss and resolve disputes. Anyone who speaks from the center of the camp must be listened to. Members of

a band gang up on wayward members to enforce rules and maintain harmony in the group. Individuals and families visit the camps of other tropical forest foragers for months at a time to socialize with family members and to look for marriage partners. These visits break up the monotony of daily life.

Relations between the Bambuti and villagers are also very important. Researchers disagree on whether this relationship is essentially dependent, independent, or interdependent. The first view sees tropical forest foragers as slaves of the villager overlords. The second sees them as fully independent if they so choose because the forest supplies them with everything they need; contact with villagers offers an agreeable change of pace but is voluntary and temporary. The third view finds a mutual interdependence between forest dwellers and villagers, with neither side holding an advantage; each has something the other wants and needs.

9 ● LIVING CONDITIONS

Traditionally, material comfort, wealth, and security are the least of the concerns of forest dwellers. They trust the forest to provide their needs, which are extremely minimal. The Bambuti need spears, bows and arrows, and nets for hunting; pots to cook in; huts to sleep under; and loincloths to wear. They trade forest products to villagers for items difficult to obtain such as salt, knives, and metal tips for their weapons.

Settlements are rustic, temporary camps situated within fifty yards (forty-five meters) of a stream suitable for drinking. Their igloo-shaped huts have open doors. Huts are made of bent saplings that form a frame onto which large mongongo leaves are tied. Mats or leaves generally serve as beds, and cooking is done on open fires near the huts. People simply relieve themselves in the forest near the camp.

After one to three months in one place, animals, fruit, and honey become scarce, and the smell of garbage and human waste becomes unbearable. The community packs up and moves to a new site.

10 ● FAMILY LIFE

Family life among tropical forest foragers is much different from that in the West. As previously mentioned, the Bambuti learn the value of interdependence and communality (living as part of a group) as children. Children call all women in the camp *Ema* (mother). Nursing goes on long after a child can walk and talk. Mothers often swap and adopt children of their sisters and close friends.

The Efe live in small camps of fewer than fifty residents. Mbuti camps usually have two to three times as many people because net-hunting, which the Mbuti practice, requires communal participation. Individual households are nuclear families (*endu*) consisting of a husband, a wife, and their children. Families are patrilineal, meaning they trace their lineage through the male line to a common male ancestor.

Marriages are exchanges between families. Mutual affection can play a part. However, generally a man offers a sister, niece, or cousin to his wife's brother or male relative. Divorce is common. A women often initiates divorce simply by packing her things (including small children) and moving back to her family's camp. If she has boys, they return to their father when they are old enough to hunt. The typical marriage is monogamous because women are scarce.

11 ● CLOTHING

Tropical forest foragers wear loincloths. Traditional cloth is made from the inner bark of vines. Men generally process the cloth, which involves pounding, wetting, and working it until it is soft and pliable. Western influence has increased the use of cotton fabrics.

The Bambuti enhance their appearance by scarification (scarring) on the face. Some women also wear bead necklaces. Both men and women file their teeth to a point, which is thought to improve their appearance.

12 ● FOOD

The Efe diet is seasonal depending on the rains, which determine hunting and gardening productivity. Typical crops include rice, cassava, and sweet potatoes. The Efe also gather honey, fruits, and nuts in the forest. Peanuts, plantains, and other foods are acquired through trade with villagers. Tropical forest foragers enjoy many forest delicacies, ranging from pangolins (an armadillo-like animal) to reptiles and insects.

Food taboos are associated with clan, sex, or individuals. Clans identify with animals that performed a kind deed or may have helped an ancestor through a crisis. They make these animals their totems and are not allowed to hunt, eat, or even be around them.

13 ● EDUCATION

The Bambuti have avoided formal education. In camp, children learn basic skills, such as tree-climbing, before they walk. Boys practice shooting bows and arrows at the age of three. As they grow older, boys accompany men on the hunt. Girls learn to gather food, cook, and make huts. This basic education is complete by the age of six or seven.

14 ● CULTURAL HERITAGE

The Bambuti have not developed a written literature and do not create visual arts. Perhaps their most important cultural legacy is their sense of family, their community reliance, and their belief in the forest. Some tropical forest foragers are accomplished storytellers and tell folktales about forest spirits and legends about ancestors. They enjoy singing and dancing, especially on moonlit nights. They stamp on the ground or on hollow logs. If they can, they borrow drums from their villager hosts.

One of the gayest and happiest dances occurs during the honey feast. Forest dwellers celebrate the honey dance after days of feasting on honey. Women form an inner ring and circle around a bonfire, while men form an outer ring and circle in the opposite direction. The men pretend to seek honey and come near the women. The women play the role of bees, humming and droning. They pick up burning branches from the fire, with which they threaten the men to remind them of the dangers of bee stings.

15 ● EMPLOYMENT

Formerly, tropical forest foragers worked just enough to supply their basic needs. Men hunted and women gathered. When they had extras, they traded them for articles and food from African villagers. The forest products they traded were generally meat, honey, fruits, and building materials. In exchange, they received plantains, yams, corn, cloth, and iron tools. Women also tended villagers' gardens, and men occasionally helped villagers clear land. While the Bambuti continue to trade, today they are more concerned with having cash. They therefore hope to get more meat than they need in their hunting. They have become

Richard Peterson

A Mbuti man works to repair his hunting net. Mbuti hunting is a group affair done with nets.

more competitive with each other so that they can sell their extra meat to get cash.

Hunting and gathering still form the core of the Bambuti's livelihood in the forest. Mbuti hunting is a group affair done with nets. The Efe men often hunt alone, either for monkeys with poison-tipped arrows, or for duikers, small African antelope, by perching in fruiting trees (which the duikers graze on).

16 ● SPORTS

Forest people do not play sports in the Western sense. They do, however, learn basic skills through mock hunts and other games. Every camp has a designated play area for children next to streams *(bopi)* that is off-limits to adults. Here children play games similar to sports that teach them about group dynamics and personal achievement. Of similar importance, the elders teach children the strategies and techniques of hunting by pretending to be animals and by showing children how to drive them into a piece of old net.

The adults also play a game (more ritual than sport) resembling tug-of-war. The purpose is to remind the community that cooperation can solve conflicts between the sexes. The tug-of-war begins with all the men on one side and the women on the other. If the women begin to win, one of them leaves to help out the men and assumes a deep male voice to make fun of manhood. As the men begin to win, one of them joins the women and mocks them in high-pitched tones. The battle continues in this way until the participants have switched sides and have had an opportunity to both help and ridicule the opposition. Then both sides collapse, laughing over the point that neither side gains in beating the other.

17 ● RECREATION

The Ituri forest is one of the world's last refuges from cinemas, televisions, and videos. The Bambuti relax after a day's hunt by sitting on homemade four-legged stools in front of their huts, talking and smoking. Tropical forest foragers also celebrate a good hunt—especially an elephant kill—with feasting and dancing. An elephant kill is an act of courage, and they know the meat and ivory will trade well.

When they move to village outskirts, tropical forest foragers socialize with villagers while trading their meat. On moonlit nights, they stay late to drink wine and dance. They put on outrageous performances to entertain villagers in exchange for beverages. A few elderly men stay behind in the camp to smoke hashish (a drug) and stand guard against thieves.

18 ● CRAFTS AND HOBBIES

Tropical forest foragers have little time and interest for crafts and hobbies. If they need a tool, they often beg to borrow it from their villager hosts. Tropical forest foragers fashion their own nets from *lianas* (vines), and make belt pouches, baskets, and mats from grasses. They make stools and chairs from sticks and branches.

19 ● SOCIAL PROBLEMS

One of the forest people's key social problems is interclan disputes over women and children. Tropical forest foragers lose about 14 percent of their women to marriage with villagers. Reciprocal marriage exchanges are therefore difficult to fulfill because families often have uneven numbers of females. Men harass, capture, and come into armed conflict with each other over "sister exchange."

Prior to independence, tropical forest foragers remained outside the mainstream of society and politics. An internal system of camp debate and consensus allowed every adult to express his or her opinion. No chief or formal council imposed rules. However, postindependence wars and nation-building drives have disrupted customary ways. Recent timber-cutting, mining, road-building, and commerce have further eroded the isolation of the forest peoples. Their values, beliefs, and way of life are in transition, causing much social instability.

20 ● BIBLIOGRAPHY

Pulford, Mary H., ed. *Peoples of the Ituri*. Orlando, Fla.: Harcourt Brace College Publishers, 1993.

Turnbull, Colin M. *The Forest People*. New York: Simon and Schuster, 1962.

Turnbull, Colin M. *The Mbuti Pygmies: Change and Adaptation*. New York: Holt, Rinehart and Winston, 1983.

WEBSITES

World Travel Guide. [Online] http://www.wtgonline.com/country/zr/gen.html, 1998.

Congo,
Republic of the

■ CONGOLESE 209

■ AKA 215

■ BAKONGO 221

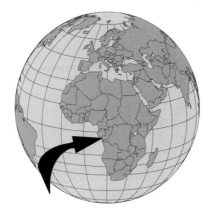

The people of the Republic of Congo are called Congolese. The population belongs to four major ethnic groups—the Bakongo, Bateke, Mboshi, and Sanga—which comprise more than 40 tribes. This chapter begins with an article on the Congolese people as a whole. There is also an article on the Aka, a group that lives in the high forest region and are possibly the Congo's original inhabitants. The Bakongo, profiled in the last article in this chapter, are Congo's largest ethnic group.

Congolese

PRONUNCIATION: kahn-go-LEEZ

ALTERNATE NAME: Congo-Brazzavillans

LOCATION: Republic of the Congo

LANGUAGE: French; Lingala; Kikongo; Sangha; Bateke; 60 others

RELIGION: Christianity (Catholicism); animism

1 ● INTRODUCTION

In October 1997, the Republic of the Congo swore in a new president after a four-month civil war. The war killed thousands and left the capital of Brazzaville in ruins. Five years after the first democratic elections, private militias (armies) installed an unelected government.

But reports of battles do not present a full picture of the Republic of the Congo. It has long been the education and banking center of the Central African region. During World War II (1939–45), it was the capital of the Free French movement led by Charles de Gaulle (1890–1970) against the Nazis and France's Vichy government (a puppet government of Nazi Germany). Its leaders were openly communist, trading vigorously with China and the Soviet Union.

The Republic of the Congo is located directly across the Congo (or Zaire) River from the Democratic Republic of the Congo (DROC, and known as Zaire until mid-1997). The river that divides the two Congos is the second-longest in Africa (the Nile is the longest). It carries the largest poten-

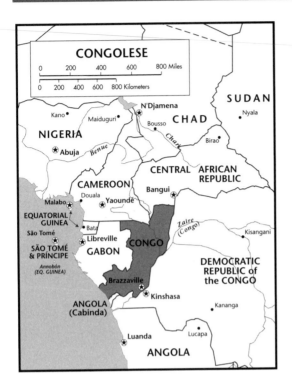

CONGOLESE

| 0 | 200 | 400 | 600 | 800 Miles |
| 0 | 200 | 400 | 600 | 800 Kilometers |

The rest is wooded savanna (grasslands), river valleys, and a small coastal plain. The Congo is about the size of the state of Montana. It is hot and very humid with high rainfall. The Congo's entire eastern and southern borders are washed by the Congo River. The role of this river in the lives of Congolese, past and present, can not be underestimated. Over 1,000 miles (1,600 kilometers) of unbroken navigable water serves as a highway for huge barges and dugout canoes, carting people and produce through Central Africa. People eat from the river, live on it in houses built high on stilts, take electric power from it, and hand pieces of it down through the generations in the form of inheritable fishing rights.

3 ● LANGUAGE

French is the administrative language of the Congo. Lingala, Kikongo, Sangha, and Bateke are the most widely spoken native languages. There are sixty other languages in the Congo, crisscrossing national boundaries. There is another kind of Congolese language though, and that is the language of the talking drum. For generations, messages have been sent from village to village by the regulated beat of special drums. These are usually situated near the village chief's compound. In the past, everyone within earshot understood the meaning of the various rhythms. There were rhythms for death, birth, marriage, or the impending arrival of a dignitary. Talking drums are still used, but they are being replaced by radio, shortwave, and television.

tial supply of hydroelectric power in the world.

The Portuguese discoverers reached the mouth of the Congo River in 1482 and began trading with the Kongo kingdom. The slave trade and ivory attracted the interest of other European countries. In 1883, explorer Peirre-Paul-Francois Camillie Savorgnan de Brazza (1852–1905) signed treaties with the Bateke, a tribe located to the north, turning over the entire region to France.

Today, the Congo continues its close relationship with France, despite achieving independence in 1960.

2 ● LOCATION

The Congo straddles the equator. Most of the land is covered by dense tropical forest.

4 ● FOLKLORE

The Congo is rich in folkloric tradition, and generalizations are difficult in a country with dozens of ethnic groups. Typically, however, heroes and personalities tend to take the form of animals. Each family, or sometimes an entire village or clan, will have its own totem—an animal whose spirit and characteristics represent the group's unity. These animals often have mystical powers and are responsible for the creation of the ancestral lineage. They are honored through storytelling.

5 ● RELIGION

The vast majority of the population identifies itself as Christian, primarily Catholic. Many continue to hold animist beliefs, believing that natural objects and phenomena have souls. They do not consider these beliefs contrary to monotheism (belief in one deity). Local animists long believed in one supreme god before the arrival of European missionaries. His name is Nzambi, and he can best be described as the omnipotent spirit of nature. One of the Congo's creation myths tells of Nzambi's great illness, back when the Earth was still completely covered with water. In his fits of coughing, he spat up the Sun, Moon, stars, animals, and people. And so the world was born by accident.

6 ● MAJOR HOLIDAYS

The Congo's national holiday is celebrated on August 15. It commemorates the country's independence from France on that day in 1960. Independence Day is celebrated in streets, courtyards, houses, and bars. Beer and palm wine are consumed in large quantities. The preferred dish on this special occasion is chicken and rice. Chicken, or any form of animal protein, for that matter, often marks a special occasion.

Other holidays include Christmas (December 25) and New Year's (January 1), Easter (late March or early April), All Saint's Day (November 1), and National Reconciliation Day (June 10).

7 ● RITES OF PASSAGE

A ritual surrounding marriage shows the traditional importance of premarital virginity for girls. This ritual, practiced less now than in the past, appears in different forms throughout the world, particularly the Near East.

Once a couple has decided to marry, both the man and the woman undergo a course in "domestic education," taught by the elders of their own gender within the family. It is assumed that the woman is a virgin, and she must receive some sexual instruction in order to contribute to a successful union. On the morning after the wedding night, the women from both sides of the family arrive early, while the couple is still in bed. They ask many specific questions about the couple's experience with sexual intercourse. If the experience did not go well, the husband has the right to ask for his "bride-price" to be returned and the marriage may be annulled.

8 ● RELATIONSHIPS

Because of the diversity of cultural heritages in the Congo, greetings are expressed in different ways. Among some groups it is common to greet close relatives not seen for a long time with a bear hug. Among friends and acquaintances, there is the two-handed shake. In neighboring Gabon, kissing alternate cheeks three to four times is common even in the villages. In the Congo this Western custom is seen almost exclusively in the modern cities.

There is a marked formality in communication among Congolese, a style that is shared throughout Central Africa. Even a business meeting should begin with a polite inquiry into the other person's well-being and that of their family, as well as some indication of the honor that their presence bestows. Public recognition of social hierarchy is very important. Agreement with an elder, boss, or anyone of higher status is valued above directness.

9 ● LIVING CONDITIONS

The Congo is a poor country by Western standards. It is far from the poorest country in Africa, however. In the late 1990s, it ranked sixteenth out of fifty-two nations according to an index used by the United Nations known as the Human Development Index for Africa. This rank indicates that Congo is a relatively wealthy nation compared to its neighbors. The wealth comes from the existence of petroleum.

R. G. Ruggiero

A man prepares fibers to weave a sleeping mat.

Outside of the cities, houses are commonly built out of mud brick and are in constant need of repair. Many people can afford corrugated zinc roofs on their homes. Those who cannot use thatch. Buildings in urban areas are usually made out of concrete blocks. There are several steel and glass office towers in Brazzaville, though they were severely damaged by the civil war in 1997.

Whether poor or wealthy, Congolese take immense pride in their homes. Mud-brick houses are ringed with handmade, well-maintained fencing. Decorative flow-

ers and bushes are planted in front yards carefully cleared of weeds and grasses in an effort to keep away snakes, rats, and insects.

10 ● FAMILY LIFE

The average Congolese woman bears six children during her lifetime. In the past, most marriages were arranged by family members. In modern times, this became much less common. Women do most of the work it takes to care for the family and run a household. They are responsible for planting, harvesting, food preparation, water fetching, child care, and housework (which can include putting on a new roof or erecting a fence). Men traditionally are responsible for hunting, clearing the forest for gardens, or, in the city, engaging in wage labor.

The word "family" has a somewhat different meaning in the Congo than in the West. Family means an extensive network of relatives, including aunts, uncles, cousins, grandparents, nieces, and nephews. The extended family plays the role in society that the state has taken over in many Western countries. Poor, sick, or disabled people are rarely sent to institutions such as nursing homes, or left to live on welfare or on the street. Their care is the family's responsibility, and the burdens of this responsibility are spread among the dozens of people who constitute a family.

11 ● CLOTHING

Generally, Central Africans take care in their dress, and Congolese are no exception. Whether a person has means or not, people in the street, the market, and in offices can be seen in pressed, colorful, hand-made clothing. *Bous-Bous,* the colorful strips of cotton cloth essential to any Central or West African wardrobe, can be dressed up or down. They also are used as head wraps and turbans by Congolese women. Office workers and bureaucrats in the cities dress much the same as they do in the West.

12 ● FOOD

While a visitor to the Congo will marvel at the abundance of greenery, this does not mean that agriculture is flourishing. Rainforest soil is very poor in nutrients. Despite additional areas of savanna and river valley, only 2.5 percent of the Congo's soil is under cultivation. Foodstuffs commonly grown on this land include bananas, manioc (cassava), peanuts, coffee, cocoa, taro (a starch), and pineapples. Some livestock is raised, but over 90 percent of the country's meat is imported.

Congolese cultures abound with food taboos (prohibitions). Many relate to village, family, or even individual totemic beliefs. It is strictly taboo for anyone to eat the meat from an animal that is his or her totem.

13 ● EDUCATION

For a long time, Brazzaville was considered the educational capital of Central Africa. Many educated people over the age of fifty who did not study in Europe (from neighboring Gabon, for instance) went to school in the Congo. The government, by its own admission, has ignored the rural economy for decades. In spite of this, there is a relatively high density of rural primary schools. Brazzaville has one university and a regionally famous painting school called L'École de Poto-Poto. Murals by Poto-Poto students can be found throughout the streets of Brazzaville. The literacy rate (percentage of those able to read and write) is estimated at 75 percent for adults.

14 ● CULTURAL HERITAGE

It is said that "Every Congolese learns to sing." Singing has long been used to make work less boring. There are songs about fishing, planting, and how to use a hoe, paddle a canoe, or pound manioc (cassava) with a giant mortar and pestle. Musical instruments include a variety of drums, the guitar, and the *sanzi,* a small wooden box with metal teeth that are plucked by the thumbs, like a hand-held piano.

Congolese are also great storytellers. Their tradition of storytelling kept histories and the arts alive before the advent of the written language. Since the introduction of French and written language, Congolese novelists, playwrights, and poets have gained celebrity throughout French-speaking Africa. Jean Malonga, Henri Lopes, Soni Laboue Tansi (1947–95), Marie Leontine Tsibinda, and Guy Menga are some of the best known Congolese literary figures.

People who have lived in the rainforest for generations know about the healing characteristics of plants that grow there. Modern pharmacists and doctors are now beginning to be study these exotic plants. A deep knowledge of the forest is a rich, yet vanishing, part of the Congolese cultural heritage.

15 ● EMPLOYMENT

During the communist regime, all land was officially state-owned. By extension, all work on the land was work for the state. This may have had something to do with the resulting underdevelopment of agriculture over the decades. Conversely, the urban bureaucratic class grew rapidly during this time. From 1960 and 1970, after seven years of communist rule, the number of people working for the new independent government grew by 636 percent. Salaries for state workers ate up almost 75 percent of the national budget. These expenditures were paid for by oil revenues and by aid from foreign governments. Since 1970, the Congo has significantly reduced the number of government employees to avoid borrowing more money from other governments and international agencies.

16 ● SPORTS

As is true all over Africa, soccer is the most passionately followed sport in the Congo. Also popular are karate, handball, basketball, and volleyball, as both participant and spectator sports. Television devotes a lot of time to sports coverage. Now, with satellite capability, even in a thatched bar deep in the brush, Congolese can follow the French Open tennis tournament.

17 ● RECREATION

Sports, singing, dancing, music, storytelling, and visiting relatives are pastimes everywhere in the Congo. In the city, there are movies, some theaters, and discotheques. Fishing is also considered recreational, as well as work. Finally, there is always the popular pastime of sitting down to a cold beer or glass of palm wine to pass the afternoon in gossip.

18 ● CRAFTS AND HOBBIES

Traditionally, Congolese art was created to serve religious or ceremonial functions, rather than for purely aesthetic reasons. Masks, weaving, pottery, and ironwork were often abstract, depicting the human head or animals. Much of the local skill in crafts has been lost. A government agency and an ethnicity museum in Brazzaville are trying to preserve the knowledge and artifacts still remaining. With an active painting and literary community in the Congo, new art forms continue to emerge.

19 ● SOCIAL PROBLEMS

In 1997, the Congo suffered four months of war in a battle to overthrow the president of its very shaky democracy. Violent death, dislocation, and general social breakdown were among the immediate problems faced by the Congolese.

There are tens of thousands of indigenous (native) tropical forest foragers (often disrespectfully referred to as "pygmies") in the Congo. They are considered to be the first inhabitants in the area. While equal rights are officially protected in the Congolese constitution, tropical forest foragers are heavily discriminated against. They have been turned away from public hospitals when seeking medical care and are not represented in government. Those working for wages do not receive equal pay for equal work. Discrimination against tropical forest foragers exists all over Central Africa.

20 ● BIBLIOGRAPHY

Biebuyck, Daniel P. *Congo: Tribes & Parties.* London: Royal Anthropological Institute, 1961.

Coppo, Salvatore. *A Truly African Church.* Eldoret, Kenya: Gaba Publications, AMECA, 1987.

Kempers, Anne Grimshaw. *Heart of Lightness.* Portsmouth, N.H.: P.E. Randall Publisher, 1993.

Warkentin, Raija. *Our Strength is in Our Fields: African Families in Change.* Dubuque, Iowa: Kendall/Hunt, 1994.

Vansina, Jan. *Paths in the Rain Forest.* Madison: University of Wisconsin Press, 1990.

WEBSITES

World Travel Guide. [Online] Available http://www.wtgonline.com/country/cg/gen.html, 1998.

Aka

PRONUNCIATION: AH-kah
ALTERNATE NAMES: Pygmies; tropical forest foragers; Biaka; Bayaka; Bambenzele
LOCATION: Northern Congo and southern Central African Republic
POPULATION: 30,000
LANGUAGE: Diaka; Bantu (Oubanguian); Sango
RELIGION: Indigenous beliefs

1 ● INTRODUCTION

In the United States, the Aka are better known as "pygmies." The term "pygmy" refers to a person of short stature (typically under five feet tall) who hunts and gathers and has a strong identity with the tropical forest. It is generally a disrespectful term that emphasizes their physical characteristics. Anthropologists suggest replacing the term temporarily with "tropical forest forager."

The main reason the Aka are short seems to be because of the absence of a dramatic growth spurt during adolescence. This is due to a lack of receptors for a particular growth hormone (IGF-I). Most mammals living in tropical forests are shorter than their savanna (grassland) relatives. This suggests that smaller size may be adaptive to the humid tropical forest.

The Aka are just one of at least ten ethnically and linguistically distinct groups of tropical forest foragers in Central Africa. (Some of these groups are the Aka, Baka, Efe, and Mbuti.) Tropical forest foragers have been living in the tropical forests for hundreds, if not thousands, of years. (Some anthropologists believe they have lived in these rainforests for more than six thousand years.) Consequently, the Aka are the "first citizens" of the Congo and Central African Republic, much like Native Americans are the first citizens of the United States.

The farming peoples of Central Africa moved into the tropical forest area about two thousand years ago and slowly established regular trading relationships with tropical forest foragers. Today, Aka-farmer relations are very complex. They attend each other's funerals, births, and marriages, and they have regular economic exchanges. The farmers see themselves as superior to Aka and talk about "their" Aka. Even though Aka-farmer trading relationships may have lasted for generations, Aka can (and do) leave the relationship any time they feel a "patron" (farmer) is not treating them well.

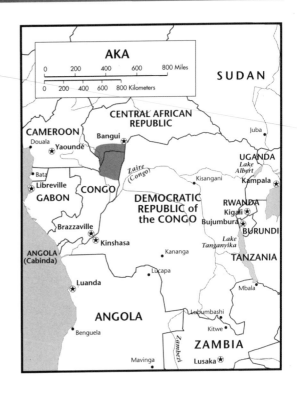

2 ● LOCATION

About 30,000 Aka live in the tropical forests of northern Congo and southern Central African Republic. Most Aka live in remote areas of the tropical forest where the population density is less than one person per square mile. Aka women average six live births during their lifetime. One-fifth of Aka children do not live to their first birthday, and close to half die before they reach age fifteen. Infectious and parasitic diseases are the most common causes of death. Due to the high child mortality (death) rate, average life expectancy at birth is only thirty-two years of age. However, if a young person lives to age fifteen, he or she will probably live to age fifty-five or older.

3 ● LANGUAGE

The Aka speak a Bantu language called Diaka, which is characterized by three tones. The language often sounds musical. Different tones can dramatically change the meaning of a word (for example, *mbongo* can mean cup, a type of bee, or panther).

Most Aka speak at least two other languages—either the Bantu or Oubanguian language of their village trading partners, and some Sango, the national language in the Central African Republic.

Aka are given personal names a week or so after birth. Personal names have meanings attached to them—for example, *Bimba* (flea), *Madjembe* (intestinal worms), *Ngunda Oti* (without hospitality). In the last case, a boy's mother gave him the name because, at the time of his birth, the boy's father's family did not provide her with much food. Sometimes Aka simply like the sounds of new words and use them as names.

4 ● FOLKLORE

Aka say that long ago they lived in villages and farmed. However, one day a woman heard bees in the sky and a group of people decided to go into the forest to see where the bees were going. They found the bees' hive and loved the honey. Finding plenty of food in the forest, they decided to stay. This is how Aka describe the origin of their life in the forest.

5 ● RELIGION

The Aka occupy a large territory, and religious beliefs vary by area. Some Aka believe in *bembe*, a creator of all living things, but those who believe in bembe indicate that he/she retired soon after creation. Djengi is the most consistently mentioned and is considered to be a powerful and generally helpful forest spirit. Communication with djengi takes place through a traditional healer (or *tuma*) who has the ability to translate the supernatural language.

Most Aka camps have a traditional healer (*nganga*). Ngangas cure all forms of illness, see into the future to help people make decisions, and see game animals deep in the forest while on the hunt. Ngangas acquire their knowledge through training and initiation.

Aka also believe that family members do not entirely leave this earth after they die. An ancestor's spirit (*edjo*) stays around, vis-

its the family, and often wants things. Many Aka believe in witchcraft, especially to explain unexpected adult deaths.

6 ● MAJOR HOLIDAYS

Aka do not use a numerical calendar, so they do not have specific dates that are celebrated each year. However, there are holidays in the sense that there are days off to relax. Such holidays occur after good hunts or when large game animals, such as an elephant or a wild pig, have been captured. Holidays also occur during the honey, caterpillar, and termite seasons.

7 ● RITES OF PASSAGE

Aka do not have much in the way of group ritual activities. At birth, parents place protective cords made from forest vines around a baby's neck, wrists, and ankles. These are to protect the baby from bad spirits and help connect him or her to the forest. At five or six years of age, boys are circumcised in a very informal and supportive manner.

During the teenage years, boys and girls get each of their top four incisor (front) teeth filed to a point. Aka believe that pointed teeth make one look more handsome or beautiful. Some Aka, primarily teenage girls, get the bottom four incisors pointed as well. Teenagers bring in new fads from other areas. Current fads include coloring teeth with a purple dye from a forest vine, piercing the nasal septum with a small twig (girls only), and shaving stripes into one's eyebrows.

The only large, group-level ritual occurs at death, when relatives travel long distances and sing and dance for days.

8 ● RELATIONSHIPS

Aka are very warm and hospitable. Relationships between men and women are extremely egalitarian. Men and women contribute equally to a household's diet, either a husband or wife can initiate divorce, and violence against women is very rare. No cases of rape have been reported.

The Aka are fiercely egalitarian and independent. No individual has the right to force or order another individual to perform an activity against his or her will. Aka have a number of informal methods for maintaining their egalitarianism. First, they practice "prestige avoidance"; no one draws attention to his or her own abilities. Individuals play down their achievements. If a man kills an elephant, he says someone else did all the work and talks about the small size of the elephant. Second, Aka practice rough joking with those who start to accumulate more than they need, do not share, or who act self-important. Third, Aka practice "demand sharing." This means that everyone shares whatever he or she has if someone else asks for it. For example, if someone were asked for the shirt he or she was wearing, the person would give it up, saying he or she really did not need it. This way most material items circulate around the camp.

9 ● LIVING CONDITIONS

Aka camps consist of twenty-five to thirty-five people living in five to seven dome-shaped houses. Houses are close to each other, and together occupy an area the size of a large living room. Each family has their own house, and everyone in that house sleeps together in the same bed. The house is big enough for one bed and a campfire for warmth during the night. The two or three adolescent boys in the camp share one house (the bachelor pad). Teenage girls each make their own small house. Houses are constructed from saplings and large leaves. Beds are made from logs, animal skins, or leaves.

10 ● FAMILY LIFE

Aka children grow up in an environment of trust, love, and indulgence. Although the mother is the primary caregiver, Aka fathers provide more care to young children than fathers in many other societies. A typical Aka childhood is free of negative forces and violence. If a child hits another child, the parent will simply move the child to another area. Corporal (physical) punishment of a child who misbehaves seldom occurs. In fact, if a parent hits a child, it is reason enough for the other parent to ask for a divorce.

During the teenage years, same-sex friends are inseparable and go everywhere together. Teenagers often travel to visit relatives and explore territories other than their own, so they may be absent from the camp for long periods. The teenage years are a time of social and sexual exploration.

First marriages occurs between seventeen and twenty-one years of age. Once a man moves his traps and spear into the house of a woman, the two are considered married; there is no formal marriage ceremony. About 25 percent of marriages end in divorce. Divorce takes place by one partner simply moving out of the house. If divorce occurs, children go with the parent they prefer.

11 ● CLOTHING

The temperature never drops below 21°C (70°F) during the day. Men and women wear loincloths made of commercial fabric obtained in trade with villagers. When Aka visit the village, they put on any Western or "villager" clothes they might have: men wear T-shirts and shorts, and women wear a cloth that they wrap around their waist.

12 ● FOOD

The Aka know more about the tropical forest than do many botanists and zoologists. They know hundreds of forest plants and animals. However, they live primarily on sixty-three plant species, twenty insect species, honey from eight species of bees, and twenty-eight species of game animals. The Aka collect roots from six species of plants, leaves from eleven species, nuts from seventeen species, and fruits from seventeen species. They collect twelve species of mushrooms, four types of termites, crickets, three types of grubs, and twelve species of caterpillars. The Aka hunt with spears for seven species of large game (primarily hog and elephant), with nets for six species of antelope, with crossbows for eight species of monkeys, and with small snare and net traps for seven species of rat, mongoose, and porcupine.

Although there is enormous diversity in the Aka diet, their favorite game animal by far is porcupine. Honey is another favorite food—the "candy" of the forest. Caterpillars may be roasted, boiled, or fried and taste like french fries.

13 ● EDUCATION

Aka do not usually attend formal schools, but they begin learning about hunting and gathering when they are infants. Parents teach babies how to use small, pointed digging sticks, throw small spears, use miniature axes with sharp metal blades, and carry small baskets even before they learn to walk. One- and two-year-olds use knives, axes, and digging sticks. They build play houses and imitate the dances and songs of adult life. By three or four years of age, children can cook themselves a meal on a fire. By age ten, Aka children can live alone in the forest if necessary. By that age they can also identify hundreds of plants and animals and they know all the important survival skills, with the exception of elephant hunting. Aka do not read or write, but they are very interested in acquiring these skills.

14 ● CULTURAL HERITAGE

The Aka have a reputation as being the best dancers in the Congo and Central African Republic. They are frequently invited to dance at festivals. Aka music is unique; it has yodeling, hocketing (tossing back and forth short notes in quick succession), and polyphonic harmonies.

15 ● EMPLOYMENT

The Aka are one of the last groups of people on earth to spend most of their days hunting and gathering. The tropical forest is not known for its abundance of wild edible foods. However, it is a land of plenty for the Aka, who have extensive knowledge of the forest. Aka actually work fewer hours per week than do middle-class Americans.

Net hunting is the most important hunting technique. It is unique among hunting techniques in that it focuses on making noise rather than stalking and being quiet. The hunt takes place at night. Families connect long nets to form a semicircle or circle. Men stand in the center of the circle and make noise to wake up and scare antelopes. Women stand by the nets, and tackle and kill antelope caught in the net. Game animals are shared with everyone in camp.

16 ● SPORTS

Forest people do not play sports in the Western sense. They do, however, learn basic skills through mock hunts and other games. Children play games similar to sports that teach them about group dynamics and personal achievement.

The adults also play a game (more ritual than sport) resembling tug-of-war. The purpose is to remind the community that cooperation can solve conflicts between the sexes. The tug-of-war begins with all the men on one side and the women on the other. If the women begin to win, one of them leaves to help out the men and uses a deep male voice to make fun of manhood. As the men begin to win, one of them joins the women and mocks them in high-pitched tones. The battle continues in this way until the participants have switched sides and have had an opportunity to both help and make fun of the opposition. Then both sides collapse, laughing over the point that neither side gains in beating the other.

17 ● RECREATION

Aka do not have televisions, radios, books, or electricity. After dark, they sit around fires to socialize, gossip, tell stories (often about gorillas or chimps having affairs with humans), and dance and sing. Dances usually occur about twice a week, but they happen every night during caterpillar season or when hunting is especially good.

18 ● CRAFTS AND HOBBIES

Aka do not have paper and pencils. Their art often takes the form of body modifications—painting, scarification (decorative scarring), haircuts, and so on. The dark juice from a fruit is used to draw designs on the face and the body that represent the sounds and sights of the forest. Scarification often takes place before a dance. Teenagers get together and cut various designs into their bodies, often around the navel. Aka use razor blades traded from villagers to cut their hair and shave their heads into some very original designs—triangles, lightning bolts, caterpillars, and so on.

19 ● SOCIAL PROBLEMS

The Aka are being affected by the global economy in several ways. European logging companies are building roads and mills to extract mahogany and other hardwood trees (most caterpillars come from these trees). Europeans and Africans are going deeper into the forest to dig for gold and diamonds. Western conservation groups are trying to establish national parks and reserves to save tropical forests, but this means that Aka often lose their lands. In addition, relations are breaking down between the Aka and farmers who have traditionally been their trading partners. The Aka are exploited by both African farmers and European investors. Aka are quiet and self-assured, and they often respond to outside pressures by fleeing deeper into the forest. Aka are not politically organized, nor do they have the literacy skills to try to eliminate these threats to their existence.

20 ● BIBLIOGRAPHY

Cavalli-Sforza, Luigi Luca, ed. *African Pygmies*. Orlando, Fla.: Academic Press, 1986

Hewlett, Barry S. "Cultural diversity among African pygmies." In: *Cultural Diversity Among Twentieth-Century Foragers*. Susan Kent, ed. Cambridge, England: Cambridge University Press, 1996.

Hewlett, Barry S. *Intimate Fathers: The Nature and Context of Paternal-lnfant Care Among Aka Pygmies*. Ann Arbor: University of Michigan Press, 1991.

Mark, Joan T. *The King of the World in the Land of the Pygmies*. Lincoln: University of Nebraska Press, 1995.

WEBSITES

World Travel Guide. [Online] Available http://www.wtgonline.com/country/cg/gen.html, 1998.

Bakongo

PRONUNCIATION: buh-KAHN-go
ALTERNATE NAMES: Kongo
LOCATION: Congo River region (Angola, Democratic Republic of the Congo; Republic of the Congo)
POPULATION: 3.3 million
LANGUAGE: Kikongo
RELIGION: Christianity; Kimbanguism; indigenous beliefs

1 ● INTRODUCTION

The solidarity of the Bakongo people has a long history based on the splendor of the ancient Kongo kingdom and the cultural unity of the Kikongo language. Founded in the fifteenth century AD, the kingdom was discovered by Portuguese explorer Diego Cao when he landed at the mouth of the Congo River in 1484. As trade developed with the Portuguese, Mbanza Bata, located south of the Congo, became the capital (later known as San Salvador). Portuguese missionaries baptized King Nzinga Mbemba (?–1550), who adopted the Christian name Afonso I. Within a few years, the kingdom was exchanging ambassadors with Portugal and the Vatican.

By the end of the sixteenth century, the Kongo kingdom had virtually ceased to exist. Invasions by neighboring groups from the east severely weakened it, and it became controlled by Portugal. In the seventeenth century, British, Dutch, and French slave ships reportedly carried 13 million persons from the Kongo kingdom to the New World. Ironically, the king and his subjects profited financially from the trade as their kingdom crumbled beneath them. In 1884–85 at the Conference of Berlin, the European powers divided the kingdom among the French, Belgian, and Portuguese. By the end of the nineteenth century, little remained of the once great Kongo civilization.

The twentieth century has seen a rebirth of Kongo nationalism and culture. The Kimbanguist religious movement gained a strong following in the 1920s and became a springboard for anticolonial sentiment. European historians and missionaries, including Georges Balandier and Father Van Wing also helped by uncovering the glorious past of the kingdom. Their enthusiasm inspired Bakongo intellectuals in the Belgian Congo to demand immediate independence in 1956. They founded a political party, whose candidates won the vast majority of municipal seats in 1959, leading to the election of President Joseph Kasavubu (1910–69), a Mukongo, as the Congo's first president.

While Kongo secessionist movements have come and gone, currently a group of fundamentalists is trying to gain independence for the Bakongo, and wants to establish a Kongo federal state composed of five provinces. It would bring together Bakongo living in the southern Congo, the Angolan enclave of Cabinda, the lower province of the Democratic Republic of the Congo (Congo-Kinshasa, formerly Zaire), and northern Angola. Its name would be *Kongo Dia Ntotela* (the United States of the Kongo).

2 ● LOCATION

The Bakongo are a blend of peoples who assimilated the Kongo culture and language over time. The kingdom consisted of some thirty groups at its beginning. Its original inhabitants occupied a narrow corridor south of the Congo River from present-day Kinshasa to the port city of Matadi in the lower Congo. Through conflict, conquest, and treaties, they came to dominate neighboring tribes, including the Bambata, the Mayumbe, the Basolongo, the Kakongo, the Basundi, and the Babuende. These peoples gradually adopted the Bakongo culture and through intermarriage blended completely with the Bakongo.

The Kongo kingdom once covered about 116 square miles (300 square kilometers). Its boundaries extended as far as the Nkisi River to the east, the Dande River to the south, the Congo (Zaire) River to the north,

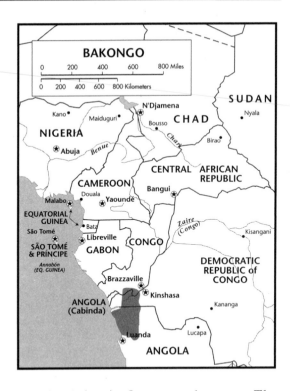

and the Atlantic Ocean to the west. The greater kingdom of the sixteenth century extended another 62 miles (100 kilometers) east to the Kwango River and 124 miles (200 kilometers) further north to the Kwilu River. Today, the Bakongo peoples still live in their ancestral homeland. It is quite mountainous and has a dry season lasting from May to August or September. Of the three ecological zones to the south of the Congo River, the hilly middle zone receives the most annual rainfall (55 inches/140 centimeters) and has relatively fertile soils and moderately warm temperatures. Consequently, it is more densely populated than the dry, sandy coastal region and the infertile arid plateau to the east.

There are about 1.6 million Bakongo living in Angola, 1.1 million in the Democratic

Republic of the Congo (formerly Zaire), and 600,000 in the Republic of the Congo, where they are the largest ethnic group. In Angola, they are the third-largest group, making up 14 percent of the population.

3 ● LANGUAGE

The Bakongo speak various dialects of Kikongo, similar to the Kikongo spoken in the ancient kingdom. These dialects differ widely across the region; some can hardly be understood by speakers of other dialects. To further its nation-building efforts after independence, the government of the former Zaire created a standardized version of the language, which incorporated elements of the many variants. Standard Kikongo is used in elementary schools throughout the Lower Province and Bandundu, and is called Mono Kotuba (State Kikongo). In 1992, Kikongo speakers in all countries numbered 3,217,000, the majority of whom lived in Angola. In the Republic of the Congo, Kikongo speakers account for 46 percent of the population.

4 ● FOLKLORE

Legends trace Bakongo ancestry to Ne Kongo Nimi, who is said to have had three children whose descendants, grouped into three clans, form the Kongo nation. The children of Ne Kongo Nimi were called Bana ba Ne Kongo, literally "the children of Ne Kongo." The abbreviation became Bakongo. Proverbs, fables, legends, and tales occupy an important place in daily life. Some popular legends only have basic elements that stay the same, since storytellers add their own spice and take great freedoms in dressing up the traditional legends. One popular character, Monimambu, is known to

the Bakongo and other peoples through oral and written literature. He is not a hero—rather he is a fictional figure with human weaknesses and feelings who has some successes but makes mistakes, too. His adventures are entertaining, but the stories not only amuse, they teach lessons as well. A favorite animal figure in Bakongo tales is the leopard.

The Bakongo recognize Dona Beatrice as a Kongolese heroine. Born Kimpa Vita, she became a Christian martyr, and later a symbol of Congolese nationhood. She lived in a time of great crisis. Rivalries had torn apart the kingdom, and the capital of San Salvador had been in ruins since 1678. In 1703, at the age of twenty-two, Beatrice sought to restore the grandeur of the Kongo. She warned of divine punishment if the capital were not reoccupied. Within two years she established a new religious teaching and renewed the Church. But her opposition to foreign missionaries led to her death. Controlled by the Portuguese, King Pedro IV arrested her. She was tried by a Church tribunal for heresy, condemned, and burned at the stake. Her idealism and sacrifice inspired a tradition of mysticism among the Bakongo, and she is considered a precursor to the twentieth-century prophet Simon Kimbangu (1889–1951).

5 ● RELIGION

The Bakongo were among the first sub-Saharan African peoples to adopt Christianity and, as a kingdom, had diplomatic ties with the Vatican. In the colonial period, Belgian missionaries established Catholic seminaries in the villages of Lemfu and

Mayidi and built mission churches and schools throughout Lower Congo.

According to the traditional religion of the Bakongo, the creator of the universe, called Nzambe, lives above a world of ancestor spirits. Many people believe that when a family member dies a normal death, he or she joins this spirit world (or village) of the ancestors, who look after the living and protect the descendants to whom they have left their lands. Spirits of those who die violent and untimely deaths are thought to be without rest until their deaths have been avenged. Sorcerers are hired to discover through the use of fetishes or charms called *nkisi* who was responsible for the death. In addition, healing practices and traditional religion go hand in hand. Traditional healers called *nganga* may be consulted for herbal treatments or to root out *kindoki* (witches practicing black magic, who are thought to cause illness through ill-will, and to eat the souls of their victims by night).

These beliefs have mixed with Christianity, and they have produced new sects. In the 1920s, Simon Kimbangu, a member of the English Baptist Mission Church, claimed to have received a vision from God, calling him to preach the Word and to heal the sick. He taught the law of Moses and spoke against sorcery, fetishes, charms, and polygamy (having more than one spouse at the same time). When he began to speak against the Church and the colonial government, the Belgians arrested him and sentenced him to death. Later his sentence was changed to life in prison, where he died in 1951. Eventually Kimbanguism gained legal recognition from the state, and its Church became a strong supporter of the Mobutu regime. Presently, some 300,000 active members belong to the Kimbangu Church, most of them living in the Lower Congo.

6 ● MAJOR HOLIDAYS

Given the political uncertainty in their countries of residence, the Bakongo celebrate secular holidays quietly these days. However, the Kimbanguists make an annual pilgrimage to the Kamba River to honor their prophet. At the river they offer sacrifices, pray, ask for blessings, and take some of the water, which is considered holy. Kimbanguists believe in Jesus as the son of God and therefore commemorate Christmas and Easter, which are major holidays.

In the Democratic Republic of the Congo, the Bakongo celebrate Parents Day, (August 1) along with their fellow citizens. On this holiday, people go to cemeteries in the morning to spruce up family graves. The grave sites may be overgrown with tall, dry elephant grass, which is burned away, creating an Armageddon-like atmosphere. In the evenings, families get together to share a festive meal with the extended family.

7 ● RITES OF PASSAGE

The Bakongo believe in a close relationship between the unborn, the living, and the dead. If they are Christian, they baptize their children. At birth, there is a ritual called a *kobota elingi* (which literally means "what a pleasure it is to give birth"), a party to which friends and relatives come to share in the parents' joy and to celebrate the continuity of the family.

Until recently, initiation *(Longo)* held an important place among the rites of passage. Longo teaches children the secrets of Bakongo traditions necessary to taking on the responsibilities of adulthood. During Longo, children learn adult behavior, including control of their physical and emotional reactions to evil, suffering, and death. The ceremonies differ in form, duration, and name among the different Bakongo subgroups. In the past they lasted up to two months. Nowadays, given Westernization and rigid school calendars, fewer children undergo the rite.

Death is a passage to the next dimension, the spirit village of the ancestors. In the past, Kongo tombs were very large, built of wood or stone, and resembled small homes into which the family of the deceased placed furniture and personal objects. The corpse was dressed in fine clothing and placed in a position recalling his or her trade. Graves these days are often marked with no more than concrete crosses, but some still exhibit elaborate stonework and stone crosses that reflect Portuguese influence. The more elaborate graves have statues of friends and family mounted on and around the tomb. Some tombs are so detailed that they truly are works of art.

8 ● RELATIONSHIPS

Bakongo are friendly people who typically greet each other both verbally and by shaking hands. The familiar greeting in Kikongo is *Mbote, Tata/Mama. Kolele?* (Hello, Sir/Madam. What news?) Respect for authority figures and the elderly is shown by holding the left hand to the right wrist when shaking hands. Men commonly hold hands in public

as a sign of friendship. Children are always supposed to receive objects with two hands.

Although young people may initiate courtship, marriage is often arranged by the family, with older siblings or extended family members suggesting possible mates.

9 ● LIVING CONDITIONS

Living conditions are poor for most Bakongo. Rural families typically live in one- or two-room mudbrick huts with thatch or tin roofs, and without electricity. Cooking is done mostly outside. Windows are unscreened, allowing flies and mosquitoes to come in. Water sources are mostly unprotected and often become contaminated. Infectious and parasitic diseases in the Democratic Republic of the Congo (DROC) cause more than 50 percent of all deaths. Children under the age of five, who make up 20 percent of the DROC population, account for 80 percent of deaths. Their daily diets generally do not have enough vitamins, minerals, or protein. Despite poor road networks, much of the agricultural produce of the Lower Congo region goes to feed urban populations in Brazzaville, Kinshasa, and Luanda.

10 ● FAMILY LIFE

The Bakongo family lives as a nuclear unit and is usually monogamous (only one husband and one wife). Although women typically give birth to as many as ten children, diseases and other illnesses cause many of the children to die while they are still infants or toddlers. Nevertheless, children are a sign of wealth, and parents consider themselves blessed to have many children.

EPD Photos

The Bakongo cut up huge banana leaves to make wrappers for pounded, seasoned squash seeds. This is a type of "fast-food" snack sold at roadside stands. Packaged banana leaves like those above can be found in the United States in specialty food stores.

The Bakongo are matriarchal. Children belong to their mother's lineage, and the maternal uncle is in charge of them even while their father is alive. The maternal uncle decides where his sister's children will study and what career they will pursue. If a man succeeds in life but refuses to help the family, he may be strongly criticized by his uncle. On the other hand, in the case of certain misfortunes, the uncle himself may be blamed—uncles have even been stoned when they were suspected of wrongdoing. However, European patriarchal ways have begun to weaken this traditional system.

11 ● CLOTHING

In ancient times, the Bakongo wore clothing made from bark softened by pounding. However, through their long association with the West, the Bakongo have adopted Western clothing. Photographs from the late 1880s show them wearing suits over their sarong (long wraparound skirts). They generally are considered to be very proper dressers by other Congolese. Women adopt the latest local fashions and hairstyles, which change every few months. The mainstay is the African sarong *(pagne)*. Many families are forced to buy used clothing at the markets; children typically wear T-shirts, shorts, and loose cotton overshirts for everyday wear.

12 ● FOOD

The Bakongo are better known for their fashions than for their cuisine. Typically, they eat three meals a day. For breakfast, a village family eats a dough-like ball made from cassava flour *(fufu)* with the previous day's sauce. Diners use their fingers, and before eating, they wash their hands in a basin of warm water. Some people may have coffee and French bread, which is baked locally throughout the region.

The midday meal is the largest of the day. Bakongo enjoy one of several sauces, eaten with fufu or with rice. Cassava leaves *(saka saka)*, pounded and cooked, are always a favorite. Dried salted fish *(makay-abu)* or sardines are added to make a rich saka saka. Another local favorite is pounded sesame seeds *(wangila)*, to which small dried shrimp are added. Pounded squash seeds *(mbika)*, seasoned with lots of hot pepper and wrapped in banana leaves, are

Heather E. Eves

Two young Congolese prepare food for the family. Cassava root (fufu), pounded and cooked, is always a favorite.

sold at roadside stands and are a popular snack for travelers. The most common dish is white beans cooked in a palm oil sauce of tomatoes, onions, garlic, and hot pepper. The beans are eaten with rice, fufu, or *chikwange* (a cassava loaf prepared in banana leaves).

Supper generally consists of leftovers, but chikwange with a piece of makayabu covered in hot pepper sauce is very satisfying, especially when washed down with beer. *Kin (Kinshasa) sept jours* (meaning "Kinshasa seven-day loaf") is a giant chikwange, so large that it reportedly takes a whole family a week to eat it.

The Bakongo are fond of palm wine. Palm juice is tapped from the top of the coconut palm trunk. It ferments within hours and must be drunk the next day. On Saturday and Sunday afternoons, people sit under mango trees, enjoying the milky, tangy drink. They also make sugar cane wine *(nguila)*, fruit wines, and homemade gin *(cinq cents)*. It is customary to pour a small amount on the ground for the ancestors before drinking.

13 ● EDUCATION

Because of their long history of contact with European missionaries, the Bakongo

227

have enjoyed relatively high levels of literacy and education. Currently, most parents want to send their children to high school and beyond, but many children from average families are obliged to drop out, at least temporarily, for financial reasons. Thus it is not uncommon to find twenty-year-olds in some high schools.

14 ● CULTURAL HERITAGE

Kongo court art ranks with that of the Bakuba of Kasai and the Baluba of Katanga, tribes of the southeastern DROC. One type of statue—the *mintadi,* or "chief"—was a large piece of sculpture designed to "replace" the chief at court while he was at war or visiting the king in San Salvador. These statues, of which few remain, were sculpted of stone or wood and showed the chief's rank. Another type—"maternity"—depicted a mother and child. In their resemblance to portrayals of the Virgin Mary, these show a Catholic influence and are notable for both their nonstylized realism and their serenity.

Kikongo has a centuries-old tradition of both oral and written literature. Kikongo verse is rich in proverbs, fables, riddles, and folk tales. Parts of the Bible were translated into Kikongo in the latter part of the nineteenth century.

15 ● EMPLOYMENT

Except for the urban migrant, most Bakongo are subsistence farmers with small patches of cassava, beans, and vegetables. Fruit tree plantations are common in some areas. Generally, farming is only moderately productive because of the dry climate and infertile soils along the coast and into the plateau regions. Along the coast, however, fishing provides a livelihood for many people. The development of industry, promised in the 1970s, never materialized.

16 ● SPORTS

In all three countries that are home to the Bakongo, soccer is the national participant and spectator sport. Boys and young men play it wherever and whenever possible. As a rule, though, people find much less time to play sports than in the West. Even on Sundays, they may farm their fields or tend fruit trees in order to have a good harvest.

17 ● RECREATION

Besides playing and watching soccer, people love to tell stories. With no electricity for reading or watching television, people grow up listening to and learning to tell tales. Nearly everyone enjoys music and dancing. Kinshasa and Brazzaville are centers for Central African music, which is enjoyed throughout the continent. Luanda is famous for its nightclubs. Young people, especially, are continually learning the latest dances. On Saturday nights, townsfolk go to cinemas or to theatrical performances. Others go to bars to dance and socialize.

18 ● CRAFTS AND HOBBIES

Traditionally, Bakongo artisans have excelled in woodcarving, sculpting, painting, and stonework. An example of their intricate carving is found in their wooden bowl covers that have human figures for handles. They also specialize in scepters (fancy royal staffs), ankle bells, cowtail flyswatters, and bottles for medicinal and magical powders, often displaying images of people and animals. Masks, on the other hand, have been less important to the Bakongo than to other people, such as the Luba.

One unique type of folk art is the fetish, which is an animal carved from wood and driven full of nails. The Mayumbe near the coast paint calabashes (gourds), decorating them with hunting scenes and colorful geometric designs.

19 ● SOCIAL PROBLEMS

The Bakongo face many of the same problems as their fellow citizens in their native countries. They must cope with uncontrolled urbanization, collapsing state health care systems, a lack of well-paid jobs, and economic instability.

Politically, Kongo nationalists have never accepted the division of their ancient kingdom at the conference of Berlin in 1884–85. They argue that the partition was a European decision in which no Congolese participated. Consequently, since the 1950s in Angola, Holden Roberto and the National Front for the Liberation of Angola (FNLA) opposed first the Portuguese and then the Popular Movement for the Liberation of Angola (MPLA) regime. Their goal was the reunification of the Bakongo spread across three countries. Their activities have resulted in repression and massacres, the most recent of these occurred in January 1993 on "Bloody Friday" when between 4,000 and 6,000 Bakongo were killed. Bakongo in Angola are also endangered because the regime links them with the National Union for the Total Independence of Angola (UNITA) rebels. Although Bakongo make up 14 percent of the Angolan population, they hold only 2.5 percent of the seats in the legislature.

20 ● BIBLIOGRAPHY

Africa South of the Sahara. London: Europa Publications Ltd., n.d.

Balandier, Georges. *Daily Life in the Kingdom of the Kongo: From the Sixteenth to the Eighteenth Century.* London: George Allen and Unwin, Ltd., 1965.

Hilton, Anne. *The Kingdom of Kongo.* Oxford: Clarendon Press, 1985.

MacGaffey, Wyatt. *Religion and Society in Central Africa: The BaKongo of Lower Zaire.* Chicago: University of Chicago Press, 1986.

WEBSITES

Republic of Angola. [Online] Available http://www.angola.org, 1998.

World Travel Guide. [Online] Available http://www.wtgonline.com/country/cg/gen.html, 1998.

Glossary

aboriginal: The first known inhabitants of a country.

adobe: A brick made from sun-dried heavy clay mixed with straw, used in building houses.

Altaic language family: A family of languages spoken in portions of northern and eastern Europe, and nearly the whole of northern and central Asia, together with some other regions.

Amerindian: A contraction of the two words, American Indian. It describes native peoples of North, South, or Central America.

Anglican: Pertaining to or connected with the Church of England.

animism: The belief that natural objects and phenomena have souls or innate spiritual powers.

apartheid: The past governmental policy in the Republic of South Africa of separating the races in society.

arable land: Land that can be cultivated by plowing and used for growing crops.

archipelago: Any body of water abounding with islands, or the islands themselves collectively.

Austronesian language: A family of languages which includes practically all the languages of the Pacific Islands—Indonesian, Melanesian, Polynesian, and Micronesian sub-families.

average life expectancy: In any given society, the average age attained by persons at the time of death.

Baha'i: The follower of a religious sect founded by Mirza Husayn Ali in Iran in 1863.

Baltic states: The three formerly communist countries of Estonia, Latvia, and Lithuania that border on the Baltic Sea.

Bantu language group: A name applied to the languages spoken in central and south Africa.

Baptist: A member of a Protestant denomination that practices adult baptism by complete immersion in water.

barren land: Unproductive land, partly or entirely treeless.

barter: Trade practice where merchandise is exchanged directly for other merchandise or services without use of money.

Berber: a member of one of the Afroasiatic peoples of northern Africa.

Brahman: A member (by heredity) of the highest caste among the Hindus, usually assigned to the priesthood.

bride wealth (bride price): Fee, in money or goods, paid by a prospective groom (and his family) to the bride's family.

Buddhism: A religious system common in India and eastern Asia. Founded by Siddhartha Gautama (c.563–c.483 BC), Buddhism asserts that suffering is an inescapable part of life. Deliverance can only be achieved through the practice of charity, temperance, justice, honesty, and truth.

Byzantine Empire: An empire centered in the city of Byzantium, now Istanbul in present-day Turkey.

cassava: The name of several species of stout herbs, extensively cultivated for food.

caste system: Heriditary social classes into which the Hindus are rigidly separated according to the religious law of Brahmanism. Privileges and limitations of each caste are passed down from parents to children.

Caucasian: The white race of human beings, as determined by genealogy and physical features.

census: An official counting of the inhabitants of a state or country with details of sex and age, family, occupation, possessions, etc.

Christianity: The religion founded by Jesus Christ, based on the Bible as holy scripture.

Church of England: The national and established church in England.

civil rights: The privileges of all individuals to be treated as equals under the laws of their country; specifically, the rights given by certain amendments to the U.S. Constitution.

coastal plain: A fairly level area of land along the coast of a land mass.

coca: A shrub native to South America, the leaves of which produce organic compounds that are used in the production of cocaine.

colonial period: The period of time when a country forms colonies in and extends control over a foreign area.

colonist: Any member of a colony or one who helps settle a new colony.

colony: A group of people who settle in a new area far from their original country, but still under the jurisdiction of that country. Also refers to the newly settled area itself.

commonwealth: A free association of sovereign independent states that has no charter, treaty, or constitution. The association promotes cooperation, consultation, and mutual assistance among members.

communism: A form of government whose system requires common ownership of property for the use of all citizens. Prices on goods and services are usually set by the government, and all profits are shared equally by everyone. Also, communism refers directly to the official doctrine of the former Soviet Union.

compulsory education: The mandatory requirement for children to attend school until they have reached a certain age or grade level.

Confucianism: The system of ethics and politics taught by the Chinese philosopher Confucius.

constitution: The written laws and basic rights of citizens of a country or members of an organized group.

copra: The dried meat of the coconut.

cordillera: A continuous ridge, range, or chain of mountains.

coup d'ètat (coup): A sudden, violent overthrow of a government or its leader.

cuisine: A particular style of preparing food, especially when referring to the cooking of a particular country or ethnic group.

Cushitic language group: A group of languages that are spoken in Ethiopia and other areas of eastern Africa.

Cyrillic alphabet: An alphabet invented by Cyril and Methodius in the ninth century as an alphabet that was easier for the copyist to write. The Russian alphabet is a slight modification of it.

deity: A being with the attributes, nature, and essence of a god; a divinity.

desegregation: The act of removing restrictions on people of a particular race that keep them socially, economically, and, sometimes, physically, separate from other groups.

desertification: The process of becoming a desert as a result of climatic changes, land mismanagement, or both.

Dewali (Deepavali, Divali): The Hindu Festival of Lights, when Lakshmi, goddess of good fortune, is said to visit the homes of humans. The four- or five-day festival occurs in October or November.

dialect: One of a number of regional or related modes of speech regarded as descending from a common origin.

dowry: The sum of the property or money that a bride brings to her groom at their marriage.

Druze: A member of a Muslim sect based in Syria, living chiefly in the mountain regions of Lebanon.

dynasty: A family line of sovereigns who rule in succession, and the time during which they reign.

Eastern Orthodox: The outgrowth of the original Eastern Church of the Eastern Roman Empire, consisting of eastern Europe, western Asia, and Egypt.

Eid al-Adha: The Muslim holiday that celebrates the end of the special pilgrimage season (hajj) to the city of Mecca in Saudi Arabia.

Eid al-Fitr: The Muslim holiday that begins just after the end of the month of Ramadan and is celebrated with three or four days of feasting.

emigration: Moving from one country or region to another for the purpose of residence.

empire: A group of territories ruled by one sovereign or supreme ruler. Also, the period of time under that rule.

Episcopal: Belonging to or vested in bishops or prelates; characteristic of or pertaining to a bishop or bishops.

exports: Goods sold to foreign buyers.

Finno-Ugric language group: A subfamily of languages spoken in northeastern Europe, including Finnish, Hungarian, Estonian, and Lapp.

fjord: A deep indentation of the land forming a comparatively narrow arm of the sea with more or less steep slopes or cliffs on each side.

folk religion: A religion with origins and traditions among the common people of a nation or region that is relevant to their particular life-style.

Former Soviet Union: Refers to the republics that were once part of a large nation called the Union of Soviet Socialists Republics (USSR). The USSR was commonly called the Soviet Union. It included the 12 republics: Russia, Ukraine, Belarus, Moldova, Armenia, Azerbaijan, Uzbekistan, Turkmenistan, Tajikistan, Kazakhstan, Kyrgizstan, and Georgia. Sometimes the Baltic republics of Estonia, Latvia, and Lithuania are also included.

fundamentalist: A person who holds religious beliefs based on the complete acceptance of the words of holy scriptures as the truth.

Germanic language group: A large branch of the Indo-European family of languages including German itself, the Scandinavian languages, Dutch, Yiddish, Modern English, Modern Scottish, Afrikaans, and others. The group also includes extinct languages such as Gothic, Old High German, Old Saxon, Old English, Middle English, and the like.

Greek Orthodox: The official church of Greece, a self-governing branch of the Orthodox Eastern Church.

guerrilla: A member of a small radical military organization that uses unconventional tactics to take their enemies by surprise.

hajj: A religious journey made by Muslims to the holy city of Mecca in Saudi Arabia.

Holi: A Hindu festival of processions and merriment lasting three to ten days that marks the end of the lunar year in February or March.

Holocaust: The mass slaughter of European civilians, the vast majority of whom were Jews, by the Nazis during World War II.

Holy Roman Empire: A kingdom consisting of a loose union of German and Italian territories that existed from around the ninth century until 1806.

homeland: A region or area set aside to be a state for a people of a particular national, cultural, or racial origin.

homogeneous: Of the same kind or nature, often used in reference to a whole.

Horn of Africa: The Horn of Africa comprises Djibouti, Eritrea, Ethiopia, Somalia, and Sudan.

human rights issues: Any matters involving people's basic rights which are in question or thought to be abused.

immigration: The act or process of passing or entering into another country for the purpose of permanent residence.

imports: Goods purchased from foreign suppliers.

indigenous: Born or originating in a particular place or country; native to a particular region or area.

Indo-Aryan language group: The group that includes the languages of India; also called Indo-European language group.

Indo-European language family: The group that includes the languages of India and much of Europe and southwestern Asia.

Islam: The religious system of Muhammad, practiced by Muslims and based on a belief in Allah as the supreme being and Muhammed as his prophet. Islam also refers to those nations in which it is the primary religion. There are two major sects: Sunni and Shia (or Shiite). The main difference between the two sects is in their belief in who follows Muhammad, founder of Islam, as the religious leader.

Judaism: The religious system of the Jews, based on the Old Testament as revealed to Moses and characterized by a belief in one God and adherence to the laws of scripture and rabbinic traditions.

khan: A sovereign, or ruler, in central Asia.

khanate: A kingdom ruled by a khan, or man of rank.

literacy: The ability to read and write.

Maghreb states: Refers to Algeria, Morocco, and Tunisia; sometimes includes Libya and Mauritania.

maize: Another name (Spanish or British) for corn or the color of ripe corn.

manioc: The cassava plant or its product. Manioc is a very important food-staple in tropical America.

matrilineal (descent): Descending from, or tracing descent through, the maternal, or mother's, family line.

Mayan language family: The languages of the Central American Indians, further divided into two sub-groups: the Maya and the Huastek.

mean temperature: The air temperature unit measured by the National Weather Service by adding the maximum and minimum daily temperatures together and diving the sum by 2.

Mecca: A city in Saudi Arabia; a destination of Muslims in the Islamic world.

mestizo: The offspring of a person of mixed blood; especially, a person of mixed Spanish and American Indian parentage.

millet: A cereal grass whose small grain is used for food in Europe and Asia.

monarchy: Government by a sovereign, such as a king or queen.

Mongol: One of an Asiatic race chiefly resident in Mongolia, a region north of China proper and south of Siberia.

Moors: One of the Arab tribes that conquered Spain in the eighth century.

Moslem *see* **Muslim.**

mosque: An Islam place of worship and the organization with which it is connected.

Muhammad (or Muhammed or Mahomet): An Arabian prophet (AD 570–632), known as the "Prophet of Allah" who founded the religion of Islam in 622, and wrote the Koran, (also spelled Quran) the scripture of Islam.

mulatto: One who is the offspring of parents one of whom is white and the other is black.

Muslim: A follower of Muhammad in the religion of Islam.

Muslim New Year: A Muslim holiday also called Nawruz. In some countries Muharram 1, which is the first month of the Islamic year, is observed as a holiday, in other places the new year is observed on Sha'ban, the eighth month of the year. This practice apparently stems from pagan Arab times. Shab-i-Bharat, a national holiday in Bangladesh on this day, is held by many to be the occasion when God ordains all actions in the coming year.

mystic: Person who believes he or she can gain spiritual knowledge through processes like meditation that are not easily explained by reasoning or rational thinking.

nationalism: National spirit or aspirations; desire for national unity, independence, or prosperity.

oasis: Fertile spot in the midst of a desert or wasteland.

official language: The language in which the business of a country and its government is conducted.

Ottoman Empire: A Turkish empire that existed from about 1603 until 1918, and included lands around the Mediterranean, Black, and Caspian seas.

patriarchal system: A social system in which the head of the family or tribe is the father or oldest male. Ancestry is determined and traced through the male members of the tribe.

patrilineal (descent): Descending from, or tracing descent through, the paternal, or father's, family line.

pilgrimage: religious journey, usually to a holy place.

plantain: Tropical plant with fruit that looks like bananas, but that must be cooked before eating.

Protestant: A member of one of the Christian bodies that descended from the Reformation of the sixteenth century.

pulses: Beans, peas, or lentils.

Ramadan: The ninth month of the Muslim calender. The entire month commemorates the period in which the Prophet Muhammad is said to have recieved divine revelation and is observed by a strict fast from sunrise to sundown.

Rastafarian: A member of a Jamaican cult begun in 1930 that is partly religious and partly political.

refugee: Person who, in times of persecution or political commotion, flees to a foreign country for safety.

revolution: A complete change in a government or society, such as in an overthrow of the government by the people.

Roman alphabet: Alphabet of the ancient Romans from which alphabets of most modern European languages, including English, are derived.

Roman Catholic Church: Christian church headed by the pope or Bishop of Rome.

Russian Orthodox: The arm of the Eastern Orthodox Church that was the official church of Russia under the tsars.

Sahelian zone: Eight countries make up this dry desert zone in Africa: Burkina Faso, Chad, Gambia, Mali, Mauritania, Niger, Senegal, and the Cape Verde Islands.

savanna: A treeless or near treeless grassland or plain.

segregation: The enforced separation of a racial or religious group from other groups, compelling them to live and go to school separately from the rest of society.

Seventh-day Adventist: One who believes in the second coming of Christ to establish a personal reign upon the earth.

shamanism: A religion in which shamans (priests or medicine men) are believed to influence spirits.

shantytown: An urban settlement of people in inadequate houses.

Shia Muslim *see* Islam.

Shiites *see* Islam.

Shintoism: The system of nature- and hero-worship that forms the native religion of Japan.

sierra: A chain of hills or mountains.

Sikh: A member of a community of India, founded around 1500 and based on the principles of monotheism (belief in one god) and human brotherhood.

Sino-Tibetan language family: The family of languages spoken in eastern Asia, including China, Thailand, Tibet, and Myanmar.

slash-and-burn agriculture: A hasty and sometimes temporary way of clearing land to make it available for agriculture by cutting down trees and burning them; also known as swidden agriculture.

slave trade: The transportation of black Africans beginning in the 1700s to other countries to be sold as slaves—people owned as property and compelled to work for their owners at no pay.

Slavic languages: A major subgroup of the Indo-European language family. It is further subdivided into West Slavic (including Polish, Czech, Slovak and Serbian), South Slavic (including Bulgarian, Serbo-Croatian, Slovene, and Old Church Slavonic), and East Slavic (including Russian Ukrainian and Byelorussian).

sorghum: Plant grown for its valuable uses, such as for grain, syrup, or fodder.

Southeast Asia: The region in Asia that consists of the Malay Archipelago, the Malay Peninsula, and Indochina.

Soviet Union *see* **Former Soviet Union.**

subcontinent: A large subdivision of a continent.

subsistence farming: Farming that provides only the minimum food goods necessary for the continuation of the farm family.

Sudanic language group: A related group of languages spoken in various areas of northern Africa, including Yoruba, Mandingo, and Tshi.

Sufi: A Muslim mystic who believes that God alone exists, there can be no real difference between good and evil, that the soul exists within the body as in a cage, so death should be the chief object of desire.

sultan: A king of a Muslim state.

Sunni Muslim *see* Islam.

Taoism: The doctrine of Lao-Tzu, an ancient Chinese philosopher (c.500 BC) as laid down by him in the *Tao-te-ching.*

Third World: A term used to describe less developed countries; as of the mid-1990s, it is being replaced by the United Nations designation Less Developed Countries, or LDC.

treaty: A negotiated agreement between two governments.

tribal system: A social community in which people are organized into groups or clans descended from common ancestors and sharing customs and languages.

tundra: A nearly level treeless area whose climate and vegetation are characteristically arctic due to its northern position; the subsoil is permanently frozen.

untouchables: In India, members of the lowest caste in the caste system, a hereditary social class system. They were considered unworthy to touch members of higher castes.

Union of the Soviet Socialist Republics *see* Former Soviet Union.

veldt: A grassland in South Africa.

Western nations: General term used to describe democratic, capitalist countries, including the United States, Canada, and western European countries.

Zoroastrianism: The system of religious doctrine taught by Zoroaster and his followers in the Avesta; the religion prevalent in Persia until its overthrow by the Muslims in the seventh century.

Index

All culture groups and countries included in this encyclopedia are included in this index. Selected regions, alternate groups names, and historical country names are cross-referenced. Country chapter titles are in boldface; volume numbers appear in brackets, with page number following.

A

Abkhazians (Georgia) [3]214
Aborigines *see* Australian Aborigines (Australia)
Abyssinia *see* Ethiopia
Adjarians (Georgia) [3]218
Afghanis (Afghanistan) [1]3
Afghanistan [1]3
Africa, Horn of *see* Djibouti; Eritrea; Ethiopia; Somalia
Africa, North *see* Algeria; Chad; Egypt; Libya; Morocco; Sudan; Tunisia
Afrikaners (South Africa) [8]93
Afro-Brazilians (Brazil) [2]11
Ainu (Japan) [5]14
Aka (Congo, Republic of the) [2]215
Albania [1]19
Albanians (Albania) [1]19
Algeria [1]27
Algerians (Algeria) [1]27
Amerindian *see* Araucanians (Chile); Cunas (Panama); Garifuna (Belize); Guajiros (Venezuela); Kayapos (Brazil); Páez (Colombia); Sumu and Miskito (Nicaragua); Tenetehara (Brazil); Xavante (Brazil)
Amhara (Ethiopia) [3]133
Andalusians (Spain) [8]132
Andhras (India) [4]96
Andorra [1]35
Andorrans (Andorra) [1]35
Angola [1]39
Angolans (Angola) [1]39
Antigua and Barbuda [1]49
Antiguans and Barbudans (Antigua and Barbuda) [1]49
Arabs *see* Bahrainis (Bahrain); Bedu (Saudi Arabia); Druze (Syria); Emirians (United Arab Emirates); Iranians (Iran); Iraqis (Iraq); Marsh Arabs (Iraq); Moroccans (Morocco); Omanis (Oman); Palestinians (Israel); Qataris (Qatar); Saudis (Saudi Arabia); Syrians (Syria); Tunisians (Tunisia); Yemenis (Yemen)
Araucanians (Chile) [2]126
Argentina [1]57
Argentines (Argentina) [1]57
Armenia [1]65
Armenians (Armenia) [1]65
Asháninka (Peru) [7]113
Asian Indians *see* Indians (India)
Asmat (Indonesia) [4]139
Australia [1]73
Australian Aborigines (Australia) [1]80
Australians (Australia) [1]73

Austria [1]87
Austrians (Austria) [1]87
Aymara (Bolivia) [1]193
Azande (Congo, Democratic Republic of the) [2]197
Azerbaijan [1]95
Azerbaijanis (Azerbaijan) [1]95

B

Baganda (Uganda) [9]98
Bahamas [1]101
Bahamians (Bahamas) [1]101
Bahrain [1]107
Bahrainis (Bahrain) [1]107
Bakongo (Congo, Republic of the) [2]221
Balinese (Indonesia) [4]143
Balkans *see* Bosnia and Herzegovina; Croatia; Macedonia
Baltic nations *see* Estonia; Latvia; Lithuania
Baluchi (Pakistan) [7]35
Bangladesh [1]113
Bangladeshis (Bangladesh) [1]113
Banyankole (Uganda) [9]105
Barbadians (Barbados) [1]133
Barbados [1]133
Basques (Spain) [8]138
Bedoin *see* Bedu (Saudi Arabia)
Bedu (Saudi Arabia) [8]41
Belarus [1]139
Belarusans (Belarus) [1]139
Belgians (Belgium) [1]145
Belgium [1]145
Belize [1]159
Belizeans (Belize) [1]159
Bemba (Zambia) [9]215
Bengalis (Bangladesh) [1]121
Benin [1]173
Beninese (Benin) [1]173
Berbers *see* Algerians (Algeria); Moroccans (Morocco); Tunisians (Tunisia)
Bhutan [1]179
Bhutanese (Bhutan) [1]179
Bolivia [1]185
Bolivians (Bolivia) [1]185
Bosnia and Herzegovina [1]201
Bosnians (Bosnia and Herzegovina) [1]201
Brahui (Pakistan) [7]41
Brazil [2]1
Brazilians (Brazil) [2]1
Bretons (France) [3]181

British *see* English (United Kingdom)
Brittany *see* Bretons (France)
Bulgaria [2]31
Bulgarians (Bulgaria) [2]31
Burkina Faso [2]39
Burkinabe (Burkina Faso) [2]39
Burma *see* Myanmar
Burman (Myanmar) [6]67
Burundi [2]51
Burundians (Burundi) [2]51

C

Cambodia [2]61
Cameroon [2]77
Cameroonians (Cameroon) [2]77
Canada [2]83
Canadians (Canada) [2]83
Cape Coloreds (South Africa) [8]100
Cape Verde [2]101
Cape Verdeans (Cape Verde) [2]101
Caribbean *see* Antigua and Barbuda; Bahamas;
    Barbados; Cuba; Dominica; Dominican Republic;
    Grenada; Haiti; Jamaica; St. Kitts and Nevis; St.
    Lucia; St. Vincent and the Grenadines; Trinidad and
    Tobago
Castilians (Spain) [8]144
Catalans (Spain) [8]150
Central African Republic [2]105
Central Africans (Central African Republic) [2]105
Central America *see* Belize; Costa Rica; El Salvador;
    Guatemala; Honduras; Nicaragua; Panama
Central Americans *see* Belizeans (Belize); Costa Ricans
    (Costa Rica); Cunas (Panama); Garifuna (Belize);
    Guatemalans (Guatemala); Hondurans (Honduras);
    Nicaraguans (Nicaragua); Panamanians (Panama);
    Salvadorans (El Salvador); Sumu and Miskito
    (Nicaragua)
Central Asia *see* Afghanistan; Azerbaijan; Kazakstan;
    Tajikistan; Turkmenistan; Uzbekistan
Chad [2]113
Chadians (Chad) [2]113
Chagga (Tanzania) [9]19
Chakmas (Bangladesh) [1]127
Cham (Vietnam) [9]191
Chechens (Russia) [7]199
Chechnya *see* Chechens (Russia)
Chewa and other Maravi Groups (Malawi) [5]205
Chile [2]119
Chileans (Chile) [2]119
China [2]131
Chinese (China) [2]132
Chukchi (Russia) [7]206
Colombia [2]177

Colombians (Colombia) [2]177
Coloreds, Cape (South Africa) [8]100
Congo, Democratic Republic of the [2]189
Congo, Republic of the [2]209
Congolese (Congo, Democratic Republic of the) [2]189
Congolese (Congo, Republic of the) [2]209
Costa Rica [3]1
Costa Ricans (Costa Rica) [3]1
Cote d'Ivoire [3]7
Creoles of Sierra Leone (Sierra Leone) [8]67
Croatia [3]13
Croats (Croatia) [3]13
Cuba [3]21
Cubans (Cuba) [3]21
Cunas (Panama) [7]64
Cyprus [3]29
Czech Republic [3]37
Czechoslovakia *see* Czech Republic; Slovakia
Czechs (Czech Republic) [3]37

D

Dahomey *see* Benin
Danes (Denmark) [3]43
Denmark [3]43
Dinka (Sudan) [8]181
Djibouti [3]51
Djiboutians (Djibouti) [3]51
Dominica [3]57
Dominican Republic [3]63
Dominicans (Dominica) [3]57
Dominicans (Dominican Republic) [3]63
Dong (China) [2]141
DROC *see* Congo, Democratic Republic of the
Druze (Syria) [8]219
Dutch *see* Netherlanders (The Netherlands)

E

Ecuador [3]69
Ecuadorans (Ecuador) [3]69
Efe and Mbuti (Congo, Democratic Republic of
    the) [2]201
Egypt [3]83
Egyptians (Egypt) [3]83
El Salvador [3]91
Emirians (United Arab Emirates) [9]117
England *see* English (United Kingdom)
English (South Africa) [8]105
English (United Kingdom) [9]123
Equatorial Guinea [3]99
Equatorial Guineans (Equatorial Guinea) [3]99
Eritrea [3]107
Eritreans (Eritrea) [3]107

INDEX

Eskimos *see* Inuit (Canada)
Estonia [3]113
Estonians (Estonia) [3]113
Ethiopia [3]121
Ethiopians (Ethiopia) [3]121
Ewenki (Mongolia) [6]46

F

Fiji [3]157
Fijians (Fiji) [3]157
Filipinos (Philippines) [7]125
Finland [3]167
Finns (Finland) [3]167
Flemings (Belgium) [1]151
France [3]175
French (France) [3]175
French Canadians (Canada) [2]89
French Guiana *see* French Guianans (France)
French Guianans (France) [3]185
French Somaliland *see* Djibouti
Frisians (The Netherlands) [6]122
Fulani (Guinea) [4]46

G

Gabon [3]189
Gabonese (Gabon) [3]189
Galicians (Spain) [8]155
Gambia, The [3]195
Gambians (Gambia, The) [3]195
Garifuna (Belize) [1]166
Georgia [3]205
Georgians (Georgia) [3]205
Germans (Germany) [4]1
Germany [4]1
Ghana [4]9
Ghanaians (Ghana) [4]9
Gikuyu (Kenya) [5]50
Gonds (India) [4]102
Greece [4]17
Greek Cypriots (Cyprus) [3]29
Greeks (Greece) [4]17
Grenada [4]25
Grenadians (Grenada) [4]25
Guajiros (Venezuala) [9]170
Guaranís (Paraguay) [7]98
Guatemala [4]31
Guatemalans (Guatemala) [4]31
Guinea [4]39
Guineans (Guinea) [4]39
Gujaratis (India) [4]107
Gusii (Kenya) [5]60
Guyana [4]51

Guyanans (Guyana) [4]51
Gypsies *see* Roma (Romania)

H

Haiti [4]57
Haitians (Haiti) [4]57
Han (China) [2]148
Hausa (Nigeria) [6]176
Hazaras (Afghanistan) [1]10
Hiligaynon (Philippines) [7]136
Hill Tribespeople (Cambodia) [2]70
Hondurans (Honduras) [4]67
Honduras [4]67
Horn of Africa *see* Djibouti; Eritrea; Ethiopia; Somalia
Hungarians (Hungary) [4]75
Hungary [4]75
Hutu (Rwanda) [8]7

I

Iatmul (Papua New Guinea) [7]79
Iceland [4]81
Icelanders (Iceland) [4]81
Igbo (Nigeria) [6]181
Ilocanos (Philippines) [7]142
India [4]87
Indians (India) [4]88
Indo-Fijians (Fiji) [3]163
Indonesia [4]129
Indonesians (Indonesia) [4]129
Inuit (Canada) [2]94
Iran [4]161
Iranians (Iran) [4]161
Iraq [4]169
Iraqis (Iraq) [4]169
Ireland [4]181
Irish (Ireland) [4]181
Israel [4]189
Israelis (Israel) [4]189
Italians (Italy) [4]207
Italy [4]207
Ivoirians (Cote d'Ivoire) [3]7
Ivory Coast *see* Cote d'Ivoire

J

Jamaica [4]215
Jamaicans (Jamaica) [4]215
Japan [5]1
Japanese (Japan) [5]1
Javanese (Indonesia) [4]149
Jivaro (Ecuador) [3]77
Jordan [5]21
Jordanians (Jordan) [5]21

K

Kalenjin (Kenya) [5]67
Kammu (Laos) [5]125
Kampuchea *see* Cambodia
Karakalpaks (Uzbekistan) [9]153
Karens (Myanmar) [6]75
Kayapos (Brazil) [2]17
Kazaks (Kazakstan) [5]29
Kazakstan [529
Kenya [5]39
Kenyans (Kenya) [5]39
Khmer (Cambodia) [2]61
Kittitians and Nevisians (St. Kitts and Nevis) [8]11
Korea, Republic of [5]91
Kurds (Turkey) [9]78
Kuwait [5]99
Kuwaitis (Kuwait) [5]99
Kyrgyz (Kyrgystan) [5]107
Kyrgyzstan [5]107

L

Lao (Laos) [5]115
Laos [5]115
Lapps *see* Sami (Norway)
Latvia [5]133
Latvians (Latvia) [5]133
Lebanese (Lebanon) [5]139
Lebanon [5]139
Lesotho [5]149
Liberia [5]159
Libya [5]167
Libyans (Libya) [5]167
Liechtenstein [5]175
Liechtensteiners (Liechtenstein) [5]175
Lithuania [5]181
Lithuanians (Lithuania) [5]181
Luhya (Kenya) [5]74
Luo (Kenya) [5]81
Luxembourg [5]189
Luxembourgers (Luxembourg) [5]189

M

Ma'dan (Iraq) [4]176
Maasai (Tanzania) [9]25
Macedonia [5]193
Macedonians (Macedonians) [5]193
Madagascar [5]199
Maghreb states *see* Algeria; Libya; Mauritania;
    Morocco; Tunisia
Malagasy (Madagascar) [5]199
Malawi [5]205
Malays (Malaysia) [5]213

Malaysia [5]213
Mali [5]221
Malians (Mali) [5]221
Malinke (Liberia) [5]159
Man (China) [2]153
Manchus *see* Man (China)
Maori (New Zealand) [6]133
Mapuches see Araucanians (Chile)
Marathas (India) [4]112
Maravi Groups *see* Chewa and other Maravi Groups
    (Malawi)
Maronites (Lebanon) [5]145
Marsh Arabs *see* Ma'dan (Iraq)
Masai *see* Maasai (Tanzania)
Mauritania [6]1
Mauritanians (Mauritania) [6]1
Maya (Mexico) [6]13
Melanesians (Papua New Guinea) [7]71
Melpa (Papua New Guinea) [7]84
Mexicans (Mexico) [6]7
Mexico [6]7
Miao (China) [2]157
Micronesia [6]21
Micronesians (Micronesia) [6]21
Middle East *see* Bahrain; Cyprus; Iran; Iraq; Israel;
    Jordan; Kuwait; Lebanon; Oman; Qatar; Saudi
    Arabia; Syria; United Arab Emirates; Yemen
Miskito *see* Sumu and Miskito (Nicaragua)
Moldavia *see* Moldova
Moldova [6]25
Moldovans (Moldova) [6]25
Monaco [6]33
Monégasques (Monaco) [6]33
Mongolia [6]39
Mongols (Mongolia) [6]39
Mordvins (Russia) [7]211
Moroccans (Morocco) [6]53
Morocco [6]53
Mossi (Burkina Faso) [2]43
Motu (Papua New Guinea) [7]89
Mozambicans (Mozambique) [6]61
Mozambique [6]61
Myanmar [6]67

N

Namibia [6]91
Namibians (Namibia) [6]91
Nentsy (Russia) [7]216
Nepal [6]99
Nepalis (Nepal) [6]99
Netherlanders (The Netherlands) [6]115
Netherlands, The [6]115
New Zealand [6]127

New Zealanders (New Zealand) [6]127
Newly Independent States (former Soviet republics) *see* Armenia; Azerbaijan; Belarus; Georgia; Kazakstan; Kyrgyzstan; Moldova; Russia; Tajikistan; Turkmenistan; Ukraine; Uzbekistan
Nicaragua [6]145
Nicaraguans (Nicaragua) [6]145
Niger [6]157
Nigeria [6]171
Nigerians (Nigeria) [6]171
Nigeriens (Niger) [6]157
Ni-Vanuatu (Vanuatu) [9]159
Nomads *see* Bedu (Saudi Arabia); Mongols (Mongolia)
North Africa *see* Algeria; Chad; Egypt; Libya; Morocco; Sudan; Tunisia
Norway [7]1
Norwegians (Norway) [7]1
Nyamwezi (Tanzania) [9]34
Nyasaland *see* Malawi

O

Oman [7]17
Omanis (Oman) [7]17
Oriya (India) [4]117
Oromos (Ethiopia) [3]141

P

Páez (Colombia) [2]183
Pakistan [7]25
Pakistanis (Pakistan) [7]25
Palestine *see* Palestinians (Israel)
Palestinians (Israel) [4]198
Pamiri [9]7
Panama [7]57
Panamanians (Panama) [7]57
Papua New Guinea [7]71
Paraguay [7]93
Paraguayans (Paraguay) [7]93
Pashtun (Afghanistan) [1]13
Pemon (Venezuala) [9]174
Persians *see* Iranians (Iran)
Peru [7]105
Peruvians (Peru) [7]105
Philippines [7]125
Poland [7]149
Poles (Poland) [7]149
Polynesia see Polynesians (New Zealand)
Polynesians (New Zealand) [6]139
Portugal [7]157
Portuguese (Portugal) [7]157
Portuguese East Africa *see* Mozambique
Punjabis (Pakistan) [7]46

Pygmies *see* Aka (Congo, Republic of the); Efe and Mbuti (Congo, Democratic Republic of the)

Q

Qatar [7]165
Qataris (Qatar) [7]165
Quechua (Peru) [7]119

R

Rajputs (India) [4]122
Rhodesia *see* Zimbabwe
Roma (Romania) [7]178
Romania [7]171
Romanians (Romania) [7]171
Russia [7]187
Russians (Russia) [7]187
Rwanda [8]1
Rwandans (Rwanda) [8]1

S

St. Kitts and Nevis [8]11
St. Lucia [8]17
St. Lucians (St. Lucia) [8]17
St. Vincent and the Grenadines [8]23
St. Vincentians (St. Vincent and the Grenadines) [8]23
Salvadorans (El Salvador) [3]91
Sami (Norway) [7]9
Sammarinese (San Marino) [8]29
Samoa *see* Western Samoa
Samoans (Western Samoa) [9]197
San Marino [8]29
Saudi Arabia [8]33
Saudis (Saudi Arabia) [8]33
Scandinavia see Denmark; Finland; Iceland; Norway; Sweden
Scotland *see* Scots (United Kingdom)
Scots (United Kingdom) [9]130
Senegal [8]49
Senegalese (Senegal) [8]49
Seychelles [8]61
Seychellois (Seychelles) [8]61
Shambaa (Tanzania) [9]39
Shans (Myanmar) [6]83
Sherpas (Nepal) [6]107
Sierra Leone [8]67
Sinhalese (Sri Lanka) [8]161
Slovakia [8]73
Slovaks (Slovakia) [8]73
Slovenes (Slovenia) [8]81
Slovenia [8]81
Somalia [8]87
Somaliland, French *see* Djibouti

Somalis (Somalia) [8]87
Songhay (Mali) [5]227
Sotho (Lesotho) [5]149
South Africa [8]93
South Asia *see* Afghanistan; Bangladesh, Bhutan, India,
    Pakistan, Sri Lanka
South Koreans (Korea, Republic of) [5]91
South West Africa *see* Namibia
Southeast Asia *see* Brunei Darussalam; Cambodia;
    Indonesia; Laos; Malaysia; Thailand; Vietnam
Soviet Union (former) *see* Armenia; Azerbaijan;
    Belarus; Georgia; Kazakstan; Kyrgyzstan; Moldova;
    Russia; Tajikistan; Turkmenistan; Ukraine;
    Uzbekistan
Spain [8]125
Spaniards (Spain) [8]125
Sri Lanka [8]161
Sudan [8]175
Sudanese (Sudan) [8]175
Sumu and Miskito (Nicaragua) [6]152
Sundanese (Indonesia) [4]155
Suriname [8]185
Surinamese (Suriname) [8]185
Swahili (Tanzania) [9]45
Swaziland [8]189
Swazis (Swaziland) [8]189
Sweden [8]195
Swedes (Sweden) [8]195
Swiss (Switzerland) [8]205
Switzerland [8]205
Syria [8]213
Syrians (Syria) [8]213

T

Tajikistan [9]1
Tajiks [9]1
Tamils (Sri Lanka) [8]169
Tanganyika *see* Tanzania
Tanzania [9]13
Tanzanians (Tanzania) [9]13
Tatars (Russia) [7]221
Thai (Thailand) [9]51
Thailand [9]51
Tibet *see* Tibetans (China)
Tibetans (China) [2]163
Tigray (Ethiopia) [3]149
Tonga (Zambia) [9]221
Trinidad and Tobago [9]59
Trinidadians and Tobagonians (Trinidad and
    Tobago) [9]59
Tuareg (Niger) [6]164
Tunisia [9]65
Tunisians (Tunisia) [9]65

Turkmenistan [9]85
Turkey [9]71
Turkmens (Turkmenistan) [9]85
Turks (Turkey) [9]71
Tutsi (Burundi) [2]57

U

UAE *see* United Arab Emirates
Uganda [9]91
Ugandans (Uganda) [9]91
Uighurs (China) [2]168
Ukraine [9]111
Ukrainians (Ukraine) [9]111
United Arab Emirates [9]117
United Kingdom [9]123
Upper Volta *see* Burkina Faso
Uruguay [9]143
Uruguayans (Uruguayans) [9]143
USSR *see* Soviet Union (former)
Uzbekistan [9]147
Uzbeks (Uzbekistan) [9]147

V

Vanuatu [9]159
Venezuela [9]163
Venezuelans (Venezuela) [9]163
Vietnam [9]181
Vietnamese (Vietnam) [9]181

W–X–Y–Z

Wales *see* Welsh (United Kingdom)
Walloons (Belgium) [1]155
Welsh (United Kingdom) [9]136
West Africa *see* Benin
Western Sahara *see* Morocco
Western Samoa [9]197
Wolof (Senegal) [8]56
Xavante (Brazil) [2]22
Xhosa (South Africa) [8]110
Yemen [9]201
Yemenis (Yemen) [9]201
Yoruba (Nigeria) [6]186
Zaire *see* Congo, Democratic Republic of the
Zambia [9]209
Zambians (Zambia) [9]209
Zanzibar *see* Tanzania
Zhuang (China) [2]173
Zimbabwe [9]227
Zimbabweans (Zimbabwe) [9]227
Zulu (South Africa) [8]117